AF556027

'THEY WILL SHOOT YOU, MADAM'

MY LIFE THROUGH CONFLICT

HARINDER BAWEJA

ROLI

For my mother, Harjeet Baweja,
the oldest in the family...

And the youngest – four generations apart –
Japman, Amyra, Rehet...

First published by Roli Books in India in 2025

Roli Books Pvt. Ltd.
M-75, Greater Kailash II Market, New Delhi 110 048
Phone: +91 (011) 40682000
E-mail: info@rolibooks.com
Website: www.rolibooks.com
Also at Chennai & Mumbai

ISBN: 9789349474314

Typeset in Century Old Style Std by Roli Books
Printed in New Delhi, India

Contents

Preface

Late one afternoon in 2017, we received an email informing us that our editor-in-chief, Bobby Ghosh would be returning to New York for 'personal reasons'. There was a sudden silence that engulfed the editorial floor of *Hindustan Times.*

There was utter disbelief too. Why would the editor want to return to the United States of America? We were a great team, doing great work, and he, I knew was completely immersed in crafting a news strategy for the newspaper. He was most definitely pushing the editorial envelope, at a time when government pressure on proprietors was steadily increasing.

As the editor in-charge of special projects, I was leading important campaigns and series that focussed attention on critical issues that were staring us in the face. That is what journalists are meant to do and we, in our own way, were trying to draw attention to subjects such as rape, racism, trolls, and hate that is eating into the innards of our society and country.

I began my career in the 1980s and worked with editors like Vinod Mehta and Aroon Purie, who gave me the space and the freedom to explore, to investigate, to be fearless, and most importantly, to be fair, just, and objective.

By the time I joined *Hindustan Times* in 2012, I had already invested about three decades in a profession that I have come to be passionate about. I was aware of the pitfalls and had heard several stories about how unhappy bureaucrats, chief ministers, union ministers, and members of parliament would call to register their annoyance with articles we had meticulously researched.

I, and my many peers, know what the intoxicating rush of a well-written and well-researched piece of journalism feels like. It is a feeling that courses through your veins and can either help you sleep well or keep you up late. Heady excitement works both ways. It helps a great deal when you also know that your bosses will stand up for you and soak in the pressure that is bound to come their way.

I was aware of stories being toned down; of some being held back and of some being 'killed'. What was dismaying was the abrupt departure of an editor-in-chief. We had started a series titled #LetsTalkAboutHate, after similarly having talked about rape, for which actor and producer Farhan Akhtar had written a moving and sensitive open letter to his two daughters. We had also done one on trolls in which several celebrities, including actor Sonam Kapoor, had shared her experience of how she handled all the hate that came her way each time she expressed an opinion on social media.

The series was doing well and the paper was getting noticed but there was a political backlash the day we started #LetsTalkAboutHate. A full page of the newspaper documented verified cases of hate crimes: of Dalits being attacked and Muslims being lynched.

Did Bobby's departure have something to do with that? That's his story to tell and I cannot completely answer that question. What I do know is that the series is no longer available for online viewing. It was pulled down before Bobby packed his bags and left for New York.

He isn't the only editor who has been at the receiving end of pressure. Pressure continues to be relentlessly applied. News organizations have been raided and many editors have either quit, with their dignity alive, or simply been pushed out. Prannoy Roy, the owner of NDTV was forced to sell his shares in the channel after persistent harassment from government agencies. Ironically, once the channel was out of his editorial control, the litany of cases against Roy were dropped and he was given a clean chit.

By 2017, I'd worked as a journalist through various political regimes including Indira and Rajiv Gandhi, Deve Gowda, I. K. Gujral, A. B. Vajpayee, and Manmohan Singh. I continue to write under the premiership of Narendra Modi.

I regret the fact that I was not a part of the media during the dark days of the Emergency, but I was emboldened and heartened by the pushback from the proprietors and editors who had the guts to churn out editions with blank pages. That was their way of holding truth to power. The Indira Gandhi government had literally switched the lights off on the media on 25 June 1975, to disable printing presses.

Six days after the darkest hour began for India's democracy, the Indira Gandhi regime came out with a list of pre-censorship guidelines. Censorship was and continues to be a slippery slope. Now, notices from central agencies like the Enforcement Directorate (ED), or the withdrawal of government advertisements that are one of the main financial sources for media outlets are fine-tuned to keep the Press in check.

During the Emergency, news organizations were categorized as 'hostile', 'neutral', and 'friendly'. Today, it is difficult to qualify for either of the first two categories. So much has been lost in the din of sensational, high-decibel debates.

Yet, I view myself as a fortunate practitioner of journalism who has had the occasion to chronicle cataclysmic events that have shaped India as a nation. I must confess – with great sadness – that the very phrase, 'Godi media', or lapdog media, is a reality that shocks and shames. Other phrases like 'sickular' and 'presstitutes' have also been hurled at us, but the brazenness with which reporters and anchors wear their political inclination on their sleeve is another discomforting pointer to how the profession has changed.

The press freedom index speaks volumes. According to the organization, Reporters Without Borders, India stood at a dismal 159 out of 180 countries in 2024, the plunge precipitous. In 2022, that rank was 150 and in 2014, it was 140.

This book, however, is not a critique of the media. It is about my own journey as a journalist.

I feel compelled to narrate my experience, though this book is not strictly what I would call a memoir. It is an examination of the many fault lines I have had the privilege of studying from close quarters.

Journalists are students of history and I have also had the privilege of meeting and interviewing a slew of people who continue to make headlines. I was a part of the very credible magazine, *India Today*, which was launched at the height of the Emergency. It soon reached dizzying heights. In the 12 years that I spent there, we did what is our essential remit: call out the powerful and speak for the powerless and the voiceless. We could do so, without being called 'anti-national'.

Tehelka, the brand associated with hard-hitting investigations, did exemplary work to expose corruption within the armed forces. It also did an important deep-dive into the Gujarat riots of 2002. My colleague, Ashish Khetan captured gory details on spy cameras. The accused – out on bail – spoke at length about how they had gone on a death spree to kill hundreds, including the former Congress MP, Ehsan Jafri.

I was also a part of a sting operation that exposed the money and muscle power that was used to try and shield the killer of Jessica Lall, a model, who was shot dead only because she refused to serve a drink in a popular restaurant in Delhi. The investigation went on to become the movie, *No one killed Jessica.*

Is any of that possible now? The answer is more no, than yes. There are several independent websites that work tirelessly to hold truth to power and do so with limited budgets. The effort to muzzle their voices is an ongoing exercise.

My previous book, *A Soldier's Diary: Kargil, The Inside Story* was written a quarter century ago. Writing books is not easy and I had sworn never to attempt another one, though I have edited and written chapters for anthologies.

This book was born out of several conversations with friends, who encouraged and goaded me to commit myself to a project that requires great discipline.

I succumbed finally, to the idea of recalling my journey which, at all times, has been challenging, frustrating, and rewarding. I have tried to do so with the objectivity that the passage of time affords. Many assignments through the battlefields of Punjab and Kashmir were disturbing and many – all these decades later – still remind me of the sheer senselessness of violence and the pain of death. I haven't been desensitized and often find myself feeling vulnerable and in despair, though I would definitely classify myself as a hardened reporter.

When I look through the rear view mirror, or the one in front, I still see conflict. I see a disturbing new India, a conflicted India.

The politics of hate has emerged as an incendiary flashpoint. Conflict bears witness to life's many changes.

I have suffered the pain of a dear friend, a Muslim, packing his bags and leaving the country in search of a fresh avenue; any avenue.

The thought of him waiting at the airport brought a sudden surge of tears that wouldn't stop. I felt like I had let him down. He, who was always the loudest in his defense of India, had begun feeling hemmed in and completely stifled. I was reminded of the time he'd told us about how he had refused to move to an official accommodation his wife was being allocated in an educational campus, because it was located in a Muslim-dominated area and he didn't want his child to grow up in a ghetto.

He, my friend, who had covered the tearing down of the Babri Masjid and its bloody aftermath, found himself giving up on the new India that was taking shape. He had once, out of sheer curiosity, asked his father about his decision to stay on in India after Partition, and the answer he had got was, 'Religion does not define nationhood.'

It does not and should not.

Religious disputes are now, however, endangering the idea of India. The mindless pursuit of digging through the rubble of history to determine the status of places of worship and the invention of new forms of strife in the name of 'love jihad', 'land jihad', and 'vyapar (trade) jihad', are striking at the very core of our foundational values.

The new India needs to have conversations. It needs to start crucial dialogues that contain conflict, not inflame it. I hope this book will spur both introspection and reconciliation. Both are important, especially because new fault lines have emerged, even as the earlier ones continue to simmer.

I understood how they simmer when, recently, while playing a game of tambola with the family, my mother called out number 84. She didn't say 'last of the fours, eighty-four', as we have always heard it being called out in clubs. She said, 'Sikh riots, 84.' I held my breath till she announced the next number and simply gazed down at the ticket. I did not have the heart to look at her. I was relieved to move on and scratch out other numbers on my ticket.

The past is embedded in the present.

My friend returned after six months. He had to. India is his home. His words haunt me every so often. 'I've earned my credentials but, in the end, I'm only seen as a Muslim. I have never felt so "othered". We are living through an unending nightmare,' he told me one day.

Justice and humanity lie at the heart of a robust democracy. Truth and reconciliation are the cornerstones that help resolve conflict. Militaries can only contain violence. They cannot provide the balm, the healing touch. Government policies, the fair churn of the administrative machinery, and the courts can nurse old wounds and prevent fresh ones from searing the country's conscience.

We cannot afford to allow our places of worship to become places of politics, and as I learnt over the years, we simply cannot afford to mix religion with politics. Conflict needs to be dialled down, not ratcheted up. Fires, when fuelled, are difficult to extinguish. I have seen so many in my journey through conflict, which started in Punjab, where politicians, including Prime Minister Indira Gandhi created the Frankenstein monster Jarnail

Singh Bhindranwale, who was smoked out and killed only after the army's tanks rolled into the holy precincts of the Golden Temple.

Four decades later, the embers continue to simmer.

Introduction

I Witness

Fault lines birth separate sets of actors, both villainous and heroic. I have had the occasion to meet them all and gain perspectives. My work – and my gender – have helped me understand how to navigate landmines, personal and professional.

1984 was a turning point for me, personally and professionally. I was barely two years into journalism when one day, Vijay Dutt, my editor at *Probe* magazine, called me to his office and said, 'Go to Amritsar.'

Amritsar, I thought to myself. The army tanks had just rolled into the Golden Temple and Punjab was under curfew. The magazine no longer exists but I had secretly wondered, then, why I had been chosen for the assignment. More senior reporters could have been tasked to travel to Amritsar from Delhi, for a story that was clearly complex.

Operation Blue Star had just ended, and Punjab was simmering with tension. Why had I been chosen to cover the aftermath of an operation that had serious consequences for the country? I was bewildered but I did not protest.

I learnt that my being a 'Sikh' had been a factor in the editor's decision to send me to Amritsar. He also felt that a woman would get better access, especially one who had grown up among soldiers, arms, and ammunition. He knew that I was a fauji kid.

Jarnail Singh Bhindranwale, the zealot, who had terrorized Punjab with summary killings of both Hindus and Sikhs, had finally been silenced. Prime Minister Indira Gandhi – who had ordered the army into the most sacred of Sikh shrines – had signed off on a risky, life-taking mission.

My mind raced back in time as I packed my bags for Amritsar.

The editor did not know that like my other fauji friends, I had grown up with a deep sense of being Indian. That was our identity. That, in fact, was our only religion. I did not protest the 'Sikh' badge just as I did not tell him that I would not like to be singled out by my gender. My eyes were set on being a part of the Punjab battlefield.

I was a journalist, not a Sikh journalist or a woman journalist.

My tryst with journalism was not part of a conscious decision. I had actually stumbled into it.

Born into an Air Force family, I had journeyed through myriad cities and different convent schools. My father would get transferred every two to three years and every so often, I'd find myself in a new school, amidst new people.

Children of defence families lead protected lives. They usually live in cantonments – not easily accessible to civilians – and grow up, like I did, amid like-minded people, who – in my growing-up years – were brought up on a very secular-centric value system. The open politicization and communalization that we see today makes me flinch.

Growing up as a fauji kid, especially in the 1960s and the '70s – when even landline phones were a rarity – gave my generation a sense of equations. What we did get accustomed to was a unique sense of identity that came attached with the uniform we saw our fathers wear each morning.

We were also children who grew up witnessing wars. I was too small when India and Pakistan waged a war in 1965, but have clear memories of the 1971 military confrontation that led to the creation of Bangladesh. We were posted in Bombay at the time and I remember the sirens, the black cardboard paper posted on the windows of our home in Navy Nagar, Colaba, and the menacing roar of fighter aircraft flying overhead.

In 1971, I had no idea that I would journey into journalism and spend more than 40 years of my work life covering different conflicts, internal and external.

As a giddy teenager, I had different dreams at different points and they varied between wanting to train as a teacher, become a psychologist, or be an air hostess.

My advent into journalism was truly an accident.

My father got posted to Delhi in 1978, the year I was to enroll in a college and I chose to do my honours in English, a language the fauj and my teachers had prepared me for.

The deep dives into books written by Thomas Hardy, Charles Dickens, T. S. Eliot, and William Shakespeare opened the windows of my mind, shaped my personality, and prepared me for a career.

Once I'd graduated from Jesus and Mary College with a degree in English literature, I still asked myself a question: Do I want to be an advertising copywriter or a journalist? The two options were the only ones on my list.

I did a one-year specialized course in both advertising and journalism and opted for the latter. It is quite another matter that I soon understood – after a few months into my internship – that real journalism can seldom be learnt in a classroom. I interned for six months at *Caravan* magazine before moving on to *Probe,* where I spent three years. In between, I did a short stint with *Surya* magazine, once owned and edited by Indira Gandhi's daughter-in-law, Maneka Gandhi.

I realized I was deeply attracted to field reporting. I had hunger in my belly and I wanted to report stories, meet people, do interviews, ask the hard questions, and feel the pressure of deadlines. I enjoyed meeting people and was far from shy. Moving from one air force station to another had helped shape my personality. Each posting entailed a process of adjustment and I had learnt to adapt to new cities, new teachers, and a new set of friends.

Packing my bags was not difficult. The trip to Amritsar, firmly set me off on my journey through conflict.

1984 was a catastrophic year for India. The storming of the Golden Temple with heavy armaments left a deep impact on the Sikh psyche. It also led to the assassination of a serving prime minister by her Sikh bodyguards.

The pumping of bullets into a frail but made-of-steel

Indira Gandhi, one of India's strongest leaders, led to the most harrowing cycle of violence which saw thousands of Sikhs being burnt alive. Delhi's by-lanes were choking with bodies and relief camps were filling up with wailing widows. The skies in the capital city bellowed with smoke.

1984 was the precise year when I started my journey through conflict, mapping India's fault lines, being a witness to contemporary history, studying fast-paced, seismic events that have altered the country, its contours, its polity.

1984 saw me delve deep into difficult, very challenging assignments that have left some emotional scars.

I'm not religious, much to my family's dislike. The savage, large-scale burning of Sikhs in 1984 after the assassination of Indira Gandhi disturbed me deeply and invoked feelings of humanity, not religion. I had just begun my journalistic career and was out on the streets of Delhi, reporting on the violence. The methodical planning and the cold-blooded killings remain a spine-chilling reminder of a deep blot on India's conscience.

Before I left home on the three mornings that Delhi burnt, I would put a large lock on the door to secure members of my family. My father, a practising Sikh and proud Indian Air Force officer, had to remove his turban and wear a helmet to reach home. That was the only way to escape the murderous mob. His uniform did not count for anything that day, as he raced from his office in South Block, hoping to reach the confines of our home in Saket, one of Delhi's many colonies. My brother, chased by one such mob, ran with all his might and hid in a water tank before returning home, shivering with cold and fright. This, though, is not entirely about them. They are both dead – one of a cancerous brain tumour and the other of a cardiac arrest.

The memories have a habit of surfacing each time I read or write about 1984. I was able to lock my home and go out and report only because a woman – who happened to be born a Sikh – could not be so identified, unlike turbaned men.

Did I want to be out only because being a woman gave me some safety from the murderous Congress-led mobs, hungry for Sikh blood?

The answer is, No.

Did I somewhere understand the meaning of what it meant to be a Sikh in 1984?

The answer is, Yes.

Did I turn to religion for solace?

The answer is, No.

Have I, over the years and decades, become religious?

The answer, again, is, No.

What I do know is that my father's psychological wound was intense. The sheer act of removing his turban left a deep impact. He drew his identity from his uniform and was a practising Sikh. The turban was also a part of his identity. He was clear in his mind, then on, that he would never retire in Delhi, where all his children lived.

My parents left Delhi in 1989 and I moved into a barsati, a two-room set on a terrace, in one of South Delhi's many colonies.

A few years earlier, in 1986, when I was looking to move

out of *Probe* magazine, I called the well-known editor Vinod Mehta and his deputy, Ajoy Bose, to check if they had any vacancies. Mehta had just launched *The Sunday Observer*, a weekly broadsheet, that instantly made headlines; not just for its format but for the fact that it was being edited by Mehta, an extremely competent, even if sometimes foul-mouthed journalist.

'We only have a vacancy in Punjab,' I was told by Bose. That was their way of putting me off, I learnt later. They didn't think I would grab the offer and soon be on my way to Chandigarh from where I filed regularly for *The Sunday Observer*.

Bose and Mehta had bargained, in their minds, that a 'woman' would not be willing to risk being stationed in Punjab. The state was in the throes of terrorism. Passengers were being pulled off buses and shot dead. Hindus were migrating out of villages and the Golden Temple complex was being slowly converted into a fortress, once again.

Punjab was teeming with stories, waiting to be told. When I arrived in Chandigarh – though I spent more time in and around Amritsar – I found I was one of only two or three women reporters. *Tribune*, the largest, most widely-circulated newspaper in the North had an unofficial policy of not recruiting women reporters. The same newspaper now has a woman editor-in-chief.

I was an oddity in Punjab. Several colleagues made me feel hospitable even though I was clear in my mind: I was a journalist, never conscious of my gender. Several other colleagues – content with filing stories based on press releases – resented my presence. According to them –

some of them, I must repeat – I was being accorded extra privileges by the bureaucracy and the politicians only because of my gender.

The Punjab posting re-endorsed what I had learnt in the lanes and by-lanes of Delhi in 1984. I had made the right decision in choosing journalism over advertising. Journalism was – and continues to be – a part of my bloodstream.

The more violence I witnessed, the more I wanted to probe. There is no greater untruth than the oft-repeated line of, 'terrorists don't have a religion'. Spending long years through various conflict zones and societies, including, Punjab, Kashmir, Pakistan, and Afghanistan, I realized that religion has a lot to do with radicalization.

Bhindranwale had a huge army of followers because he spoke a certain language. In Afghanistan, the Taliban has weaponized religion and in Kashmir, many militants sounded the death knell for its rich, syncretic traditions by aiming their guns at Kashmiri Pandits.

The terror exports from Pakistan, who crossed the line of control (LoC) into Jammu and Kashmir; or came to Mumbai across the high seas to enter the city and carry out one of the most audacious attacks on Indian soil were bred in madrasas and mosques, and brainwashed in the name of Allah.

As I covered the momentous events, spanning four decades, I learnt that violence was not about the number of victims it claimed. The headlines didn't lie in, '10 killed in Punjab's Tarn Taran'. They did not lie in, '4 soldiers ambushed in Poonch', or '25 killed in serial bomb blasts'.

Violence has a sociology and deep psychology. Insurgencies are fuelled by political misadventures. They are aided by human rights violations, rigged elections, and by international players – who in the name of geostrategy – are willing to arm and sustain terror outfits.

In 2003, the United States invaded Iraq on a false premise. The country – it has been now proven – had not acquired 'weapons of mass destruction' as claimed by the George Bush administration. The US, also guilty of arming Osama bin Laden, one of the most Machiavellian terrorists, turned around and erased New York city's iconic twin towers in an attack that stunned the entire world.

I began to understand – while stationed in Punjab – that while Bhindranwale was dead and gone, his notorious legacy was still alive. He had been buried, but the fires he lit in the minds of the youth and large swathes of the Jat population that empathized with his version of violence, were very much alive.

The Punjab fault line was deep and the demand for Khalistan, raised by Bhindranwale, still has political ramifications. The consequences, in fact, are now playing out in the international arena, affecting geostrategic ties, including between India and the US and between India and Canada.

While in Punjab, I also understood that I had a voracious appetite for adventure. The hunger to report dangerous, life-threatening conflicts is accompanied by a hard-to-describe adrenalin rush. It has its perils, though it helps inculcate courage, determination, and the firm belief that the pursuit of a story will yield results.

What I was not prepared for was the sheer viciousness that came my way, only because I was a woman. I did not want to be seen as anything other than a journalist but life is not always what you want it to be.

I found love while I was posted in Punjab. A chance meeting with an Aide-de-Camp (ADC) to Punjab Governor Siddhartha Shankar Ray, who I sat with as I waited to go into the governor's office for an interview, led to a meaningful, exhilarating relationship that was to end in marriage over a two-year span.

One morning, however, I was rudely awakened by the constant ringing of the doorbell of the flat where I lived in Chandigarh. I opened the door to find two burly, pot-bellied inspectors from the Punjab Police. Surprised to find the police at my door, I asked them what they wanted.

'Complaint *hai*,' one of them said.

'Complaint, what complaint?' I asked. Several thoughts raced through my mind. Was their visit connected to a story I had written? Was the police upset that I had interviewed militants ensconced in the Golden Temple?

'There is a lot of noise at your home late in the night,' one of them said adding, 'complaint *hai* that senior IPS and IAS officers visit you at night.'

My legs were knocking and I stared at them in disbelief, but quickly gathered my guts and the courage that comes from covering conflict, to say, 'Can I have a copy of the complaint?'

The minute they said they could not share a copy, nor let me see the piece of paper one of them was holding in his hand, I told them to leave. They must have been surprised by my reaction.

I shut the door on their faces and took a few minutes to gather myself. I had learnt how to handle militants. I had also taught myself how to manoeuvre and avoid crowded places, like markets and cinema halls, for that is where bombs claimed maximum victims. I had, however, not anticipated an attack that would be so personal and petty.

The lesson from this attack set me firmly on the road to freedom.

I quickly got ready and went to the secretariat which housed the office of Julio Francis Ribeiro, the then director general of Punjab Police. I told him what had happened and his response changed my perspective in life. I learnt a lesson in courage. I learnt to spread my wings and fly, undeterred, unafraid, unfettered.

'I am sorry that the Punjab Police came to your door. Even if officers are visiting your home, it is not the police's business,' Ribeiro said. He called me a few days later to tell me that the governor's office had acted on a complaint filed to his office by a male journalist.

Why would the governor waste his time on such complaints?

As the governor of Punjab, major power rested with Siddhartha Shankar Ray. He knew me well and had no problem with me or my reporting. He was generous with his time and even invited me to the Raj Bhawan to meet his wife, Maya.

The problem arose when his ADC broke the news of our impending marriage. By then, the ADC – and let him stay unnamed – wanted to quit the army and had sought his boss' help. Ray burst a blood vessel when he learnt that one of his staffers was marrying a journalist. He couldn't have state secrets leak out, he apparently said.

The ADC, focussed on leaving the army, lacked the spine to go ahead with a marital commitment, but that is only a side story. The thought that journalists – in this case, me, – needed partners to source information, was insulting. It was a personal and professional affront.

I had not learned my journalism in the diploma classroom. We learn it through field reporting. Information is not stored only in official files marked 'top secret' and 'confidential'. It is gathered through hard work. If, over the years, I've been called 'danger junkie' and 'bullet Baweja', it must have come through the willingness and determination to navigate conflict zones. It came through risk-taking abilities and the ability to listen patiently to players across dividing lines.

I had little trouble in packing my bags and leaving Chandigarh for Delhi in 1988. A year later, my parents would make the same city their home but my heart lay in exploring another universe. The pettiness of the very masculine mindset of the city – in the late '80s at least – had to be left behind. In fact, I was determined to do so, even though I would no longer see friends like Bittu and colleagues like Kanwar Sandhu and Vipul Mudgal as frequently as I'd got accustomed to. They were always there to hold my hand and lend me a shoulder. They remain a part of my life; a part of my inner circle of friends.

Within a year of my returning to Delhi and being a part of *The Sunday Observer*'s Delhi office, I got a call from *India Today* magazine. The Kashmir insurgency was taking root and my experience of the Punjab battlefield would stand me in good stead.

The insurgency in Jammu and Kashmir was vastly different from Punjab. The 'khadkus' or terrorists in Punjab were quite different from Kashmir's 'mujahids'. This was particularly true in the early years of Kashmir's long and continuing tryst with violence. As chapters in the book will detail, I was more frightened of Punjab's gun-wielding militia than I was of Kashmir's Kalashnikov warriors. Punjab's terrorists were brutal and cold blooded, quite unlike the local Kashmiri militants who were later joined by hard-core mercenaries exported from Pakistan.

My first trip to Srinagar was in December 1989, a few days after Rubaiya Sayeed, the daughter of Union Home Minister Mufti Mohammad Sayeed had been kidnapped and released in exchange for jailed militants.

The mood on the streets was upbeat. Slogans of '*hum kya chahte... azadi*' rent the air and young men, cradling AK-47s, mingled openly in the processions that became a routine. I could not understand why mothers were smearing mehndi on the palms of their young sons and willingly sending them to training camps across the LoC into Pakistan. They were celebrating the fact that their sons would soon sport weapons.

No country worth its salt and sovereignty gives in to the threat from terrorism. Countries, however, often make the fatal mistake of crossing the line, forgetting that their guns are pointed at their own people.

Kashmir was famous – sometimes infamous – for its cordon and search operations. Soldiers belonging to the Indian Army, Border Security Force (BSF), and the local police – on receiving intelligence inputs regarding the presence of militants in Srinagar's colonies – would lay a cordon (surround the area), use a loudspeaker to summon the men to a side and then storm into homes to check for hidden weapons.

Reporters must learn the fine art of neutrality. It is particularly important in a conflict zone. The civilians – non-combatants – need a patient hearing. They are the real victims of violence and the people's voices must be heard the loudest. The militants and secessionists must know that a journalist will meet officials from across the spectrum, including the armed forces with whom their 'war' is, and vice-versa.

The politicians, equally, must understand that journalists will point to their mistakes. Earning the neutrality badge is tough and each player grants it grudgingly. Each side has its own version of what they perceive as the truth – their truth – and slowly, very slowly, it grows into trust. Publicity is each side's oxygen and they slowly let you into their circle.

One morning I was in one such 'circle', sitting with a senior BSF officer, just before he briefed his company commanders, who were setting off on cordon and search missions across Srinagar's various localities. 'This is Kashmir. The local population is hostile. They are not on our side. Use the "danda" if you have to. That is the only way they will give you information on the militants, but be careful, don't beat them so much that the civil rights activists start making a noise.'

Here was a senior official, the rank of an inspector general, briefing his troops, while a board outside his heavily guarded complex was advertising the slogan of, 'We are here for you.'

The use of the 'danda' often led to larger protests. I went to a colony in downtown Srinagar to cover the aftermath of one such operation. Many youth had been picked up and the women were agitated. One woman held me by my hand and took me into her room which had been ransacked. The cordon and search party had suspected that she had given shelter to one of the militants. Furniture lay strewn in the rooms and the floor of her kitchen was littered with utensils. The drum in which she stored rice – not larger than the size of a bucket – had been turned over. 'What did your Indian Army expect to find here?' she asked. 'Can I hide a man in this? Can I even hide a weapon in this? Is this how you think we deserve to be treated? Is this how you will end militancy?'

Each one of her questions led to further questions: Is this how the armed forces hoped they would be able to quell an insurgency? Were they tackling it or fuelling it? The 'danda' and the overturned rice container pointed to the fault line. I was only its chronicler.

Jammu and Kashmir has witnessed episodic shifts since 1989 when the insurgency took root. In 2025 – as I write this – its history and geography both lie altered.

Article 370, which gave the state its special status, was abrogated by the Narendra Modi-led government on 5 August 2019 and the state cleaved into two union territories (UTs). But do the people in the two UTs of Jammu and Kashmir and Ladakh feel like they are a part of the 'Union' or do they feel that the 'Territory' – which is their home – is being viewed as a piece of real estate by political rulers in New Delhi?

In the '90s, when I was still earning my spurs as a conflict reporter, news had a different pace. Broadcast journalism had not burst into our homes. When I was reporting out of Punjab and then Kashmir, we did not have the luxury of mobile phones, social media accounts, and hashtags.

When I was on my way back from the colony where the very angry and wounded woman had taken me into her kitchen, I learnt another lesson that comes only through active field reporting.

A photographer colleague and I were making our way back to the hotel, through downtown Srinagar, when we suddenly heard the staccato sound of gunfire. The sun was setting and we had to get back to the hotel before it became totally dark. Kashmir had various kinds of curfews and we were out on one such day.

The Jammu and Kashmir Liberation Front (JKLF) had called for all civilian cars to stay off the roads after 5 p.m. We were on the wrong side of the deadline. As we heard the burst of gunfire, I urged our driver to stop the car, thinking we had zipped past a security picket – sandbagged bunkers in which soldiers stood guard, the nozzle of their weapons visible through a small mesh window. My driver's reply astounded me. *'Yeh doosri side ka fire hai.'* The militants had fired, he said. How did he know? I asked.

Kashmiris had learnt to identify the sound of weapons. The militants and armed forces used separate makes and civilians had learnt to tell the difference.

A minute later, as we continued driving, we were actually stopped by the BSF. I jumped out of the car and said, 'Press, press,' showing him my *India Today* identity card. He looked at our car. A bullet had grazed it and another one was lodged on the side. We were lucky the bullet had not shattered the window to claim one of us as collateral damage.

'This piece of plastic won't save you your life. Do you realize your car was targeted?' he said, very agitated. His voice, in fact, was loaded with contempt.

Civilians had been warned not to be out after 5 o'clock in the evening and we were out in a white ambassador taxi. The militants had opened fire at a white ambassador – a symbol of officialdom.

'Should we escort you to your hotel, Madam,' the BSF inspector offered. I thanked him and said we would move on. He was making room for my gender. Not many women reporters were regular visitors at the time. I was acutely conscious of not being part of a security escort. That would've ensured a safe passage back to the hotel, but in Kashmir, where information networks are strong, it would have chipped at the very valuable asset of being – and seen to be – neutral.

Kashmir was never short of surprises. The next day, when my photographer and I were at the Srinagar Idgah, a large graveyard that came to be called the resting place of 'martyrs', we were approached by a group of men. 'Were you in downtown Srinagar yesterday in the white ambassador?' one of them asked.

We are in trouble, I thought to myself, wondering what lay ahead. With some dread and what seemed like many seconds later, I answered in the affirmative. 'We have come to apologize,' he said. 'We opened fire from the first floor of a building but stopped just before firing the next round because we then saw the number plate of the car and realized that it was a taxi,' he said, much to my alarm.

Conflict zones are risky.

They are also murky.

Kashmir became murkier after the infiltration of foreign terrorists. Pakistan's military establishment was training and sending merchants of death across the LoC. Some, like Maulana Masood Azhar came by air from Dhaka, on a Portuguese passport, and checked into New Delhi's government-owned Ashoka hotel.

The stodgy, 5 feet 3 inches, Maulana had failed to train as a militant. He told his interrogators, after he was arrested in 1994 that it was because of his 'poor physique'. His physical frame was not what mattered. His indoctrinated brain and the dangerous ability to motivate young minds to wage jihad, made him invaluable to his masters in Pakistan. Several of his speeches have been recorded and widely circulated.

I gleaned a glimpse into his mind by reading his interrogation report. Azhar was tasked to reach Kashmir from Delhi but he first went to Ayodhya, where one of the cassette recordings, quote him saying, 'I remember the day I was standing there. In front of me lay the Babri Masjid in ruins. Angrily, I was stamping the ground, squashing the Indian soil with my shoes and saying, O Babri Masjid, we are ashamed, O Babri Masjid, we are sorry....'

Azhar's mission in Kashmir did not last very long. He was arrested within a month of his arrival. He had been sent to inject a jihadi fervour into the insurgency which had started as an indigenous battle for 'azadi'.

I happened to be in Srinagar when Azhar was arrested and paraded before the media. He was a big catch and we were invited for a special press conference. When I asked him a question, he refused to answer or look at me. His religion forbade him to make eye contact with women.

Despite being in custody, he had no reservations in narrating what he had done in the previous two days in the Valley. He was fortunate, he said, that Allah had chosen him for what he called an Islamic duty and his only regret was that he had been captured and not killed. Had he been tortured, I asked? Driven by rage – he broke his own rule – and looking me straight in the eye, said sarcastically, 'No, the army has been showering me with petals.'

Azhar spent five years in a jail in Jammu before he was released in exchange for passengers aboard IC 814, the Air India flight that had been hijacked on Christmas Eve, 1999, from Kathmandu and finally taken to Kandahar where the Taliban were in power. He was flown to freedom by the Indian government, then headed by A. B. Vajpayee. Jaswant Singh, the then minister of external affairs travelled in the same plane in which Azhar and two other, equally dreaded terrorists were being flown to Kandahar.

Azhar's arrest and release were important milestones in my own understanding of how terrorist networks operate; how valuable they are to their handlers in Pakistan. The ISI's hand was guiding not just Azhar and his army, but the Taliban too. I also understood their worldview of women; and their ability to bring nations to the precipice of war.

After he landed in Kandahar where the Taliban greeted him and sped him away in a convoy, he clearly already had plans. His eyes were set on India and he soon announced the formation of the Jaish-e-Mohammed (JeM, or army of the prophet), in 2000.

The JeM literally exploded in front of the Jammu and Kashmir assembly, not long after Azhar's release. A year later, the state saw its first suicide bombing – an act in which men are willing to convert their bodies into missiles. The attack took a heavy toll, killing 39 people.

More recently, on 22 April 2025, terrorists walked out of the woods in Pahalgam and killed 25 tourists and a local horseman. Blood was spilled once again on Kashmir's soil. The terrorists had aimed their guns not just at Hindu tourists – and they did so after determining their religion – but also to provoke a dangerous communal conflagration. The killings in Pahalgam were different from the attack on 14 February 2019, when a JeM suicide bomber blew up a convoy of trucks carrying Central Relief Police Force (CRPF) troopers in Kashmir's Pulwama. As many as 40 were killed.

Soon after the Pulwama attack, the Narendra Modi government re-drew the security matrix by conducting air strikes deep into Pakistani territory in Balakot, where the JeM runs a training camp. It did the same after the Pahalgam attack through Operation Sindoor. An intense tit for tat military exchange of drones and missiles brought both countries to the precipice of war in May 2025.

Terrorism has changed. India's response to terrorism, too, has changed, and I've had the chance to study the seismic shifts from close quarters. I've been witness to the new red lines being drawn by the Modi government, who authorized the defence forces to aim their missiles at the headquarters of the Lashkar-e-Taiba (LeT) in Muridke, on the outskirts of Lahore, and at the JeM headquarter in Bahawalpur, in the heart of Pakistan's Punjab. On 7 May 2025, when images of the destruction at Muridke were flashed on television screens, my mind was immediately flooded with memories of my trips to the LeT headquarter. I remain the only Indian journalist to have walked into the heavily guarded complex.

One conflict zone took me to another and along the way, I also got a glimpse of how intelligence agencies work.

Intelligence agencies keep an eye not just on insurgents and politicians but also on each other. Research and Analysis Wing (R&AW) wants to know what the Intelligence Bureau (IB) is up to and the IB is curious about what information the 'sister agency' is gathering. In Kashmir, I was often asked whether I'd been to the 'neighbourhood'. The office-cum-residences of both agencies are only a few buildings away from each other.

The competitive streak also extended to the different security and paramilitary forces that are a part of the counter-insurgency grid. Each force, be it the army, the BSF, and the local police would try and get militants to surrender. Numbers mattered. I remember getting access to a group of surrendered militants who complained that they had been beaten up by members of one of the above mentioned forces because they had not surrendered to them but to another agency.

The surrendered militants soon became a potent force and were brazenly used by the army to counter the pro-Pakistan Hizbul Mujahideen (HM). Internecine warfare added a new set of guns. The local population was now caught between three sets of players: the terrorists, the surrendered militia, and the armed forces.

Fault lines birth separate sets of actors, both villainous and heroic. I have had the occasion to meet them all and gain perspectives. My work – and my gender – have helped me understand how to navigate landmines, personal and professional. Being a woman helped me gain access to homes and families willing to pour their hearts out.

Journalists are students of contemporary history. I definitely consider myself to be one. I am fortunate to have crisscrossed from Punjab to Kashmir, Pakistan to Afghanistan. I've seen the transition of the Babri Masjid into a Ram Temple.

I am privileged to have had rare insights into how militant minds work; how soldiers brave hostility from amongst their own people and how they lay down their lives. I witnessed their raw courage in Kargil's frigid heights when India was forced to wage a short but sharp war in the barren mountains in 1999.

I am privileged, also, to have been given permission to visit Muzaffarabad, the capital of what India calls 'Pakistan occupied Kashmir' (POK). The chance to breach the armed gates of the Lashkar headquarters in Muridke, barely two weeks after the dastardly 26/11 attacks in Mumbai, India's financial nerve centre, remains one of my most coveted assignments. As does the access I got to underworld don, Chhota Rajan, who is now lodged in the safe confines of Delhi's Tihar jail.

I have witnessed how journalism has evolved, how my own country has transformed.

As a young reporter in Chandigarh, I did not even have a typewriter. I remember handwriting my stories and taking a rickshaw to the post office, where a friendly telex operator would help send my reports to the telex machine in Delhi's *Sunday Observer* office. The one message I did not want Delhi's telex operator to convey was simply this: 'garbled garbled'. The story, punched onto a thin strip of white paper, had to then be transmitted again.

No phones, no fax machines, no WhatsApp groups, no Google alerts. It was journalism at its most challenging, frustrating but purest best. A far cry from today's breaking news, screaming anchors, twitter trolls and for so many – the giddy rush of counting likes, reposts, and quote tweets.

Crosschecking facts entailed repeated trips to government offices where officials were always busy in meetings. Now, each time I do a Google search, I stare in sheer wonderment. So trained are we in the art of fact checking, journalists of my generation are not content with the first item Google throws up.

Check once, check twice, check thrice.

As I look back on four decades of work, I feel compelled to tell – and retell – some of my most iconic assignments. Each story has left an indelible impression that mirrors my journey. Each story factors in my personal experience whilst also recording events and battles – many epochal – for the sheer depiction of how governments – both at the state-level and at the Centre have responded to threats and challenges.

The responses – honed and chiselled at times and plain blunderous in some instances – have shaped India and its march through the decades.

My chapters detail slices of contemporary history. The stories are by no means an encapsulation of everything that the country has seen.

The book is about what I have seen; about what I have witnessed. I am fortunate to have had the chance of recording some of the seismic shifts. Interestingly, while a lot has changed in the last forty years of my work life, there are several issues that continue to simmer. They continue to challenge. They beckon attention.

My first visit to Afghanistan was in 1996, when the Taliban first captured Kabul and decorated their Kalashnikovs with roses. They are back in power, as I write this book. They were reluctant to talk to a woman then and they will definitely not speak with me now. Their ideology remains unchanged. Their edicts for women are as suffocating today as they were in 1996. In fact, they are worse. Afghanistan is full of Masood Azhars who will not look women in the eye, or let them out to study and work. They are now not even allowed to pray out aloud.

To end, I'll cite just one more example. The aspiration of some youth to undertake dangerous, often perilous journeys to make it to Western shores, measures equally, if not higher, on the Richter scale. The ambition to better one's life – by selling one's fortune – continues to burn with equal zeal.

My first sting operation in Belgium exposed how illegal immigrants were being transported to the United Kingdom in lorries. The operation was done while on a scholarship to London. In 1994, a television channel hired me and a colleague, also a part of the Chevening scholarship programme. The news channel needed journalists who could speak Hindi and Punjabi. The languages helped us penetrate the vast network of agents. My colleague and I posed as a couple who wanted to cross the channel from Belgium into the United Kingdom. 2024 exposed how 'donkey flights' were carrying immigrants hoping to cross the border from Nicaragua into the US. The modus operandi has changed and the costs are higher. The agents I met in Brussels charged £2,000 British pounds. The agents in Punjab, Haryana, and Gujarat are now billing their clients ₹40 to 60 lakhs (£40,000–57,000).

None of the journalistic assignments have been easy. Each one that I have chosen to detail have been risk-laden but eye-opening. They've quenched the thirst for first-hand knowledge and fed the hunger for a greater understanding of India's ground realities, some bitter, others tragic and some that have courage stamped all over them.

For the most part of my 40 years, I have been a print journalist, except for a two-year stint in television. I tried my hand at television after having spent a quarter century in print and for me at least, the medium appeared shallow. It did not allow me the space or the time to pursue and dig out stories. I am a passionate consumer of news – you could even call me a news junkie – but I was happier being a byline. I did not – and still do not – want my face to be my calling card.

I'm not sure why – and I do not protest – but I'm still sometimes referred to as 'Mr Baweja'. I'm often mistaken to be a man. I know so from the comments section that online pieces now afford.

In my words – and through my experience – here are some steps in my life through conflict.

The Punjab Battlefield and the Shadow of Khalistan

One evening in 1987, months before Operation Black Thunder, I was granted an interview with Jagir Singh in room number 14. The room also served as 'Daftar (office) Khalistan' and Jagir Singh of the Panthic Committee was both feared and dreaded. We sat on the floor, face to face, and he patiently answered my questions, justifying the call for Khalistan.

The Golden Temple, set in the midst of the serene waters of the holy sarovar (reservoir), glistened in the sharp afternoon sun. Its mesmerizing beauty and reverence, had for long borne mute testimony to its own defiling. The sanctum sanctorum in the Harmandir Sahib continued to echo to the sweet, lyrical, sounds of kirtan, but all around it, the place of worship, most sacred to the Sikhs, was slowly being weaponized and fortified.

The Akal Takht, the highest seat of temporal power, lay straight across the Harmandir Sahib. It is here that the Granth Sahib, the holy book, is brought every night to rest. It was also where Jarnail Singh Bhindranwale, the Sikh preacher-turned zealot, grew to command a formidable band of well-armed terrorists. He made the Akal Takht his home, assuming perhaps, that this was one address no one in the Indian government would dare attack.

No one dared, until 1984, a year that stands out for being one of the most catastrophic in contemporary history.

1984 saw the storming of the Golden Temple through an operation called Blue Star. It also bore witness to the assassination of a sitting prime minister, Indira Gandhi, and the murderous assaults on innocent Sikhs across India. The carnage, triggered by calls for revenge, left close to 3,000 dead in the national capital, under the very nose of the Congress government. Flesh-hungry mobs had a free run of the streets. Armed with iron rods and petrol bottles, they pummelled and killed without fear.

A few months before the stench of death wafted through Delhi's alleys, Indira Gandhi had given the go-ahead to the Indian Army for an all-out operation against Bhindranwale. The rise of the 'Sant', as Bhindranwale was called, was as terrifying as it was meteoric.

He and his band of blind followers had stamped their power through gruesome killings of both Sikhs and Hindus. The Hindus, in particular, had been targeted through a series of massacres. Hindu passengers were made to get off buses and as they lined up on the side of a road, they were riddled with bullets, till they fell in a heap. The zealot who grew in stature and went beyond being just a preacher at the Damdami Taksal seminary in Chowk Mehta, near Amritsar, spread terror by singularly aiming his guns at the Hindu community.

On the night of 5 October 1983, a group of turbaned terrorists hijacked a bus in Kapurthala, and forced six Hindu passengers out. They lay dead in a matter of minutes. The massacre stood out for its savagery. It was also an attack that forced Prime Minister Indira Gandhi's hand. She decided it was time to place the state under President's rule. Chief Minister Darbara Singh, who spoke openly against Bhindranwale was made the sacrificial goat.

Political misadventures – crafted with electoral strategies as their core – don't always produce intended results; they flame fires that cannot be controlled. Indira Gandhi and her then home minister, Gaini Zail Singh – who later went on to become the president of India – had allowed Bhindranwale to grow in stature. They thought he would be the perfect foil against the Akali Dal which held political sway over Punjab.

It was during those terrifying times that I started making forays into the battlefield of Punjab.

It became clear in 1981 that the political players, including those from the Congress and the Akali Dal, were fanning flames that would be difficult to control. The Congress gave Bhindranwale a free run in the hope that he would outshadow the Akali Dal. The Akalis, however, had no choice but to support the 'Sant' and his army. Not doing that would weaken them politically. Their own vote bank, comprising the peasantry, was enamoured by Bhindranwale and totally taken in by the fervour with which he ignited the claim that Sikhism was under threat. The resistance from the Akalis was minimal.

There were several windows of opportunity to control the fire but politics and politicians came in the way of conflict resolution. One such window of opportunity presented itself in 1981 after the killing of Lala Jagat Narain, a high-profile editor, but it was squandered. The death knell came soon after.

Bhindranwale was released within a month of being arrested for the killing of Jagat Narain, the founder-editor of one of Punjab's most widely read Hindi newspapers, *Punjab Kesari* on 9 September 1981. Within four days of Narain's brutal killing, All India Radio announced that a warrant had been issued to arrest Bhindranwale, who at the time, was addressing a congregation in Chando Kalan, Haryana. By the time the police arrived here, the 'Sant' had already fled and reached the gurdwara at Chowk Mehta, where he had learnt his scriptures. His followers gathered in large numbers to prevent him from being arrested. He agreed to hand himself over, but on his own terms. The police allowed him to address a congregation before he surrendered. He whipped up a frenzy before being escorted to jail. His supporters retaliated by opening fire. Eleven casualties were reported in the firing between the police and Bhindranwale's armed supporters. The 'Sant' spent less than a month in Ferozepur jail where he insisted on being guarded and served food only by Sikhs with long beards.

The 'Sant' was in jail but Delhi was still playing political games. On 14 October, Zail Singh informed Parliament that there was no evidence to link Bhindranwale to the chilling murder of Lala Jagat Narain. Once free, Bhindranwale went to Delhi to celebrate. He was accompanied by close to a hundred supporters who openly brandished their weapons. Home Minister Zail Singh made no attempt to rearrest him; nor did Prime Minister Indira Gandhi. The senior-most politicians of the country catapulted Bhindranwale into a hero. The genie was now out of the bottle.

Bhindranwale, a village preacher from Moga, who had come to Amritsar via the Damdami Taksal, knew exactly when to turn the heat on. After his return from Delhi, he moved into the Golden Temple complex. The holy precincts of Sikhism's most sacred shrine were soon converted into a military fortress. Arms were being brought in right under the nose of the local police. The judiciary too was affected.

I remember judges unwilling to hear bail applications of arrested terrorists, unless they were brought in blindfolded. The capitulation of the state was evident. Harchand Singh Longowal, president of the Akali Dal was clearly uncomfortable with the 'Sant's' growing might but was too timid to take him on. The negotiations between the Akalis and the central government did not yield political dividend. The least they expected was for Chandigarh to be declared the capital of Punjab, but Indira Gandhi vacillated between choosing to conclude her negotiations with the Akalis and the inevitable option of smoking the 'Sant' out of his bastion.

Captain Amarinder Singh, an articulate, well-connected Congress MP, also a descendent of Patiala's royal family, is a living witness to Mrs Gandhi's many vacillations. In 1982, she sent for him and asked him if he knew Bhindranwale and Longowal. She was keen on negotiating with both and Amarinder said that while he knew Longowal, because he was from the village next to his mother's, he had never met Bhindranwale. The meeting concluded with Mrs Gandhi asking him to find a way of connecting with the 'Sant', who, by then, was getting shriller.

'I approached Bhindranwale through SSP, Punjab Police, Simranjit Singh Mann. With Simranjit's father, S. Joginder Singh Mann and my brother Malwinder, I went to Rode village and met Bhindranwale. I told him I had come on Indira Gandhi's behalf, to see how we can take the parleys forward. He said he was willing to speak to the government,' Amarinder told me in an exclusive interview for this book in March 2025.

Amarinder met the man who was holding Punjab – and New Delhi – hostage, several times. 'We held several secret meetings at a factory located in a village called Channo on the Patiala-Sangrur border. Bhindranwale would come in a cavalcade of buses. He was cautious. I never knew which bus he would emerge from.'

Indira Gandhi used Amarinder, who in turn worked closely with S. Ravi Inder Singh of the Akali Dal, his personal friend and then Speaker of the Punjab assembly, to discuss several demands the Akalis were making under the Anandpur Sahib Resolution. The demands included making Chandigarh the capital of Punjab. It also included a water-sharing agreement to address the grievance that Punjab had to feed Haryana's water demands. The other demands were the live broadcast of kirtan from the Golden Temple and granting Amritsar the status of a 'holy city'.

Amarinder kept briefing the committee set up by Mrs Gandhi. The committee included three senior cabinet ministers: P. C. Sethi, R. Venkataraman, and P. Shiv Shankar. Negotiations were being held at several levels and Amarinder was central to all. He was talking to Bhindranwale and also briefing the cabinet ministers who were holding talks with senior Akali leaders including Prakash Singh Badal, Harchand Singh Longowal, Balwant Singh; the Shiromani Gurdwara Prabandhak Committee (SGPC) president, Gurcharan Singh Tohra; and Surjeet Singh Barnala.

In addition, he was working closely with a committee of secretaries looking into the issue, which included Mrs Gandhi's Principal Secretary Dr P. C. Alexander, the Cabinet Secretary C. R. Krishnaswami Rao Sahib, and the Home Secretary T. N. Chaturvedi.

The parleys spanned two years, beginning in 1982 and continuing till four months before the army marched into the Golden Temple. Amarinder revealed several crucial details to me in the course of our lunch meeting in March 2025. 'Indira Gandhi wanted her son, Rajiv Gandhi to meet Bhindranwale and I set up the meeting twice. The first time [in 1982], I picked up Rajiv and we drove to the Safdarjung airport where a special aircraft was to fly us to the Ambala Air Force station, where Bhindranwale was already waiting for us. We were recalled before we could reach the airstrip. I had to make up a story and told Bhindranwale that we couldn't make it because the plane had developed a technical snag.'

Within a fortnight, Amarinder picked up Rajiv Gandhi

again. They were to, once again, go to the Ambala Air Force station where Bhindranwale had already reached. This time, Amarinder was sure they would make it for the meeting. They were airborne, and on their way, but the pilot got a radio message asking him to return. Why was the second meeting also aborted? 'Mrs Gandhi was told by Punjab Chief Minister Darbara Singh that there were plans to lay an ambush and that her son, Rajiv would be killed,' Amarinder told me. 'How do you know?' I asked him and his reply was simple: Rajiv had shared the information with him. Indira had lost her younger son Sanjay Gandhi in an air crash and was scared of losing Rajiv too. Amarinder also suspects that Darbara Singh, who had favoured Bhindranwale's arrest, wanted to get back to his bête noire, Zail Singh and that he was the one who told Mrs Gandhi to not let her son walk into the trap.

Political rivalries add to conflict. Political games of one-upmanship make conflict murkier.

Indira Gandhi's prevarications did not help the Akalis counter Bhindranwale, who continued to inflame passions. The secret parleys continued till the very last minute and included a meeting in which Rajiv Gandhi met Badal and Tohra. Once again, Amarinder was the one who brought the two sides together. According to Amarinder, 'Mrs Gandhi had agreed to transfer Chandigarh to Punjab and had also committed to a water-sharing formula [with Haryana and Rajasthan]. The terms of the agreement were to be announced a day before her birthday on 19 November, but she reneged after Bhajan Lal, chief minister of Haryana and Shiv Charan Mathur, chief minister of

Rajasthan, got wind of the impending announcement and threatened to resign.'

The 'Sant' who had been given freedom from arrest by the Congress soon became a Frankenstein monster. He openly mocked Indira Gandhi, after being let down twice by Rajiv Gandhi. He also knew that he had reduced the Akali Dal – and in turn, the SGPC ostensibly in charge of running the Golden Temple complex – to mere dummies. Stalwarts like Longowal, who headed the Akali Dal and Tohra, who held sway over the SGPC, were just pawns on a chessboard.

By this time Bhindranwale had by his side, a fine military mind and a legendary officer called Major General Shabeg Singh.

Shabeg Singh had gone on to worship Bhindranwale after he was dismissed from service just one day before he was to retire. He fought to clear the charges levelled against him and did so successfully, but by then, a deep sense of humiliation and betrayal took him closer to the belief that he had been discriminated against only because he was a Sikh. Before the ignominious dismissal, Shabeg had been celebrated for having played a decisive role in the 1971 war, by training the Mukti Bahini. That was the year Bangladesh was liberated. It was a high point in Mrs Gandhi's premiership and she earned the title of 'Durga'.

History is not always kind to those who help script it. An interview given by Beant Singh, Shabeg's brother, to *The Times of India* in December 2021, helped shed light on just how humiliated the war hero felt when he was dismissed from service without a court martial. Shabeg, busy providing training in guerilla warfare to the Mukti Bahini, could not find the time to attend his own brother's wedding. Stating that his brother was patriotic to the core, Beant said that Shabeg didn't think twice about cutting his hair to train the Mukti Bahini, the resistance force drawn from within the ranks of Bangladesh's military force. Known as S. Beg amongst the resistance force, the Major General crossed the line – literally so – to join Bhindranwale to avenge the deep sense of humiliation he felt. Shabeg had won his cases in court but wanted to, according to his brother, 'cause much more financial damage than the central government had caused him by depriving him of his retirement benefits.'

Military advisor to Bhindranwale, Shabeg Singh was instrumental in fortifying the Golden Temple, sandbagging it and deciding exactly where the 'Sant's' troops would be positioned. Every tower, crevice, and manhole had been made battle ready.

The face-off between Bhindranwale's army and the Indian Army was inevitable. Indira Gandhi had no option – after last ditch efforts at a negotiated settlement failed – largely because she lacked the nerve to go ahead with it. She was forced to fight a battle that would be her last.

It was, in fact, clear on 25 April 1983 that the battle was beyond the scope of the local police. Avtar Singh Atwal, deputy inspector general (DIG), Punjab Police, had gone to the Golden Temple to offer prayers. As he left the compound that day, the 40-year-old senior police officer was shot dead at the main entrance of the temple at 11 a.m.

He was holding the *karha prashad* in his hand when he died. His body lay on the steps, while the killers strolled back into their fortified bastion.

Atwal's body lay at the entrance of the Golden Temple for several hours. His driver and security officials had fled and so had other policemen deployed in the vicinity. The terrorists had killed the DIG, sending a chilling message that they had succeeded in sinking the panic-stricken administration into a policy paralysis. The already delicate situation in Punjab was to take a turn for the worse.

Darbara Singh was still the chief minister when Atwal was killed. He was expressly told by his bosses in New Delhi to not send the police force into the Golden Temple. Mrs Gandhi was aware of the sensitivities of sending uniformed personnel into what the Sikhs perceive to be their Vatican. Punjab slid quickly into the morass of violence between Atwal's killing and the proclamation of President's rule that saw Darbara Singh's tenure come to an end on 6 June 1983.

Exactly a year later, Indira Gandhi's army was rolling its tanks into the Golden Temple to silence the 'Sant' she had lent a halo to. It would not be wrong to say 'Indira Gandhi's army' because the Supreme Commander was kept in the dark about the orders she had given to the army. Zail Singh, by then, was the president of India. He had no inkling about Operation Blue Star. He confirmed this in his memoirs.

Several books have recounted the details of Operation Blue Star, including *The Punjab Story*, published by Roli Books. An anthology, the chapter by Subhash Kirpekar has excerpts from the last interview given by Bhindranwale on 3 June 1984. Kirpekar, who reported for *The Times of India*, had gone to the Golden Temple, like hundreds of other pilgrims, that same day, to commemorate the martyrdom of Guru Arjan Dev.

The last interview makes for foreboding reading. It was recorded hours before a lethal blow was to be dealt, not just to the Golden Temple, but to Punjab and the Sikh psyche. The exchange of sporadic fire had begun and the army was at the temple's vicinity.

Q What do you think of the army takeover in Punjab?

A It is done to suppress the Sikhs. But the government will not succeed. Previous regimes have also never succeeded in such efforts.

Q Do you believe that the army will enter the Golden Temple?

A No, the army will hang around this place like the CRPF and BSF have done for the last two years. Except truth and justice, nothing but evil is expected of this government. It is premature to say anything about the timing of the entry [of the army] and its possible impact. Their behaviour and intentions will be known in a few days.

Q Will you not be outnumbered by the army which has superior weapons too?

A Sheep always outnumber the lions. But one lion can take care of a thousand sheep. When the lion sleeps, the birds chirp. When it awakes, the birds fly away.

Q Did you listen to the prime minister's speech yesterday?

A No, there is no need to; it is not important.

Q Do you support the creation of Khalistan?

A I never opposed it; nor have I supported it [looks at me rather jubilantly to see if I am impressed by his taciturn reply].

Q But is it your contention that the Sikhs cannot live in India?

A Yes. They can neither live in nor with India. If treated as equals, it may be possible. But frankly speaking, I don't think that is possible.

Q What can be done to stop the slayings of people, including journalists, in Punjab?

A [Raising one eyebrow] Ask those who are responsible for it.

Q If some harm were to befall you, who would be your successor?

A [With a quizzical look in his eyes] Time will tell. I can't name anyone. It is not an elective post. I think whosoever attains the status of God will come up as my successor.

Q Do you fear death?

A [Eyes nearly blazing with anger] He is not a Sikh who fears death and he who fears death is not a Sikh.

Bhindranwale then introduced his military advisor, Shabeg Singh to Kirpekar. On being asked how soon he expected the army operation to start, Shabeg's reply was terse. 'Maybe tonight,' he said.

That evening, the foreboding evening of 5 June, as the sun set on Amritsar, the Golden Temple was glinting in the fading light. It glowed for a few more hours before the electricity supply to the city was cut off. The shadows had lengthened.

The army was at the doorsteps of Sikhism's holiest shrine.

Both sides were battle-ready. One side was being commandeered by Major General Kuldeep Singh Brar. His division had been called in from Meerut. The other side, who had fortified the complex, was being commandeered by Shabeg Singh. Ironically, they had fought together in 1971, for the liberation of Bangladesh. Both had earned their spurs; Brar as a Colonel and Shabeg as a Brigadier.

In June 1984, Shabeg found himself in direct battle with Brar, one of the officers he had trained at the Indian Military Academy in Dehradun.

Punjab – and India's – watershed moment was upon it.

Brar's brief was given to him in no uncertain terms, by his boss, Lieutenant General K. Sundarji, heading the Western Command on the outskirts of Chandigarh, in Chandi Mandir. Mrs Gandhi had conveyed her concerns to the then army chief, General A. S. Vaidya: no bullets were to be fired in the direction of the Harmandir Sahib or towards the Akal Takht. The terms of Operation Blue Star were clear; the army was expected to flush out Bhindranwale and his men – dead or alive – without firing a single shot in the direction of the sanctum sanctorum.

Terrorists don't play by rule books. On the night of 5 June 1984, the Indian Army realized that they too could not stick to the redlines dictated by Mrs Gandhi's government. The chasm between what was desired and what actually transpired was miles apart. It would eventually widen the gulf between Punjab and Delhi; between the Sikh community and the Congress party.

Major General Brar has shared details of Operation Blue Star with several journalists, including me. (He later wrote a book on the operation, titled *Operation Blue Star: The True Story*.) His account of what he shared with me is gripping.

'That morning before we went in, I addressed all the troops. I went from battalion to battalion starting at six o'clock in the morning. They didn't know what was going to happen,' he told me, continuing, 'I told the troops that tonight we would be going in for an operation inside the Golden Temple. Don't talk about it as it's a secret. I want you to understand that it is an operation against our own people who have gone astray. Therefore, it's not that we are disrespecting the holiness of the shrine. The shrine is no longer holy. It has already been defiled.'

As a Sikh himself – though clean shaven – he was aware of the sensitivities of the situation. He communicated that by saying, 'If any of you don't want to go in because of religious sentiment, please stand up. I can assure you that you will not be asked to take part in the operation and no action will be taken against you.'

Not all troops who were sent in, were Sikh. Brar, Commander 9 Division, continued to speak to all of them, reminding them that when they joined the forces, 'We swore that regardless of caste, creed, religion, we are

Indians, and our constitutional duty is to look after the independence and integrity of India.... We have been given an order and we have to carry it out, but in spite of that, if you are emotionally disturbed, you don't have to go inside...,' he reiterated.

Brar briefed battalion after battalion along the same lines. When he reached the third battalion, a Sikh officer, Captain Jasbir Singh Raina, got up, and Brar remembers saying, 'Don't worry, son. You don't have to go in.' Raina, apparently replied, saying, 'Sir, you misunderstood me. I want to be the first one to go in. I want to get to the Akal Takht and I want to get Bhindranwale.' Earlier, Raina had risked going into the temple in civilian clothes to get an assessment of how the temple had been fortified.

'You're a very brave officer. I salute you,' Brar said, deciding that Raina's platoon would be the first to enter the Golden Temple.

It was.

What ensued was something neither Brar nor anyone – above or below the chain – had anticipated. The platoon came under heavy machine gun fire. Bhindranwale's trained army was lying in wait and the sound of heavy fire rent the air. Raina had multiple gunshots on both legs. Brar told Raina's commanding officer, Colonel Israr Khan, to evacuate him immediately, but Raina used his elbows to keep inching towards the Akal Takht.

Brar knew then, that the plan to enter the temple and swim across the sarovar towards the Harmandir Sahib had failed. The militants holed up inside the complex had a clear view of the incoming troops and they were not going to give up. The troops were pinned at the parikrama that circumambulates the sarovar.

The ferocity of the fightback had not been anticipated. Under Shabeg's military guidance, the terrorists were firing from little holes drilled into walls, without giving away their positions.

Heavy army casualties led to a change of plan. The operation had to be concluded before day break. All hell had broken loose and the clock was ticking. The night, even though moonlit, was the only camouflage.

In the end, as we know from several documented accounts, the army had to bring in an armoured personnel carrier (APC) and drive in tanks that had already been positioned around the Golden Temple complex.

The army had to set aside the two main preconditions dictated by the political masters in New Delhi. It could not prevent the Harmandir Sahib from being pierced by bullets, nor could the operation conclude without the Akal Takht being pulverized. The main gun of the tank had to fire at least 20 rounds – some accounts peg the figure at 60 – to silence the terrorists holed up inside the Akal Takht.

Sikhism's highest seat of temporal power was pummelled and at least 200 bullet marks pockmarked the golden sheath of the sanctum sanctorum. One bullet had also pierced the Granth Sahib, the holy book, inside the Harmandir Sahib. The only rule Bhindranwale and his band of followers had not traversed was to make the Harmandir Sahib their hiding hole. Even the zealots acknowledged the sanctity of the Sikh sanctorum.

It was well into the morning of 6 June that the guns

were finally silenced. Two days later, the country's first Sikh head of state, President of India, Giani Zail Singh visited the complex, when he was shot at by a sniper. The army was still moving from room to room, looking for arms, ammunition, and explosives.

Had Bhindranwale died or had he escaped through a passage behind the Akal Takht? The question was soon answered when his body was identified by his cousin, who ironically, was a junior commissioned officer (JCO) in the Indian Army. Shabeg's body too, was found.

The body of Bhindranwale, the preacher who had created a state within a state was laid out on a slab of ice, as the administration prepared for the cremation. The 'Sant' who had stirred the war cry for Khalistan, a separate state, had ironically not travelled the distance to actually announce it. In all his interviews, his ambivalent reply always was, 'I have never opposed it, nor have I supported it.'

Cremating the dead was an arduous task. The bodies had begun rotting in the unforgiving June heat. The army kept finding more bodies as they went from room to room along the parikrama. The army also rescued frightened women and children, who were hiding in the buildings at the back, in the Serai block, where Longowal and Tohra were holed up, all through the operation, unsure whether they would survive the onslaught.

The psychological blow rendered by the use of tanks within the Golden Temple complex was the opening of a new chapter in the politics of Punjab – and the country.

The Sikh psyche was badly bruised and became all

too apparent with the resignations of senior IAS and IPS officers. Simranjit Singh Mann, who Amarinder had approached, was amongst the first to resign. Close to 3,000 army men also deserted the ranks in a bid to reach Amritsar. They wanted to see the extent to which their 'Vatican' had been destroyed. The mutiny, born out of a lethal mix of high emotions fuelled by wild rumours, led to armed Sikh soldiers abandoning the units where they were posted.

Reports of soldiers abandoning their posts led to tense moments. For the first time since 1947, tanks and machine guns were deployed at Amritsar's borders. The city had to be sealed. The army leadership in the city quickly turned the turrets of the tanks – earlier facing the Golden Temple – towards points from where the city of Amritsar could be accessed. Desertions are serious business. They added not just to army leadership's tensions but to civil strife and came as a pointed reminder of just how deep the wound was. The deserters were marching from states as far away as Rajasthan and Bihar. Major General Brar, who led the operation, later wrote in his book, *Operation Blue Star: The True Story*: 'The revolts could easily have been controlled but for a serious and glaring failure of commands in those units and commands where they surfaced. Military leaders, particularly at senior levels, failed to take Sikh troops into confidence....' By the time the book hit the stands, Brar was a Lieutenant General.

The desertion was not an ordinary law and order aberration. As per army records, as many as 49 deserters were killed at various roadblocks en route to Amritsar and 19 were reported missing. The remaining (2,900 had deserted) were arrested and discharged from the army. A few years later, as a part of a healing touch policy, the families of those killed and those missing were awarded a compensation of ₹1 lakh each.

Back in Amritsar, the army was asked not to vacate the Golden Temple in a hurry after Blue Star. They were needed to maintain security and ensure that militants did not return with their guns. Mrs Gandhi asked the army to stay, also because she did not want photographs of the heavily-damaged Akal Takht to stir passions, but it was too late. Rumours are a lethal weapon and the army and the administration had a tough time controlling the hordes of people marching towards Amritsar, where entry into the Golden Temple was restricted. A prominent Sikh minister in the Union Cabinet, Buta Singh was tasked to get the Akal Takht repaired. He chose a Nihang Sikh named Santa Singh. The decision was taken quickly because the Akalis wanted to preserve and showcase the damaged Akal Takht as a symbol of the Indian Army's aggression.

When I entered the Golden Temple complex for the first time, a few weeks after Operation Blue Star had concluded, I held my breath. The destruction was on full display. The few pilgrims who had gained access – through organized entries – were weeping inconsolably, caressing the walls of the complex like they would the cheeks of a baby. Others were kissing the parikrama, tears rolling down their eyes. The memory is still vivid four decades later. Women, old and young, were putting pieces of debris into bags to take home as a reminder of the attack on their faith.

Santa Singh and his followers, dressed in flowing blue robes were at work at the Akal Takht. They would begin work only after imbibing milk boiled with marijuana – a ritual that caused a lot of consternation because the faithful believe that the Gurus had banned all forms of intoxication.

The hurry to present a repaired Akal Takht was not the only problem. In the months after Operation Blue Star, the army was told to hunt down militants who may have escaped. Code-named Operation Woodrose, the exercise was meant to 'prevent the outbreak of widespread public protest' but it only alienated the Sikh community further. If the aim was to comb the countryside and hunt down militants, it did not succeed.

Quite like the army deserters, there were many amongst the ranks of the police who were feeling outraged. Two amongst them were posted as Prime Minister Indira Gandhi's guards. On the morning of 31 October 1984 – five months after tanks had barrelled the Golden Temple complex – Beant Singh and Satwant Singh took aim at the prime minister of India as she emerged from her residence into the lawn. Her personal secretary, R. K. Dhawan, couldn't believe what he was witnessing as she fell to the ground. No ambulance was available at the prime minister's residence. Dhawan and Sonia Gandhi, her daughter-in-law, bundled her into an ambassador car and drove straight to All India Institute of Medical Sciences. By the time she was officially declared dead, a huge crowd had started gathering outside the hospital.

The hospital lay en route between my father's office

and our home. That day – when he was forced to take off his turban to ensure he stayed alive – was a day when memories were etched, not just for us as a family, but for thousands of others. For the next three days, fires raged in several colonies of Delhi as Sikh after Sikh was dragged out and killed in one of the most horrific carnages independent India has seen. In my introduction to this book, I have written about how I started to become aware of my Sikh identity only after the 1984 violence. While searching through the debris of my emotional journey, I must also add that while I understood why the community felt injured and assaulted by the army action within the precincts of the Golden Temple complex, I did not feel religiously stirred. I understood early in my life, through conflict, that terrorists know they're signing their own death warrants, the minute they choose to pick up a gun.

The wound – irrespective of how I felt – was deep and it manifested itself in violent ways. Two years after Blue Star, on 10 August 1986, armed motorcycle assailants shot and killed former army chief, General A. S. Vaidya in Pune. The assault on the holiest Sikh shrine – necessitated by political prevarication – had far-reaching consequences and the state stayed in its pincer hold.

Operation Blue Star had killed Bhindranwale but given birth to terrorists in the hundreds. Elections were held in Punjab in September 1985 and though the Akali Dal won a decisive victory, they were unable to defuse the inflamed passions under Chief Minister Surjit Singh Barnala. His government announced several measures, including financial packages for victims of terrorism and rehabilitation schemes for the army deserters, but failed to rein in the radicals.

In early 1986, I packed a suitcase and moved to Chandigarh as a correspondent for *The Sunday Observer*. Punjab was a busy beat and several pan-India and international organizations had offices headquartered in the state. There was seldom a day when a Punjab story did not appear on the front pages of newspapers. *The Sunday Observer* was an important newspaper. It was India's first Sunday broadsheet and while Vinod Mehta worked his editorial magic, Rekha Khanna burnt the midnight oil. In charge of the paper's marketing, circulation, and production, she ensured, week after week, that the edition was available at newsstands across the country, as soon as copies rolled out of the printing press.

I was stationed in Chandigarh but made fortnightly trips to Amritsar. The Golden Temple was slowly being fortified again. Before I made Chandigarh my home for two years, I had also flown to Amritsar from Delhi in January 1986. Members belonging to the Damdami Taksal and the All India Sikh Students Federation (AISSF), both central to Bhindranwale's journey through violence, were back in the Golden Temple complex. Deeply upset over the facelift of the Akal Takht by Santa Singh, the two organizations decided it had to be torn down and rebuilt. Kar Seva, according to them, was the only answer to 'Sarkar Seva'.

On 26 January 1986, while the rest of the country was celebrating Republic Day, the Damdami Taksal and the AISSF gathered in front of the Akal Takht and organized a Sarbat Khalsa (a congregation of Sikhs). In what can only be described as a coup, they announced the removal of the official SGPC, a body elected to manage the gurdwaras and the community's religious affairs and announced the formation of a five-member Panthic Committee. Jasbir Singh Rode, Bhindranwale's nephew was appointed as the jathedar, or the head of the Akal Takht. The radicals were back. The radicals, in fact, did not allow the complex to slip out of their control after Blue Star. At one of the Sikh congregations, months after the bloody operation, I was rescued by Amarinder Singh, after there was a stampede-like situation. He was kind enough to literally pick me up before I was trampled and drive me back to the safety of my hotel. He quit the Congress after Blue Star. 'I had told Mrs Gandhi that I would leave if troops were sent into the shrine,' he told me, adding, 'I discovered that the army had gone in while playing golf at Naldehra, near Shimla. I went to meet Indira Gandhi and after making me wait, she said, "So you've resigned," and walked off. Rajiv heard me out and said, "It's your decision." He was more understanding.'

In 1986, I stood in front of the 'sarkari' Akal Takht as it was brought down by heavy machinery. The new, more militant SGPC now called the shots. It was clear that the state had lost control once again. Bhindranwale was being eulogized and the imprint of the terrorists was clearly visible, as the state slipped backwards and into an abyss.

The Hindus were back to being targets and Punjab was witness to more of the infamous bus massacres in which passengers belonging to one faith were lined up and mercilessly shot dead.

Khalistan had reared its head again. Bhindranwale, who often gave the call for Khalistan, never took steps towards formally announcing a separate state, for all the years that he had held sway. But on 29 April 1986, the Panthic Committee made the declaration for Khalistan at a well-attended press conference at the Golden Temple complex. Operation Blue Star had provided fuel for the open proclamation, though the announcement did not come with any geographical description. It was aimed, perhaps, at providing ideological ammunition.

In 1986, at the height of violence in Punjab, Julio Francis Ribeiro took over as the state's director general of police (DGP). He had also taken on the militants through a policy referred to as 'bullet for bullet'. Even as he tried to raise the flagging morale of the Punjab Police, the militants continued with their frenzied killings which led to a large number of Hindus fleeing their homes. The Sikh-Hindu ratio in the state was 58:42, when I was stationed there as a correspondent, but rural villages soon saw an exodus.

The Hindu-Sikh divide had sharpened after the carnage in Delhi following Mrs Gandhi's assassination. The two communities who were wholly integrated till the advent of Bhindranwale, now had their own reasons for feeling scared. Violence continued to wrack urban centres and rural swathes of Punjab. Posters asking Hindus to leave began to appear on village walls and several Hindu traders were targeted and killed. The targeted killings continued and July 1987 saw its worst, most bloody 24 hours, within the span of which, two horrific bus massacres took place.

On 6 July 1987, terrorists belonging to the Khalistan Commando Force, stopped a bus in the dead of night at Lalru, a town that separates Haryana from Punjab on the Grand Trunk Road. The bus, on its way to Rishikesh from Chandigarh, was hijacked and taken off the main highway, where soon, 38 Hindu passengers lay dead. The terrorists were in control and the police helpless spectators.

The very next day, on 7 July, Khalistani terrorists struck again and killed 34 Hindu passengers in Haryana's Fatehabad. I was in Chandigarh at the time and clearly remember a bus survivor recalling a terrorist aboard the Lalru bus, asking, 'Where is your Ribeiro now?' I took the question to Ribeiro himself – who I met often – and he said wryly, 'The police can only fight terrorism, not solve it. The bullet for bullet policy will continue.' By then, Barnala's government had been dismissed and Punjab had once again come under President's rule.

More troops were sent to Punjab but the scars worsened with the deployment of the CRPF. While the Punjab Police was seen as pro-Sikh, the paramilitary – dominated by non-Sikh troops drawn from several states – became a refuge for the Hindus.

At a village on the outskirts of Amritsar that I visited in 1986, I saw an urn containing the ashes of a young man. Fear had forced his Hindu family to flee before they could immerse their son's ashes. On the way back from the village I was stopped by two gun-wielding, strapping Sikh terrorists. On demanding – and hearing my name – they cautioned me with a frightening, 'Don't you see how the Sikhs are being treated? Have you forgotten your religion?

Focus on the atrocities against your own community.'

As I have recounted in the introduction, I identified myself as an Indian and not as a Sikh. The encounter with the two terrorists, who asked me to focus on 'my own community' reminded me of the fact that I had left the Air Force life – and a value system that was deeply secular – far behind and was well on my way into my own journey through conflict.

The 'khadkus' of Punjab were very different from the militants of Kashmir; especially the homegrown ones. I was lucky not to have become another statistic. They did not know that the anti-Sikh riots had stirred me emotionally but had not converted me into a regular practitioner of religion.

I did not tell them. They were beyond simple lessons of humanity. It was pointless telling them that religion needs devotional space in private chambers of the heart and ought not to be mixed with politics either, for it only ignites conflict.

Conflict is a great teacher and I learnt several lessons. The first lesson came early in my journey, during my posting in Punjab.

I was inside the Golden Temple complex through 1986 and 1988, when another operation, this time, called Black Thunder was put into motion. The complex had been overrun by militants once again and each room around the parikrama had become home to terrorists belonging to different groups.

One evening, I was granted an interview with Jagir Singh, a wanted terrorist and important member of the panthic committee, in room number 14. The room, which lay at one end of the parikrama, also served as 'Daftar (office) Khalistan' and Jagir Singh was both feared and dreaded. We sat on the floor, face to face, and he patiently answered my questions, justifying the call for Khalistan. There had been a lull in the vicious cycle of violence in the days preceding our interview and I asked him about it. He fell completely silent, as if lost in thought. 'Is that what you think?' he asked, after a long pause, adding, 'On some days you feel more hungry. It is not necessary to eat two chapattis for every meal.'

After the interview, I went to meet Satyapal Dang, a Communist Party of India (CPI) leader who was under heavy security because of his open criticism of how the terrorists were defiling a place of worship. While still with Dang, his phone rang and I could see anxiety writ large on his face. He put the phone down, looked at me and said, 'Eight people have been shot dead in Amritsar.' I froze. My mind travelled back to the 'chapatti' connotation. There may have been no connection between the question I had asked Jagir Singh and the killings, but I made a mental note: refrain from asking questions about the number of killings; focus on the sociology and psychology of violence instead.

Every conflict zone has its own sociological and psychological script. Each also has a different ideology that births diverse sets of terrorists. Punjab's militants were adept practitioners of violence in the name of religion. They were also deft at seeking the safe confines of gurdwaras to carry out nefarious agendas.

Unlike in 1984, the temple had now become the headquarter of several militant organizations, many in conflict with each other. All the rooms were occupied by members of groups such as the Khalistan Commando Force, Khalistan Liberation Force, and Babbar Khalsa, among others. Neither had a stand-out commander that matched the stature of the 'Sant', or his ability to unify the disparate groups.

Operation Black Thunder is often referred to as Black Thunder 1 and 2. The first, conducted between 30 April and 1 May 1986 was necessitated by the open declaration of Khalistan at a press conference on 29 April. Barnala was forced to agree to a flushing-out operation involving the local police and commandos drawn from the National Security Guards (NSG). Amarinder Singh, who was agriculture minister in Barnala's cabinet, resigned once again after finding out about troops entering the holy precincts from his tailor. Barnala, the chief minister was weakened after he was declared a 'tankhaiya' (outcast), by the SGPC.

My focus, however, is on the operation that commenced on 10 May 1988, because it helped lead Punjab out of the cycle of violence.

Operation Black Thunder 2 was conducted under the full glare of the international press. Punjab was under President's rule once again and Siddhartha Shankar Ray was the governor.

Every morning, we, the media, would wake up and make our way towards the rear of the complex from where we had a good view of the Harmandir Sahib. The Press was at a safe distance from the firing power of the terrorists holed up within the holy precincts of the Golden Temple, and of the NSG who had been flown to Amritsar to lay a siege and fire if they saw any movement.

The operation had to be launched, because quite like how DIG Atwal was shot dead at the stairs of the Golden Temple in 1983, the terrorists holed up inside the shrine, aimed their guns at another officer in May 1988. The CRPF's DIG, S. S. Virk came to the temple on 9 May, after receiving information about militants constructing a fortification within the complex. Terrorists holed up inside, took aim and an injured Virk had to be rushed to hospital where his jaw had to be reconstructed.

The date of Operation Black Thunder was preordained. The State had to move in and the NSG, already prepared, arrived quickly.

Ribeiro had moved on to become the advisor to Governor Ray and the famed K. P. S. Gill was now the director general of the Punjab Police. Ved Marwah, who headed the NSG, had a fair idea of the fortifications after he had requested the Indian Air Force to undertake sorties to ascertain the strength of the terrorists. He also had videos of how Bhindranwale and Shabeg had fortified the temple in 1984. Brar's army had done its homework.

There was no way another Blue Star could be repeated. The temple had been fortified once again but lacked Shabeg's military precision. The strategy to clear the complex was changed. Rajiv Gandhi, Indira Gandhi's son was now the prime minister, and he knew that the political, psychological, and human cost of invading the shrine was not worth the risk. He had lost his mother and was acutely aware of the anger and alienation an entry would entail. And thus a whole new strategy was crafted.

Unlike in 1984, when telephone lines were cut, in 1988, they were used to communicate with the terrorists. The terrorists inside the Golden Temple, were told to walk out without their weapons. Close to 150 did as they were told, but much to the anxiety of the police and the NSG, about 47 used the ceasefire window to dash into the sanctum sanctorum. Before the ceasefire announcement, the NSG commandos shot anyone who dared to come out of their room onto the parikrama. Jagir Singh, who I had interviewed, came out of Daftar Khalistan in search of water and was shot immediately. His body lay rotting on the parikrama in the oppressive May heat.

I saw Operation Black Thunder live. The NSG had to wait for three days before the final batch of militants, who had taken refuge inside the sanctum sanctorum, were forced out. Gill decided to tire them out. Electricity and water supply were cut. For three days, the terrorists had no food or water in the scorching month of May.

Finally, they emerged, in a single file, their arms raised above their shoulders. The abject surrender was captured and broadcast on television screens around the world. The terrorists were not saviours of the faith. They had, in fact, desecrated the holiest spot in the Golden Temple.

I was amongst a group of journalists who hung around for a few hours after the terrorists had surrendered. Journalism teaches you perseverance and tenacity and both stand you in good stead. Gill was also still there and we had several questions: Would the militants have booby trapped the precincts before surrendering? How was he going to go ahead with the mopping-up of the Golden Temple?

We persuaded him to allow us – only a few journalists had stayed on – into the Golden Temple before the troops went in. 'What if the people blame you and say your troops planted weapons inside,' we told him. He excused himself and went to make a telephone call. He could not have let us in without permission from the Centre, which was monitoring the operation from Delhi. The wait was agonizing because it was close to twilight and soon it would be dark.

Gill came back about half an hour later and told us we could follow him in but warned us of the risks. Electricity had still not been restored and many of us walked in, not sure of how to evade landmines, in case, any had been laid to trap the troops. Adrenalin is a heady concoction. It drives war correspondents to undertake dangerous assignments.

Gill led the group. He was a practising Sikh and his uniform was a part of his religion. I had met him several times before that hot 19th May afternoon, when Black Thunder ended. 'We have to take the battle straight into the terrorist camp,' he would often tell me. Gill always made time for journalists, even when he was caught in the midst of unsavoury controversies that included him pinching the bottom of a fellow woman bureaucrat in 1988. I spent several evenings chatting with him over large mugs of beer. He had great capacity – not just for beer – but for deep conversations, devious strategies that included blatant disregard for human rights, he believed firmly that terrorists deserved none whatsoever. In the late 1980s, Punjab was flush with stories of how terrorists were hunted down and killed. Capturing them alive and putting them through the due process of law was not Gill's hallmark. His deputies knew that well. Officials would often privately tell us about how their bodies were tied to boulders and drowned.

On 19 May, when we entered the Golden Temple, I walked with trepidation, stepping on glass shards and ammunition empties. Gill made us crouch as we approached the Harmandir Sahib for fear that some terrorists may still be hiding inside.

I was shocked to see mounds of human faeces, liquor pouches, and sacks full of hair. Even for an atheist like me, it was too much to absorb.

The stench was unbearable. The holiest of Sikh shrines had been completely defiled. The terrorists had relieved themselves in the large vessels meant for *karha prasad*. Some had clearly cut their hair in a bid to evade identification. Many rooms in the parikrama were full of torture implements. The terrorists who had surrendered with their arms up, revealed later, that many suspected informers had been lashed and killed in those very rooms. Their bodies were thrown into gutters. That evening as Gill walked ahead of the media group into the Golden Temple complex, he earned his spurs. He did not know either, if the militants had mined the precincts before surrendering.

He walked straight, without once crouching or lowering his head. A few evenings later, when I met him again, for a one-on-one chat, I asked why he walked like he was taking part in a parade. 'The turban must always be held high,' he replied.

Gill was fearless but that was also a flaw that drove him and his chosen group of officers to commit large-scale human rights violations. The top cop often found himself on the wrong side of the law he was supposed to uphold, but one of his greatest failings was that he paid scant respect to it. In an earlier posting in Assam, he was dragged to court for kicking a demonstrator to death, but later acquitted.

By the early '90s, people in Punjab feared the police more than the terrorists. Black Thunder had provided the impetus to go after terrorists and Gill did that with impunity.

By then, Gill had earned the reputation of being a super cop. Few knew that he was an ardent reader and could recite Shakespeare with the same ease as he could wield torture implements.

Years after his controversial but successful tenure in Punjab, he became advisor to Narendra Modi, then chief minister of Gujarat, after the 2002 riots. In 2007, he flew to Chhattisgarh to join Chief Minister Raman Singh, to root out Maoist rebels.

He spoke to me often about his time in the red corridor state and not one to mince words, said: 'After three or four days into my stint, Raman Singh told me to relax and enjoy my stay. I had drawn up an elaborate plan on how to deal with the threat from Naxals but it was never implemented. I remember calling for a meeting – not in the capital city of Raipur but in the interiors – and many officers came in civvies and in unmarked vehicles. They were trying to pass off as civilians. This is not a response that is going to raise the confidence of the people. Policemen can only die in such a situation. The paramilitary forces are stuck in a terrain they don't know, just like the Americans are in Iraq and Afghanistan.'

Gill's plan for Chhattisgarh also involved a human approach and I have often wondered why he didn't apply the same yardstick to Punjab, where his deputies often breached the law. After violence ebbed in the state, the judiciary and the human rights bodies found their voices. At least five Punjab Police officers chose death by suicide after they found themselves hounded by cases pointing to their excesses.

Conflict is as bloody and murky as it is tragic.

Several strains of the conflict are still visible in the rubble of history.

In 2023, a spark was ignited in Punjab when a radical preacher, Amritpal Singh, who fashioned himself after Jarnail Singh Bhindranwale, flew in from Dubai where he had lived since he was 19. Heading an organization called 'Waris Punjab De' (the inheritors of Punjab), the 30-year-old Amritpal organized his dastar-bandi (a turban-tying ceremony) at Bhindranwale's village, Rode.

Like Bhindranwale, Amritpal tried to assemble a Molotov cocktail of religion and politics as its essential ingredients. He garnered some support by giving sermons on his self-professed goals: practising a purer form of Sikhism, addressing sacrilege cases, solving the problem of drug addiction amongst Punjab's youth, and storming a police station.

He was quickly chased down and arrested, under the National Security Act (NSA), but won the Khadoor Sahib Lok Sabha constituency while in jail in Assam in 2024. He won by a margin of 1.97 lakh votes but was careful not to use the word 'Khalistan' in any of the posters or speeches made by his aides on his behalf. His victory pointed to an uneasy fact: the sentiment for Khalistan was easy to stir. The same sentiment perhaps led to another electoral victory. Sarabjeet Singh Khalsa, the son of Beant Singh, one of the bodyguards who killed Indira Gandhi, won the Faridkot Lok Sabha seat as an independent candidate. He campaigned on how the Granth Sahib had been desecrated during the rule of the Akalis and how protesting farmers had been called terrorists and Khalistanis by the Narendra Modi government. The government had rolled back the farm laws but Punjab remembered how the farmers were forced to make the highway their home for almost a year.

History holds grim lessons. The appetite for Khalistan is now largely confined to the diaspora and has stoked diplomatic fires affecting relations between India and Canada, and the United States of America. Both Canada and the USA have accused India of using its intelligence agencies to sanction assassinations of members sympathetic to the Khalistani cause.

The American courts are pursuing the case of an alleged plot, hatched by Indian intelligence agencies, to bump off one of the main leaders of the Khalistan movement,

Gurpatwant Singh Pannun of Sikhs for Justice (SFJ), in New York. The plot involved a former R&AW officer, Vikash Yadav, a fact New Delhi was forced to admit to. The government, however, maintains that he is no longer on their rolls.

While New Delhi was forced to set up a committee after Washington shared details of the plot, it chose to brush off similar charges made by Canada in regard to the killing of Khalistani separatist Hardeep Singh Nijjar. Relations between India and Canada are tenuous. Both countries expelled each other's diplomats and relations continue to be strained even though a new dispensation has replaced the Justin Trudeau administration.

Whether Prime Minister Mark Carney and his Liberal party will be able to negotiate India's sensitivities vis a vis the Khalistani lobby which remains active and articulate is a question that can only be answered in the future. The Indo-US relationship, which has become about tariffs and illegal immigration too, will be tested in the future. Also at test is US President Donald Trump's offer to negotiate the issue of Kashmir between India and Pakistan. India has always been averse to the idea of third-party mediation but the fact of the matter is that Trump announced the ceasefire after the Pahalgam killings led to a tense standoff between India and Pakistan in May 2025. While the Indian government maintains that it paused Operation Sindoor after a reachout from Pakistan, Trump has been reiterating his desire to resolve the conflict, suggesting that India and Pakistan could even meet for 'a nice dinner'.

We don't know how far US will now take the Pannun case and to what extent it will damage the India-US relationship. Will Donald Trump exact a price in different ways? That too, is a question for the future. What we do know is this: the Modi government must control its testosterone levels and not let the adrenalin damage India's growing global influence. As we know, such hit jobs don't come without political clearance. There are provocations from Khalistani elements based abroad but the solutions lie in extradition treaties, not hit jobs. Many who purport the slogan of Khalistan were not even born in 1984, the catastrophic year that changed India in several ways.

The past continues to intervene in the present.

Thirty-eight years after Operation Blue Star, Lieutenant General K. S. Brar, was attacked on a London street, in 2022 by four people, including a woman. 'There were four assailants. One attacked my wife and three lunged at me with their kirpans. I was able to fend them off. They looked to be in their early 30s and were certainly born after Operation Blue Star,' Brar recalled in a recent conversation with me. His security has been further tightened. 'I am virtually living inside a prison,' he said, wistfully.

The rubble of history is unkind. The embers of conflict are easy to stoke. That is a definitive lesson I've learnt through my own life through conflict.

The Underworld and a 'Bhai'

I had not just accompanied the underworld kingpin's aide to a casino. I had also visited Chhota Rajan's home.

In about two hours and ten minutes, Bombay, as it was called then, was brought to its knees. On 12 March 1993, a series of powerful bombs exploded at 12 different locations, many iconic. The Bombay Stock Exchange and the Air India building were among the targets.

Cars and scooters laden with explosives kept erupting to claim innocent lives. In the span of a few hours, the death toll was already a bloody roll call: 257 killed and hundreds injured.

I rushed from the *India Today* office, then located in Delhi's Connaught Place, to North Block, which houses the offices of the home ministry. Rajesh Pilot, the minister of state for internal security was preparing to leave for Bombay. He would take a commercial flight, he told me, in case the special plane did not leave the same day.

Pilot waited to brief Prime Minister P. V. Narasimha Rao, who was in Sikar, Rajasthan, where he had gone for a public engagement.

I was sitting in Pilot's office when he asked his staff to connect him to his wife, Rama. 'I will not be able to keep my promise of returning home early. I am leaving for Bombay,' he told her. Putting the phone down, he looked at me and said, 'Today is our wedding anniversary.'

The celebrations could wait. There were a million instructions to be issued. Maharashtra was the home state of his boss and Union home minister, S. B. Chavan, who signalled that they leave for Bombay the next day. He was not keen on Pilot seizing the initiative and going alone.

In a few hours, instructions went out at breathtaking speed. By 5 p.m., as I reported for *India Today* magazine, high-level teams of the Intelligence Bureau (IB), R&AW, Central Forensic Science Laboratory, and ballistic experts from the NSG were rushed to Bombay.

The country had been placed on high alert, the army alerted and security beefed up in communally-sensitive areas. A minor outbreak of stone throwing at Mahim was quickly brought under control. By the same evening, all police officers and junior ranks on leave were recalled and directed to check basements of high-rise buildings dotting Bombay's skyline. Air India was instructed not to accept cargo or courier until further orders. Security was heightened at airports and railway stations.

Rajesh Pilot was still waiting for word on the special plane. The wait did not last much longer. Prime Minister Rao told both, Chavan and Pilot to leave for Bombay. Pilot allowed me to travel with him and I was soon on board the special flight.

In January 1993, two months before the blasts ripped through Bombay, riots had wracked the city soon after the demolition of the Babri Masjid in Ayodhya on 6 December 1992.

The demolition shaped contemporary political history in several ways. An honest appraisal – and only an honest one – can do justice to our understanding of how India evolved and devolved after frenzied kar sevaks climbed atop the domes of the masjid and brought them down one by one. The Ayodhya skyline was as grey that fateful evening as Delhi's was in 1984, when my father was scurrying home on his scooter.

At *India Today*, we worked day and night to bring out a special issue titled 'Nation's Shame'. Our bureaus in Delhi and Bombay kept up its reportage of the demolition, the subsequent riots, and the bombs that exploded in the very heart of India's financial capital.

The serial bombings announced the hellish power of dreaded gangster and underworld don, Dawood Ibrahim. Dawood had left the country in 1986, after he was wanted in a murder case. He was known to be a part of the underworld that constantly raised its head in Bombay, but 12 March 1993 would firmly set him on the way to being designated a global terrorist.

What made Dawood shift from gold smuggling and

terrorizing real-estate tycoons and Bollywood producers to planning and executing a crippling blow to India's second most important city?

In a column in *Hindustan Times*, colleague and well-known television journalist, Rajdeep Sardesai asked some pertinent questions. '...Why had Dawood, who in October 1992 was seen waving the Indian tricolour during an India-Pak cricket match in Sharjah and had offered gifts to the Indian team if they won, been transformed into the man who bombed Mumbai six months later? Why had a Dubai-based smuggler become a Karachi-based terrorist? Was the demolition of the Babri Masjid the turning point?' he asked.

The demolition was a definitive moment. It changed India's secular destiny. It gave rise to the Bharatiya Janata Party's (BJP) saffron agenda and its promise of constructing a grand Ram temple. It also mirrored the changes in the underworld and how its trigger-happy henchmen operated.

Chhota Rajan alias Rajendra Sadashiv Nikalje, another underworld kingpin, had risen quickly from being a bootlegger and a muscleman providing cover for shady financial land deals to becoming a close aide of Dawood.

Claiming to be upset over the serial bombings in Bombay, Rajan distanced himself from his mentor, calling him a traitor. Dawood had taken shelter in Pakistan, where he has been well looked after by his ISI masters, but the question in 1993 was, where exactly is Rajan? How was he so successful in using his henchmen to still wield influence in Bombay?

Rajan had billed Dawood a traitor and was not going to let him go gently into the night. On 13 November 1995, Thakiyudeen Abdul Wahid, the managing director of East West Airlines, was on his way home in Bombay, when he was brutally shot dead. A close lieutenant of Rajan, it was later revealed, had pumped 30 bullets into Wahid. The managing director paid with his life because Rajan believed that Dawood had invested money in the airline.

The answer to the question of where Rajan was operating from, came in the form of a phone call, a few months after Wahid's killing.

One morning, in early 1996, the *India Today* receptionist greeted me, like she always did, with a big smile and a message that left me frozen on my feet. 'Some Chhota Rajan had called. He wants to talk,' she said.

Chhota Rajan had called?

The information was not easy to soak in.

'He wants to talk?'

'Where was he calling from?'

'Has he left a number?'

The familiar rush of adrenalin was slowly creeping in, even as I asked myself why the underworld kingpin would want to reach out to the media?

I took the piece of paper on which the number had been neatly written down and went to the library to do some research. Every morning, the library staff would cut stories, culled out of newspapers, and punch them into boxed files, marked subject-wise. Going through the files was the only way to do research. There were still no Google engines weaving instant magic.

Slowly, the penny dropped. Chhota Rajan was trying to make a determined bid for leadership of the Mumbai underworld. Wahid's sensational murder had put the spotlight on him and the Mumbai police was squarely pointing a finger in his direction. Image is as important as muscle and Rajan was, perhaps, taking the interview route to make some explosive revelations. According to one of the clippings in the library file, an unidentified Dawood aide had queered the pitch by saying the killing could also be a handiwork of the D-Gang.

Aroon Purie, the owner and editor-in-chief, was a brilliant boss. Travelling long distances was never a problem. He encouraged and taught us how to practise journalism at its best. He definitely taught me how to pursue a story. Credibility and integrity were the magazine's second names, and he had no reservation in signing off on the interview with Chhota Rajan. 'Hit left, hit right, hit centre. Be thorough,' he would often tell us in the newsroom.

Babbar Sher, is how we referred to him. The magazine had no competition in the '90s and the world of news was ours to explore. Not a single story – in fact not even the letters to the editor page – went to the printing press until Purie had read and cleared it.

I called the number scribbled on the piece of paper the receptionist had given me. One of Rajan's aides answered and helped me fix a date for the interview that would take place in Kuala Lumpur (KL) in 1996. I had one condition: The interview would have to be tape recorded. I was not flying to Malaysia to speak to a fugitive to take pen-and-paper notes.

The underworld dons were sniping at each other and the cat and mouse game between Dawood and Rajan had the Mumbai police on its toes.

My trip to KL began with my baggage not showing up. Rajan's aide was at the airport to receive me. My hotel had been booked and paid for by *India Today*, but before I could check in, I needed some toiletries and a fresh set of clothes.

When would the interview take place?

Do we have a time?

I was full of questions and Rajan's aide said, 'Would you like to go to Genting. It has some good casinos....' I looked at him in complete disbelief, and then thought to myself, *Maybe Rajan will show up at some casino.*

Genting is about an hour's drive from KL and as we wound our way up, my heart was pounding. It was still pounding when we returned from the casino. I didn't have my interview yet but I was richer by a few dollars, having tried my luck at a few gambling tables of the many casinos. Betting on the blackjack table and the slot machines paid dividends and the aide, looked on, amused.

I gambled with a close aide of an underworld don, I thought to myself as I switched off the lights in my hotel room that night.

The wait was not too long.

I got the first ever, exhaustive interview with Rajan and he had a lot to say. In fact, he made several claims that got spooled into the recorder, as he spoke. He linked Dawood to the Bombay blasts (which the police was already doing), but he gave details which only he could have known. Till the serial blasts shook Bombay, Dawood and Rajan had not formally split. They broke up only after the mayhem; in fact, because of the bloody, life-consuming mayhem.

I remember the underworld kingpin as an amiable person, fluent in what is often referred to as 'Bombaia Hindi'. His voice was deep but never threatening. I was not uncomfortable being around him briefly, when he showed up at a restaurant, or later, when we recorded larger sections of the interview through a device attached to the landline phone in my hotel room.

I reproduce some portions, not all. The full interview is still available in the *India Today* archives.

Q Why did you leave Dawood?

A He is not a man worth talking about. He betrayed both me and the nation. He got three of my men killed to try and reduce my power. He killed them in the worst possible fashion – by befriending them first, inviting them over and dining them....

Q And why do you say he betrayed the nation?

A He was the brain behind the Bombay bomb blasts in which hundreds of innocents lost their lives.

Q You are making a very serious charge. How do you know that he was involved in the blasts?

A Because at that time [March 1993] I was in Dubai and Dawood was in Karachi. He returned two–three days after the blast and was inundated with calls congratulating him. I asked him about his involvement and, of course, he denied it. You see, by March we were in any case falling out with each other. Differences had crept in after the killing of my three associates and I was not part of the many closed-door meetings in which Tiger Memon and Dawood were together. There was also talk of landings [of explosives] in my presence.

Q Why were you not part of the conspiracy?

A I was not in the inner circle anymore and if I had any idea, I would not have allowed it to happen. Perhaps Dawood suspected that.

Q How could you have prevented the blasts, said to have been planned with the help and support of Pakistan? It wasn't a one-man operation.

A I would have told the department or contacted someone in the Indian government. I would also have put my own men on the job.

Q How did you finally leave the gang and escape from Dubai? They must have been keeping an eye on you.

A Not just that. My passport had gone to the Indian Embassy for renewal and I never got it back.

Q But didn't you have a receipt?

A I had a receipt. In fact, I still have it, but Dawood told me that the embassy had instructions not to renew my passport. The truth, however, is that he got it renewed but never gave it back to me. Along with mine, he had given his brother Noora's passport, which came back renewed. It was his way of pressurizing me. Anyway, it may be news to him, but I still have an Indian passport issued in Dubai.

Q How could he get it renewed? You mean he had contacts even in the Indian Embassy?

A Yes, money means a lot in this business and can buy you anything.

Q So how did you leave Dubai?

A I got myself another passport. But don't ask me how, because I will not spell it out.

Q You finally parted company after the blasts and have now become his opponent. The Bombay police believe that your gang is behind the killing of Thakiyudeen Wahid, the managing director of East West Airlines.

A I gave the instructions for Wahid's killing. He was Dawood's financier in India. I got him killed because I wanted to take revenge on Dawood for the bomb blasts. Before that, Sunil Sawant, another very close associate of Dawood, was bumped off on the streets of Dubai. I want to eliminate all the people who have let down the country by conspiring to blow up Bombay.

Q But Dubai is supposed to be Dawood's headquarters. He has been controlling the Bombay underworld from there for so many years.

A Dawood is only a media don and he has been in Pakistan for over two years now, not having the guts to go back to Dubai. I have my contacts and resources and have proved that I can get him, even if it means planning an operation in Dubai. Sawant was Dawood's main hitman and we got him despite all his security guards. Now I am looking for Dawood.

Q But you say he is in Pakistan...

A So what? I know where he is, and we have already made

one attempt on his life in Karachi. There are smugglers in Pakistan who are opposed to him because he is stepping on their turf. He might think that Pakistan is safe because it is an Islamic country, but there are people there who want him as badly as I do. I will not rest till I finish him off. He is my nation's enemy and has to be taught a lesson.

Here was an underworld don, openly talking about his plans to eliminate his former boss.

Rajan needed to be asked the hard questions too. He, after all, was also a killer, a black marketeer, a thug, a mercenary....

I continued with my next question.

Q How are you any different? After all, you are also working against the nation.

A I have never harmed the nation. My fight is against Dawood.

Q But you are also a killer, a criminal...

A I am killing Dawood's men. In fact, I am making the police's job easier and am doing the country a good turn by getting rid of those who conspired to destabilize it.

Q It seems odd that you should go on about the country when you admit that you will continue to indulge in killings. What about Wahid's killing?

A I gave the instructions for Wahid's murder. He was Dawood's financier in India.... East West Airlines is, in fact, owned by Dawood. Wahid used to come to Dubai – where I also met him – often and Dawood told me that he was starting an airline. It was important to kill Wahid for that was another way of reducing Dawood's power.

Did I have a headline? Rajan was confessing to Wahid's killing. His voice was there... on tape... on record... undeniable....

My field training was kicking in... never let the interviewee get away with claims.

Question, cross-question....

Interviewing is an art and journalists are its practitioners. There is a way of asking the hard question, without the screaming and the screeching. I usually soften the 'target' with easier questions in the beginning, before plunging in with the harder, accusatory ones.

Q The Bombay police has announced an award of ₹2 lakh for anyone who provides information on Wahid's killers. Why don't you claim the award?

A I don't want that money. It is compensation enough that the operation was successful. There can be no greater satisfaction than that.

Q Apart from killings, what are your other activities? The police believe that you smuggle narcotics.

A I have never touched drugs in my life. I don't believe in earning money through spoiling people's lives and hurting them.

Q You have hurt Wahid's family.

A What about the hundreds who were killed in the blasts and what about their families? They were truly innocent. Wahid should never have involved himself with Dawood.

Speaking on behalf of Wahid's family and calling out the fact that he had hurt them, stood us in good stead. They were upset when the interview was published but we were able to explain that we, in fact, had pointed to the fact that family members had been pained.

Q You were also very close to him [Dawood] till only two years ago...

A Yes, and that is the only regret I have. Not that I am part of the underworld but that I associated with a man like Dawood.

Q Are you sure he is in Karachi?

A Yes. Initially, just before I left Dubai, I had his telephone number there and even called him to see if I had been given the correct number. That number has obviously changed but I know from my sources that he is still there. The number, in fact, was given to me by Sawant. I called him once to wish him on his birthday [26 December]. He does travel out of Pakistan once in a while, but Karachi is his base.

Q You are involved in the property business in Bombay in a big way. According to estimates, you make several crores through contract killings, property business, and protection money.

A Several crores a year, not in a day.

Q What will you do with so much money?

A I need the money to weaken Dawood's gang.

Q You can weaken him by surrendering and cooperating with the police...

A I don't trust the government because a lot of them are mixed up. Dawood is capable of buying officials and turning them against me.

Q You must be using the same tactics – building contacts in police and political circles.

A I don't believe in using money because the person who takes money from me can sell himself to anyone, Dawood included. Nor do I have any political godfathers. Yes, I am a supporter of the BJP and the Shiv Sena. One of Dawood's aides said recently that Bal Thackeray was number one on their hit list. All I want to say is that if necessary, we will provide protection. No one can touch Thackeray saab. Dawood won't be doing his own Muslim brothers a favour by trying to touch Thackeray, for then all hell will break loose.

Q So, you have approached the Shiv Sena.

A No, I have not. But they only have to give us a hint and we will be at their service.

Q So is it true that there is some sort of a communal divide even in the underworld?

A Not in my mind. I still have a lot of Muslims working with me and I consider all Muslims my brothers. Dawood too has Hindus, even in his inner circle, like Sharad Shetty and Anil Parab.

Q Why are you talking of religion and Hindu-Muslim amity? As far as the police is concerned, you are an underworld hitman who has jumped bail.

A All of us in the underworld are hitmen. And why can't I speak on behalf of my country? I am not interested in destabilizing the country through blasts and provoking communal riots.

Q So killings are okay if the aim is settling personal scores?

A I have been let down by Dawood. That doesn't hurt me as much as the blasts do. I will stop only after I have finished Dawood and Tiger Memon [a co-conspirator in the Bombay blasts] and I have set a target of a year for myself to accomplish that.

Q How do you manage to remote control?

A It is the age of communication. The telephone is my weapon.

Q Have you met Tiger Memon?

A Several times. He used to come to Dubai often to meet Dawood. He also came to attend my wedding in 1988. Dawood and Tiger have a long association. He was in Dubai even during the riots and before the blasts; Tiger and Dawood went to Karachi together....

Q Dawood has established and earned for himself the title of don. You talk very confidently of catching up with someone who was once your boss.

A I am very confident. It is you press people who have made a petty smuggler and criminal out to be a don. Today it is not his writ but mine that runs in Bombay. Dawood, in fact, is under pressure. His men are hiding in Bombay and if we can penetrate Dubai too, which was once his unchallenged domain, then what kind of a don is he? He is now only a fugitive who won't be able to run for too long.

Q You are also on the run. Are you scared of Dawood?

A I am not scared of him. In fact, I'm prepared to take him on face to face. If I am in hiding, it is only because I have an unfinished agenda. The day I get him, I will come back to India and surrender. You might think I am in hiding but as far as I am concerned, I am being practical. Why should I offer myself to them when I know that they must also be in search of me? After all they have managed to kill my friends and associates too.

Q How long will you continue to hide? Aren't you fed up with the kind of life you're leading? Running from the law is also an offence.

A I cannot surface as long as there is a threat to my life. I will return once my task is over and then I am willing to face trial and go to jail if necessary. But only after I have taught Dawood a lesson.

The interview was done in 1996 when not too many photographs of Rajan were in the public domain. His aide, who had picked me up from the airport, then took me to Rajan's apartment where I poured over several albums, including one containing his wedding pictures. The aide generously gave me photographs that are now a part of *India Today*'s photo archives.

I had not just accompanied the underworld kingpin's aide to a casino. I had also visited Rajan's home. He was obviously not there. Like terrorists, kingpins keep changing their locations. They are afraid of being hunted down, not just by the Interpol but their rivals too.

Rajan finally landed in Tihar jail in 2015 without completing the mission he so wanted to. He could not eliminate Dawood despite having the active support of the Intelligence Bureau.

The years, 1993 to 2015, are the subject of a separate book, but I'm not done with this chapter yet.

After my return from Kuala Lumpur, Rajan started calling me once a week on my residential landline number. He had forewarned me and laughingly said, 'I will call you as Chetan.' Each time he called, I recalled a cherubic face, a squat man who had a fondness for gold.

'Hello didi, Chetan *bol raha hoon*,' he said, each time.

(Hello didi, Chetan speaking.)

'*Mere liye koi kaam*?'

(Is there anything I can do for you?)

What work could I possibly have of a fugitive sailing the high seas in Southeast Asia....

I would dutifully report the conversation to my colleagues – now amongst my best friends – at the *India Today* office and they would jokingly name people who were troubling them at work.

The weekly calls were becoming discomfiting. One day, I finally told him to stop calling, saying, 'I am a journalist and my phone is probably being tapped.'

What I did not know – but realized soon enough – was that Rajan was the one who had already been virtually adopted by some officers of the IB. Even in his interview to me, he had tried to paint himself in 'nationalistic colours' and spoken openly about working in the interest of the country. He had, without qualm, sided with Bal Thackeray, the Shiv Sena supremo.

I had the occasion to interview Rajan twice more. In 1998, after the sensational killing of Nepal MP Mirza Dilshad Beg, a close associate of Dawood, Rajan gave me a telephonic interview. I was still with *India Today*. Fugitives change not just their location but also their contact numbers. A high-ranking official from the IB shared his number after some persistence from me.

Rajan was becoming media-savvy and knew that his sensational disclosures would make headline news. He provided me with yet another one by admitting to Beg's killing.

Q The suspicion is that you killed Mirza Beg?

A Yes, I gave the orders for his killing. The men who pulled the trigger were my hit men. They shadowed him and found out his schedule.

Q Why did you have him killed?

A He was the conduit for the ISI [Pakistan's spy agency, Inter-Services Intelligence]. He was the main person supplying weapons and explosives, including RDX. He was also a close contact of Dawood Ibrahim's and anyone who aligns with Dawood is my enemy. With Beg out of the scene, it will not be easy for Dawood to operate from Nepal.

Q What was the immediate provocation?

A All of Dawood's hit men were Beg's guests. He used

to give them shelter, entertain them and then even help them in getting Nepalese passports. Through the ISI, he was spreading terror in India. Check with the intelligence agencies and they will tell you that his name crept up each time an incident took place. He also had a hand in the Coimbatore blast where L. K. Advani was the target. He was harming my country by assisting the ISI.

Q You are no better. You are also part of the underworld.

A I only kill those who are anti-India. The killings of Salim Kurla and Mohammad Jindran were also at my behest. They were killed because they were accused in the Bombay blasts. I will kill all the accused one by one. Let no one think that they can repeat such incidents or get away with such crimes.

Q The case is in court and the law will deal with them.

A The court is only giving bail orders. Some are even getting police protection. The accused must be killed.

Q If you are pro-India as you make yourself out to be, why don't you surrender instead of continuing to hide in Malaysia?

A How can I do that? You want my enemies to rejoice.

Q So you sit in Malaysia and issue death warrants.

A I am not killing innocents.

Q Did the Indian authorities seek your help for Beg's execution?

A No. But if I am approached, I will not hesitate to help.

The fact of the matter is, he did not hesitate to help. He was approached and was more than willing to help.

Rajan, over the years, had perfected the art of using media interviews as effective weapons.

The quest for Rajan's interviews and the killing of J. Dey, a senior journalist in Mumbai, are well documented for his sheer lethality and his ability to manipulate the headline. Dey, also an author of a book on the underworld, had enviable contacts that helped him document how the dark world operated. He was pumped with bullets while driving home on his motorcycle, in June 2011. His book was titled, *Khalas – An A to Z Guide to the Underworld.*

Did Dey pay with his life because he knew too much? What we do know is that Jigna Vora, a journalist paid a heavy price for being a crime reporter. She was falsely accused of conspiring with Rajan in Dey's killing and ended up spending months in jail. Her book, *Behind Bars in Byculla: My days in prison* inspired the Netflix series titled, *Scoop*.

Scoops are an intrinsic part of a journalist's life. *The Times of India* definitely had one through a front page report that revealed details of how Rajan's sharpshooters Vicky Malhotra and Farid Tanasha were being coveted by Ajit Kumar Doval, a retired director of the IB and the current National Security Advisor (NSA) to Prime Minister Narendra Modi. The plan entailed targeting Dawood in Dubai where his daughter was marrying the son of famous Pakistani cricketer, Javed Miandad.

The scoop laid bare an intricate maze of open secrets. While Rajan had boasted of contacts in the government, the specifics had, until then, not been revealed. The nexus between some sections of the Mumbai Police and the D-Gang was also, till then, part of popular corridor gossip. Did the Mumbai Police deliberately throw a spanner?

Former home secretary and BJP MP, R. K. Singh put the controversy to rest through an interview he gave to *India Today* channel in 2015. 'An operation to eliminate Dawood Ibrahim was being planned, before it was blown by actions of some Mumbai cops. Ajit Doval was involved in the operation,' he said.

The plot dated back to 2005. Doval had retired as director of the IB in January that year. The same year, it was revealed that Dawood's daughter Mahrukh was to marry Junaid, Javed Miandad's son.

The IB had specific information regarding the wedding. The nikaah was to take place in Mecca on 9 July. A reception had also been fixed for 23 July, to be held at the swanky Grand Hyatt hotel in Dubai. Doval, an expert in covert operations – and a Kirti Chakra awardee, for his crucial intelligence gathering in Punjab – clearly thought this was the best chance to take a shot at India's most wanted. The gamble was simply this: it would be difficult for a father to stay away from blessing his soon-to-be-married daughter.

Who better to outsource the operation to than Chhota Rajan himself. Rajan tasked two trusted deputies: Vicky Malhotra and Farid Tanasha. Rajan had several scores to settle with Dawood, including an attack in Bangkok in 2000, when the Karachi-based don's henchman got within sniffing distance of the on-the-run Rajan. He sustained three bullets but survived. His escape from the hospital was engineered and aided by the intelligence agencies.

Rajan was not extradited to India. The agencies still needed him.

Intelligence operatives will tell you – and I have interacted with many across Punjab, Kashmir, and Pakistan – that best conceived plans can falter. They may be thoroughly planned and plotted but at just that nth second comes a twist that can turn the secretive operation on its head.

Unknown to Doval, or the IB, the Mumbai Police learnt of Malhotra and Tanasha's presence in India and their numbers were tracked. A senior official was despatched to Delhi to track the gangsters based on their location. By then, mobile numbers were common, and surveillance techniques had advanced.

Home Secretary R. K. Singh believes the Mumbai police officers deliberately sabotaged Operation Dawood because of their close ties with the gangster. The Mumbai Police, however, have their own version of what is easily one of the biggest intelligence exposes. A seemingly ugly turf war brought the curtains down on one of the most audacious plans to nab Dawood.

The team that came to Delhi from Mumbai, found the Malhotra–Tanasha duo involved in a deep conversation with a third person at an upscale hotel in Lutyens' Delhi. Was the third person the 'Sir' they had been speaking to in the telephone conversations that had been tracked? The intriguing voice did not show up results for voice sample matches.

We know that 'Sir' was none other than Doval. The details are available in a book titled *Madam Commissioner*, by retired IPS officer Meeran Chadha Borwankar. Released in October 2023, Borwankar recounts in the book how the team from the Mumbai Police followed the 'agents' after they left the hotel and got into a car.

The car was intercepted, and the duo were arrested. The agitated stranger – or Sir – introduced himself as the former director of the IB and asked to speak to the officer who was in charge of the operation.

When Borwankar finally spoke to Doval, the former IB director insisted that Malhotra be let off. According to the IPS lady officer, when she refused, she was told, 'I will teach you a lesson.'

Borwankar claims in the book that she retorted by telling the stranger that she would teach him a lesson instead. Was Borwankar taught a lesson? The officer, who had the seniority to be appointed the first woman director of the Central Bureau of Investigation (CBI), retired as DG, Police Research Bureau and National Crime Record Bureau.

Even though the former home secretary mentioned Doval by name, the former director of the IB has always maintained that he was at home that day, watching television. No spook will reveal actual details. The last thing they want is for their cover to be lifted. Doval has never made a mention of the famed encounter.

I have known Doval for several years. I first met him in the '80s, when he was posted in the Indian high commission in Islamabad and then in Srinagar. We have had several conversations on terrorism and counter-terrorism, which I am not at liberty to reveal. Intelligence officials are not allowed to go on record and journalists, me included, gain their trust by keeping theirs.

Doval did consent, however, to give me an interview after he retired as the IB's top boss. By then, I was working with *Tehelka* magazine and the interview is available on the website of the Vivekananda International Foundation, an institute he helped found. In a rather candid interview, Doval answered questions pertaining to several crisis points: the release of Masood Azhar, the intelligence failures that led to the hijacking of IC 814, and Kargil. We also discussed Dawood and Rajan.

Q Let's talk about Dawood. We haven't been able to get him after so many years.

A We should have been able to get him. After all, he has been protected by a sovereign state.... We can get him if the victim state decides to take some initiative – military or covert – any initiative that does not involve the cooperation of another state. The basic point is somebody is sheltering him.

Q Why are we not planning a covert operation?

A No comments.

Q Why don't we still have any concrete evidence of the fact that he is in Pakistan? Like a photograph, maybe?

A Yes, we have. We have given the governments of Pakistan and other governments photographs of Dawood in Pakistan. Maybe his Pakistani passport. His movements and his photograph and his address.... Maybe the house in which he lives. There is a photograph where he is in the lawn. Even that has been given. Maybe a national identity card of Pakistan; even that has been given.

Q So, how can Pakistan get away?

A They are a sovereign country.

Q What does America have to say? They are involved in a global war against terror. What do they tell us in the face of all this evidence?

A They have designated him a global terrorist. They are doing everything that's to be done to deal with an internationally designated terrorist.

Q But nothing stops America from picking up people it wants from 'sovereign' nations. They have done that in Pakistan?

A Certainly, if Dawood Ibrahim was Osama bin Laden, then, probably, with the same evidence, much more would have happened. That's the reality. That's how the entire game is played in the international community.

Q Are we not playing that game well? Or are they not listening to us?

A Pressure has been there on Pakistan, but it has still not responded. Successive governments have been putting a lot of pressure. The NDA government gave a list of 22 persons to them. Their addresses and details were shared. The material about their involvement in India was given. They have built up a huge impact over there. They have built commercial interests there. They have bought ships and shopping plazas there.

Q So we have the proof, but we don't have Dawood?

A That's what I said. Knowledge doesn't mean that it will be acted upon.

Q So America is not pushing the envelope because it needs Pakistani support right now?

A America is willing to push Pakistan up to a point. But not to the point where it meets our requirement. The obstinacy of Pakistan is so high, the advantage of Dawood to them is so high that they would probably not give him easily.

Q Has Dawood not become a liability for Pakistan?

A He is a liability as well as an asset. On balance of consideration, he is more of an asset. The advantages are more than the costs involved.

Q What are the advantages of keeping him? Why would Pakistan want to shelter a global terrorist?

A For any covert action that they may have to carry out, not only against India but globally, he [Dawood] is a person who has got terrorists with money power, who has got his underworld contacts, who has got contacts with gunrunners, who can leverage the counterfeiters, position the people, position the assets. Take the Kandahar hijackers. They land up in Bombay. Why did they come to Bombay? Because they wanted the Indian driving licence so that they can travel around. It is delivered in their house, the flat they are living in. Because Dawood can get it done.

Q So Dawood helped them?

A Yes. So there are a large number of people who come on subversive missions, on sabotage missions. The devil lies in the detail. Who can give you that critical help at the micro level? Who can send you a taxi to pick you up from the airport, take you from the airport where you are safe, get you a document you require, hire a lawyer in case you are arrested, bribe somebody and get you released? Now that covert capability puts ISI in an advantageous position.

Q To what extent can he still run his underworld apparatus in Mumbai? Is he in control?

A As far as the apparatus is concerned, he is still very much in control.

Q But the underworld war seems to be on the decline...

A The pressure on him is on the decline. It's a world of its own, where there are ups and down. May be, Dawood realizes that he may like to come back to India. Probably he may be thinking that things may change in Pakistan and globally. He would also like a certain amount of....

Q Has he sent such feelers?

A I am not aware of it but I am aware of how their minds work. They would like to have a certain amount of stability.

Q He will have to spend the rest of his life in jail. Would he be willing to do that?

A I don't know. It depends how many cases are pending against him. After all, when the Bombay blasts happened, he was not here physically. So, it's a matter of judicial pronouncement against him. The best course for him would be to come to India. After all, how far and how long is he going to run? And even if he is never caught, his entire life would be spent…. Indian system is very liberal. Judiciary is very independent. He can get the best of the lawyers. Be a good Indian citizen. He may also not be happy at being [branded] as a traitor for himself, his family.

Q **It is part of the charter of intelligence agency to try and get a man like Dawood even if it means using a rival like Chhota Rajan. To what extent has that strategy succeeded? How close has that reached?**

A No comments at all. I don't discuss operations.

I had also done one more interview with Chhota Rajan in the mid-2000s, soon after telephonic conversations between Bollywood stars Salman Khan and Aishwarya Rai were leaked to the media. In the tapes, Khan could he heard alluding to Dawood Ibrahim.

I had lost contact with Chhota Rajan. Sourcing his number took only a little bit of persistence. I got it, once again, from a senior IB official. Despite the botched-up operation, the intelligence agency was clearly still in touch with him.

Unlike Doval, Rajan was willing to answer questions.

Q **One of your associates, Vicky, was apprehended recently. He was in the company of a senior Intelligence Bureau officer. You obviously have links with intelligence agencies...**

A There is no dearth of patriots in this country. Difficulties

[Vicky's arrest] are encountered even when we intend doing something good for the country.

Q So you do have links with the IB. Are you providing them information about the D company?

A We help a lot. Not only Dawood, there are other problems also, but I don't want to talk about it. It will only alert the enemy. There are other problems concerning the country which we want to resolve. If we do it together it will be easier to handle. Together, we can do a lot of things.

In the interview, while he conceded help from the IB, he also said, 'I should get support from all quarters, some support me and some are against. If I have majority support, I will do something, I will do wonders, will do it early and come back... threat to my life as some of the Mumbai Police personnel are acting on behalf of Dawood and are being used by him.'

In the end, Rajan had to come back to India. Delhi's Tihar jail, where he is currently lodged, is perhaps the safest place. It is certainly beyond the reach of the Mumbai Police that outed both Doval and Rajan.

Rajan's return was carefully planned after intelligence agencies learnt that the kingpin's location – he was in Australia by then – had been shared with the D-gang, by one of his aides.

Sleuths are known to shield their contacts. Rajan was finally extradited from Indonesia. Australia did not want blood being spilt on its streets and so the don took a flight to Bali from Sydney.

Rajan, most wanted by the Mumbai Police, where over 70 FIRs are registered against him, is in a jail in Delhi, where he is wanted in about seven crimes.

The one person who will know where Dawood is, is Javed Miandad. I'd managed to record a telephonic interview with him, soon after his son married Dawood's daughter. I asked him straight, about his son marrying a designated terrorist's daughter, and he said, 'I am not concerned about Dawood or who he is. I am only interested in the happiness of our children. They should be happy with Allah's blessings. That is all.... Just because she is someone's daughter, will you say, let her die? Even you people [Indians] leave things to kismet.'

The underworld's influence in Mumbai is greatly reduced but Dawood remains amongst India's most wanted. He remains at the crosshairs of a dark, spooky world involving, crime, cricket, politics, and terrorism.

'Bhai' Chetan alias Chhota Rajan's world has shrunk within the safe confines of a prison. He may have forgotten me, but he remains, forever etched, as part of my journalistic journey.

The Grand 'Hero' of Kashmir's Liberation Movement

'Why don't we talk about the moon and the stars today...
Why do you always talk about work...
I believe you had a good time at an army dinner last night?' The liberator, who had thousands chanting after him, was taunting me, trying to scare me.

The Kalashnikov rifle was Kashmir's chosen weapon and one of its earliest wielders was Yasin Malik, the leader of the popular Jammu and Kashmir Liberation Front (JKLF).

Jammu and Kashmir was engulfed in secessionist flames in 1989, soon after the abduction of Rubaiya Sayeed, daughter of then Union Home Minister Mufti Mohammad Sayeed. Malik was the architect behind the dramatic kidnapping that changed the contours of the Kashmir insurgency and catapulted it into a popular movement for 'azadi'.

Malik was born in 1966 in Maisuma, a colony in the densely populated area of downtown Srinagar. It was like a little protest capital where crowds would gather before marching onwards. At the time, people marched in the thousands, to the heady slogan of,

Hum kya chahte... Azadi...
Azadi ka matlab kya...
La ilaha illa Allah...
(Freedom, freedom is what we want...
What does freedom mean?
There is no god but Allah)

Maisuma was the 'Gaza' of Kashmir and the lean looking, kurta-pyjama clad Malik, its chief inhabitant and Pied Piper. He commandeered and thousands flocked out of their homes to be a part of some of the most relentless anti-India protests. The protests only gathered steam after the V. P. Singh government – of which Sayeed was the home minister – caved in, rather quickly, to release arrested militants in exchange for Rubaiya.

My first visit to the turbulent Valley was in 1989. The 23-year-old daughter of the home minister had just been released in exchange for five militants and Srinagar was throbbing with excitement.

The Farooq Abdullah-led state government, which had been forced to release the militants – despite the chief minister's protestations – was near absent. The administration was gripped by fear as it watched its people take to the streets in the thousands. This was the time when another slogan was added to the chants of azadi: '*Jo kare khuda ka khauf, utha le Kalashnikov.*' (Those who fear God, should pick up the Kalashnikov.)

The militants had succeeded in getting five of their

comrades released in exchange for the home minister's daughter and the entire Valley was celebrating. The release also proved to be a tipping point that tilted the scales fairly and squarely in the direction of the armed struggle that had reared its head in Jammu and Kashmir.

A few years before the dramatic kidnapping, Malik was a mere nobody. He was one of the campaign agents for the infamous 1987 assembly elections that are often pinpointed to as the spark that lit the raging fires that have since engulfed Jammu and Kashmir. The popular perception that the blatant rigging of the election gave way to an insurgency is a subject that has been analysed in detail.

In 1987, Malik was campaigning for Mohammad Yusuf Shah, one of the candidates of the Muslim United Front (MUF), a conglomerate of parties demanding a referendum to break away from India. Instead of the MUF emerging victorious, the Farooq Abdullah-led National Conference–Congress stood accused of rigging and stealing the mandate.

The political engineering sparked unprecedented anger in the region. Hundreds of Kashmiris, Malik included, crossed the LoC to train as militants under Pakistan's watch. Mohammad Yusuf Shah alias Syed Salahuddin, the MUF candidate who lost the election, is ironically still based in Pakistan. He is a popular showpiece for Pakistan's Inter-Services Intelligence (ISI), who often showcases him to highlight the point that the freedom struggle in Kashmir has an indigenous face.

Malik returned from Pakistan in 1989 to ignite the militant movement. The JKLF, of which he was an important part, became the first *tanzeem,* or outfit to declare an armed rebellion against the Indian government.

Ironically, Mufti Sayeed, a Kashmiri, helped that process. He'd been sworn in as the Union home minister on 2 December and found himself in the thick of a crisis barely six days later when he got news that his daughter had been dragged out of a Matador car and whisked away. The young medical intern at Srinagar's Lalla Ded Memorial Women's Hospital, was on her way home, when she was forced out of the mini-van on 8 December.

Mufti was, at that precise time in the evening, chairing his first security meeting as home minister in New Delhi, when he learnt of the kidnapping. He knew what a grave mistake he was making by reacting as a father, rather than as the all-important home minister, but he buckled under the weight of parental emotion. He admitted as much to me several years later when in an interview, he told me that surrendering to the demands of the militants was a regret he would 'take to his grave'.

But at that moment, his first and only response was to get his daughter out at any cost and for this he used every connection. They ranged from IB officials to high court judges to ministerial colleagues like I. K. Gujral and Prime Minister V. P. Singh as well.

The exact sequence of events was revealed to me by Dr Farooq Abdullah, then the chief minister, who in a bold interview said: '...in the middle of the night, then Prime Minister V. P. Singh called me saying, "Doctor Saab we are sending a team. Please help release her." At five o'clock in the morning, I find at my door Mr Gujral, Arif Mohammed

Khan, and M. K. Narayanan. These three fellows sat down in the hamam which was the warmest room.

'It was December and these guys were shivering. I gave them kahwa to warm them up and told my chief secretary and Mr [A. S.] Dulat [then IB chief in Srinagar] to brief them.' The delegation was told it would be a huge mistake to release militants. 'I told them the release would be a "nail in India's coffin".'

Arif Mohammed Khan, a minister in V. P. Singh's government, suggested that the delegation fly back to Delhi to brief the PM and tell him to use diplomatic pressure to get Rubaiya released. According to Abdullah, 'Mr Gujral said no, no, we have got the authority and if he [Farooq Abdullah] does not release the militants then we are going to dismiss him.'

I asked Farooq Abdullah if they said they would dismiss him as bluntly as that and he replied, 'Yes, straight to my face and I said, wonderful, if the Government of India wants to sink India, then go ahead and give it to me in writing. I told my chief secretary to please take a note that such and such a team has come, that they have the PM's and cabinet's orders that the five militants have to be released at all costs. Whatever the cost to the country and therefore whatever the onus, whatever happens here, to the country will be because of the Government of India. Get them to sign this.'

New Delhi buckled quickly. The home minister's daughter was released on 13 December in exchange for five imprisoned JKLF terrorists – Abdul Hameed Sheikh, Ghulam Nabi Bhat (brother of JKLF founder Maqbool

Bhat), Noor Mohammad Kalwal, Mohammad Altaf, and Javed Ahmad Zargar.

Kashmir was in the throes of an insurgency and Yasin Malik, Rubaiya's main kidnapper was giving it direction. A month after the kidnapping, on 25 January 1990, he aimed his guns at Indian Air Force personnel at Rawalpora, on the outskirts of Srinagar, killing four and injuring 22. The Valley was his domain, and he was on a high after making the Government of India buckle and release the five militants.

Malik and his accomplices were soon arrested and the CBI filed a chargesheet in 1990 itself. The case, however, went cold and I discovered in 1994 that the intelligence agencies were in touch with him. They even helped him move from a Delhi prison to a hospital in the capital for heart treatment.

Crucial conversations took place between the sleuths and the terrorist. He was allowed a safe passage back to Srinagar in June 1994. The intelligence operation obviously had political sanction.

I had been making regular trips to the troubled Valley since December 1989 and wanted to see how the people would respond to the return of a man they worshipped and saw as their liberator.

I booked a seat on the same Delhi–Srinagar flight as Malik. A helpful IB officer had provided me a landline number for Malik. He gave me his flight details and promised to give me an interview after reaching Srinagar.

What was the deal? Why was a chargesheeted terrorist – accused of killing four IAF officers and kidnapping a home minister's daughter – being flown to freedom? Malik was out on bail, but would he be able to bail the government out and nudge other separatists to the negotiating table? Had the government undertaken a risky gamble? What if the relentless anti-India protests were to rock the streets of Kashmir again?

Malik landed in Srinagar as a changed man. The terrorist, booked for killings and a kidnapping, said he was now a disciple of Mahatma Gandhi and the principle of non-violence. He was giving up guns, he announced.

The government had released Malik in the hope of reviving a political dialogue. Malik, one of the founders of the militant movement was back and the entire route from the airport to Maisuma was teeming with people who came in busloads. They came laden with visible emotion.

As far as the locals were concerned, their hero had returned. They came out in large numbers, showering him with petals and sweets, even though the JKLF had not officially organized any rally or procession.

Officials admitted, and I wrote so in an *India Today* story, that the outpouring was 'the largest gathering since the pro-azadi rallies of 1990….' Just before he was released on bail, his doctor had pleaded that he was a dying man, but the ailing Malik, treated for a heart disease, was transforming himself from militant to politician.

He was mobbed the minute he stepped out of the airport. I was astounded and kept taking quick notes and adding to my questionnaire. The promised interview was to take place after the welcome procession would wind its way to Maisuma where a stage had been set up.

The Centre had its own reasons for releasing Malik and pausing the cases against him. Between 1990 and 1994, local Kashmiris had started questioning the purpose of the armed struggle for freedom. Many amongst the militant ranks were resorting to exactly what they were accusing the security forces of: rapes and extortions. Insurgencies often fall prey to a process of criminalization and in Kashmir, the torchbearers of azadi were being accused by their own populace. There were also reports of militants knocking on civilian doors and taking shelter at gunpoint.

The groundswell of support was thinning. From the government's point of view, the risk was worth taking. The common man was agitated about the direction the movement had taken; economic activity was suffering and as a senior home ministry official put it, 'The Kashmiris will never turn to India, but they may settle for an honourable way out. It's better than living under the fear of the gun.'

The mood of the people was undergoing a perceptible change over the previous year. They had suffered hardships to support a shut-down call given by the Hurriyat Conference – an umbrella organization comprising separatists – after security forces had laid siege around Srinagar's revered Hazratbal shrine in October 1993. The separatists would often call for a curfew, or a shutdown and the local population was feeling the economic pinch of having to keep their businesses shut.

Though the militants, who had taken shelter inside, came out of the shrine only on the understanding that they would be released, the people had felt let down. The common Kashmiri was not aware of the deal that had been struck. Reports of the militants vacating the Hazratbal shrine were viewed as an abject surrender.

Kashmiris have always kept their ear close to the ground, domestic and international, and were surprised and angered when Iran, in an effort at balancing its 'India-Pakistan' relationship, asked Pakistan not to put a human rights resolution to vote at Geneva. The resolution was meant to call out alleged violations by security forces deployed in Kashmir. The US' shifting stand on Kashmir was also noticed. President Bill Clinton had openly reaffirmed the US' faith in the Simla Agreement of 1972, which called Kashmir a bilateral dispute between India and Pakistan. Earlier, the US had often reiterated the need for Kashmiri aspirations to be factored into any resolution. And in Pakistan, Prime Minister Benazir Bhutto's statement that her country does not favour a plebiscite as they could lose if the option of independence was given to the people of Kashmir, confirmed what the people suspected all along – that Pakistan was using them and may not, when the crunch comes, support the azadi movement.

It was this mood that the Centre was trying to cash in on, when it let Malik out. Jammu and Kashmir was under Governor's rule and Malik was released in the hope that he would fill the existing leadership void and channelize the anti-Pakistan feeling towards a political dialogue. The JKLF – always a proponent of the slogan for independence – still commandeered popular support and the hope was that Malik would be able to rally people around him. By then, Farooq Abdullah, the former chief minister, had left his state far behind and moved to London.

Conflict zones are murky. There are never any fool-proof scripts. Gambles can never be pre-scripted. They always come with a risk factor. Malik received a welcome so overwhelming, so tremendous, there was no room for him to scale down his demand for independence, even if he had wanted to.

The procession from the airport took seven hours to cover a distance of about 16 kilometers. At each step, every kilometer of the way, the Valley witnessed the revival of the slogan for independence. It also gave a boost to the JKLF, which in the past two years had lost out to the pro-Pakistan groups, particularly the Hizbul Mujahideen (HM). Pakistan's ISI had injected its own jihadis into Kashmir, to keep the JKLF's influence under check. It was their way of keeping their 'Kashmir should secede to Pakistan,' strategy alive.

Malik had his own calculations. He was playing to his own script. New Delhi was helping him make the transition from being a hard-core militant to an overground political leader, and though he openly said he was eschewing violence, he was acutely aware that the Hizbul was watching; perhaps thinking of setting up death squads to aim their guns at him.

Malik needed to re-establish himself. He had agreed to hold unconditional talks with New Delhi and the minister of state for internal security, Rajesh Pilot, had responded by saying the government had an open mind. A nervous Pilot had even sent Wajahat Habibullah, former divisional commissioner of Kashmir, to meet Malik. Habibullah returned saying that Malik favoured a political dialogue.

As the cavalcade wound its way towards Maisuma, I was unaware of what lay ahead or the unpleasant discovery I would make.

Malik had a lot on his ambitious plate. He also had a lot at stake. He could scale down the demand for independence only at grave risk to his life. He could also be branded as an Indian agent. He had to guard against the Hizbul's firepower and tread cautiously in his quest to position himself above other secessionists.

Mirwaiz Umar Farooq, a part of the Hurriyat Conference was also a respected religious head. He was coronated as the Mirwaiz at the age of 17, after the assassination of his father, Mohammad Farooq, in 1990. The young Mirwaiz's Friday sermons at Srinagar's Jamia Masjid were a huge draw. Few in Kashmir missed the fact that Malik's cavalcade went way past the Mirwaiz' residence and he turned back to visit Umar Farooq at home, only after the latter personally sent for him. The Centre was keen on using Malik to counter Hurriyat Conference leaders like Mirwaiz and Syed Ali Shah Geelani, who were perceived to be tilting towards Pakistan. Unlike the JKLF, which stood for independence, the other separatists spoke a language that pleased their masters in Pakistan.

When the procession finally reached Maisuma, I glanced at my questionnaire again. The interview was to follow the first address he was expected to make after returning from Delhi's prison. As soon as Malik took the stage and before he could even utter a single word, he swerved and fell. The sheer fatigue of the seven-hour journey in an open jeep, constantly waving and shaking hands with people lining the roads, led to him fainting on stage, in front of a huge gathering of people.

I did not have my interview. I'd booked myself on the same flight as Malik and travelled Srinagar's streets, but the Pied Piper was laid out in a hospital bed, where he stayed, for a few days. His aides, who travelled with me on the same flight from Delhi, promised to call my hotel and intimate a time.

The wait was gruelling. I kept adding to my questionnaire. A day later, an aide finally called to tell me that Malik would give me the interview in the hospital. He also gave me a clear message: Please come after dinner because there are too many visitors during the day, and it would be difficult for 'Yasin Saab' to focus on the interview.

Stepping out after dusk was fraught with risk. I was well aware of that but was willing to take my chances. I still had my press card and knew that while it would enable me to explain my late-night outing to edgy soldiers, it would not be a shield if a bullet were to come our way.

In the course of my journey through conflict, I'd learnt a few key 'must do's'. It was important to engage the same driver on every trip. That helped build a relationship and my driver became a trusted companion; an important local guide, who would help me out of many distressing, life-threatening moments.

The drive from the hotel to the hospital through dark, deserted streets is a memory that has stayed in my mind. In Srinagar, young boys happily threw cricket balls and bricks at streetlights. Those were the orders from the militants who had a run of the streets. The nights were always eerie. One had to drive cautiously. Driving past security bunkers was an ordeal. A torchlight breaking the darkness of the night was a clear signal that we had to stop. Usually, the press card helped, even though the driver – a local Kashmiri – was always looked at with suspicion.

I was glad to finally enter the porch of the hospital. Malik's aides escorted me to his ward, where he lay behind hospital curtains. He greeted me and seemed in no hurry to start the interview. There were still people around him and I waited while he spoke to them in Kashmiri, a language I could barely comprehend. It is often said that you have to be born a Kashmiri to be able to speak it and in all my years of reporting from there, I get the drift but have learnt only five proper sentences.

Malik's sister was by his side, and he finally turned his attention to me. After asking him how he was feeling, I wished to move on with the interview. To my utter shock and acute discomfiture, the 28-year-old grand hero of the liberation movement, who had just arrived to a tumultuous reception, extended his hand towards me and said, '*Mujhse dosti karogi*?' (Will you be my friend? Well, that is the literal translation but does not convey the tone of what he was implying.)

I froze on the stool. This is not what I was prepared for. This is not why I had risked the late-night drive. I shifted uncomfortably on the stool and muttered, 'So should I start the interview?'

'But what is your hurry?' he asked, his hand still outstretched. He spoke English well, but had chosen Urdu while extending his hand, asking for 'dosti'.

Dread was slowly creeping into me. I felt trapped and hapless. He reminded me of a chief minister in Punjab who had hugged and held me in a tight embrace and whispered, 'Next time, don't bring your photographer along. Come without a male bodyguard.'

'Can we start?' I remember telling Malik and he relented as his sister said something to him. He kept looking at me and finally answered the questions. The interview is a part of *India Today*'s archives.

Q What are your priorities now?

A My first task will be to purify the movement. There is no change in the goal but criminals, who have entered the movement and are giving us a bad name, have to be weeded out. It needs a daring initiative and I will do it even at the cost of my life.

Q What do you see yourself as – a militant or a politician?

A It depends on the situation.

Q So you kidnapped Rubaiya Sayeed and killed five IAF officers because the situation demanded it?

A Yes, I picked up the gun and indulged in many actions because that was the need of the hour.

Q And you killed innocents?

A The IAF officers were not innocents. They were defence officers of another country. Kashmir is neither a part of India nor Pakistan. And why are you talking only about the IAF officers? I was involved in other actions as well.

Q But Kashmir is part of India.

A We don't share that view.

Q Will you use the gun again?

A It's a nonsensical question. I may be the chief of the organization but the executive powers rest with the high command. They will decide.

Q Are you willing to hold talks with the Centre?

A Yes, if there are no preconditions, and we are treated equally. Both India and Pakistan, frankly, have misled their countries. Neither knows what the real situation in Kashmir is, because it's not [Narasimha] Rao's and [S. B.] Chavan's sons who are getting killed. Kashmir is not a law and order problem.

Q But countries, including the US, are backing the Simla accord.

A The US is also saying that the wishes and aspirations of the Kashmiris have to be taken into account. If India and Pakistan miss the present opportunity, diplomatic pressure will peak and there can also be international intervention.

Q Does it mean you are willing to discuss autonomy?

A Independence remains our goal. Autonomy is not an issue.

Q Were you released following an understanding with the Centre?

A I am out on medical grounds and my medical report was written not by a Kashmiri but by Delhi doctors.

Q Will you participate in polls?

A I don't believe in the electoral process, nor do the Kashmiris.

Q Will the JKLF indirectly support the National Conference if elections are held?

A The JKLF also has people who earlier had affiliations with the Congress (I) but that doesn't mean we'll help the Congress (I). Let's see who comes out and votes.

The interview was done, and I was in a hurry to get back to my hotel. We were well into the night and the city was asleep.

'Meet me the next time you come to Srinagar,' Malik said, as I picked up my bag to leave.

On my way back to the hotel, through the same deserted streets, I wondered: Is this the man New Delhi has set its sights on? Will he be able to deliver on his promise of a dialogue? Will he be able to pave the way forward for a beleaguered state caught in the vicious cycle of violence?

For New Delhi, Malik's release was being billed as a refreshing change. For the government, the prospect of a dialogue was better than the firefighting operations that Kashmir was inexorably caught in.

I reached the hotel to the staccato sound of bullets. The sharp, screeching sound came from some distance away. It was a sound Kashmir's journalists were getting accustomed to.

On my return to Delhi, I told my friends at *India Today* about my encounter at the hospital. 'You like playing with fire, you junkie,' one said, while another felt that I should definitely reach out to Malik for another interview, on my next trip to the Valley.

I was a frequent traveller to the troubled Valley and it was only a matter of time before I made contact with him for a second interview. Malik called me to his house in

Maisuma. He was seated on a Kashmiri carpet. His sister, who he lived with, was nowhere in sight, while four armed JKLF gunmen stood in guard, just outside the room.

I sat down and took out my notebook. Malik was in no mood for an interview. The conversation kept getting more and more personal and extremely discomfiting. The gunmen at the door paced up and down, shuffling their feet. They were on duty to protect New Delhi's trusted lieutenant and the people's hero.

I'm not sure if they could hear what their boss was saying.

'Why do you always want to talk about work?' he asked.

'I am a journalist and I'm here for an interview....'

'Why don't we talk about the stars and the moon today?' he asked....

The shuffling of JKLF's loyal gunmen was audible. The door of the room was ajar.

'Can we start the interview?'

'I believe you had a good time at an army dinner last night?'

The liberator, who had thousands chanting after him, was taunting me, trying to scare me.

'Yes, I was at an army dinner last night and will meet them again. If they tell me, you were at Yasin Malik's yesterday, I will tell them the same thing; that I will continue to meet people from across the spectrum. That is my core job as a journalist,' I said in a firm voice.

There was no uncertainty to what I was conveying.

'Again, you're talking about work. Let's discuss poetry,' he said, while asking for some tea to be served.

'Can I start the interview?' I asked again.

'*Mujhse dosti karogi*?'

It was clear that there was going to be no interview. I politely finished my tea, got up, walked tentatively past the gunmen and made my way back to the hotel. The receptionist told me that Malik's sister had called and handed me a phone number on a slip.

I did not return the call.

I had seen a side to Malik few would have known even existed. It is impossible for me to read any news related to him without the memory of my own experience creeping in. Sitting opposite him on the carpet, with him insisting on talking about the moon and the stars, was a difficult half an hour.

Covering a conflict zone comes with a myriad complexities. It takes a physical, psychological, and emotional toll. Over the years, I found myself getting sucked into the lives of a violent society. I visited the Pandits living wretched lives in tents in Jammu, after they were forced out of their homeland. I watched as the young chose the path to violence and homes got shattered with the death of loved ones. I remember Kashmiri men leaving home only after they'd put their address in their pocket so at least their bodies would reach the right home if they were struck by flying shrapnel and bullets. I remember a five-year-old pleading with his mother to lift the heavy tombstone under which his father lay buried, so he could come back home.

The responsibility of showing the way out of senseless killings was entrusted to Yasin Malik, who soon found that espousing Gandhian principles was easy; finding peace was not. True to his promise to Rajesh Pilot and Wajahat Habibullah, he declared a ceasefire.

Pakistan did not want this. Within a few months of his return to the Valley, Malik was expelled by Amanullah Khan, the Muzaffarabad-based chairman of the JKLF. I had met him in Rawalpindi, in Pakistan, on a previous trip, and interviewed him again on the news of Malik's expulsion, for *India Today* magazine.

Q **Why did you expel Yasin Malik?**

A I had been suspecting for a long time that he had an understanding with the Indian government to stop militant activity. Militancy is our life. Such a person is not fit to head our organization. Under him, a popular organization like the JKLF was being reduced to a mohalla in Srinagar. His attitude towards his colleagues was that of a fascist.

Q **Malik says you have an understanding with Indian intelligence agencies.**

A I have devoted my whole life to working for the liberation of my country. India got the Interpol to issue a warrant against me and it got my American visa cancelled. How can I be an Indian agent?

Q **Now you have been expelled [Amanullah was based in Islamabad... he and Malik fell out after he came overground after his release] and Srinagar has been made the JKLF headquarters.**

A If Rajesh Pilot or Krishna Rao expel Narasimha Rao tomorrow, will it make any difference? It is just a joke. Yasin Malik has been expelled by me under our constitution. And that's it.

Q **You have been accused of running the JKLF through remote control. Malik says that has ended.**

A Where did Yasin himself come from? I created the JKLF, and the JKLF created Yasin. We brought him here, trained him and sent him back. What is he talking about? He is the one who bargained away the armed struggle.

Malik's release led to several peace initiatives; each attempted by different governments; from Narasimha Rao to A. B. Vajpayee and Manmohan Singh. He was wooed by several intelligence officials including A. S. Dulat, an IB officer who retired as the chief of R&AW, and Ajit Doval. Dulat remembers Malik as a cocky, cigarette-puffing man who had his feet up on the table when he went to meet him just before he agreed to go to Srinagar to declare a ceasefire.

The Che Guevara of Kashmir – as he was once called by Kashmiri journalist, Basharat Peer – now stands convicted for life in terror funding cases filed by the National Investigations Agency (NIA).

The 'convict' who pleaded guilty to charges of terror funding is lodged in Delhi's Tihar jail. He is also being tried for the kidnapping of Rubaiya in 1989 and for the attack on Indian Air Force personnel in Srinagar's Rawalpora. Four air force officials were killed and 22 injured when they were fired upon at a bus stop. One official has identified Malik to be amongst those who opened fire on them. Similarly, Rubaiya, whose sister Mehbooba Mufti later went on to become Jammu and Kashmir's first woman chief minister, has identified Malik as her abductor.

Malik, once used to being under the constant gaze of popular, public attention, is now entangled in legal battles. He got some attention after he went on a hunger strike in Tihar jail in 2022, alleging unfair treatment. He was also in the spotlight in 2020, after he released an open letter, through his family.

The contents read like a self-appraisal. 'When we, the non-violent political activists of Kashmir, failed to find any space for peaceful democratic politics, we got compelled to tread an armed path in 1988 under the banner of Jammu Kashmir Liberation Front (JKLF). The whole world knows that Kashmiris have no history of violence and also that starting an armed struggle was not our desire, but it was rather a compulsion.'

He also pointed out facts as he perceived them, through the same open letter, released just before he had started another hunger strike in Tihar, where he is incarcerated in Prison No 7.

'From 1994, after the declaration of my unilateral ceasefire, I and my colleagues in JKLF have remained firm on the non-violent struggle. There is not a single piece of evidence about me or my JKLF colleagues who have ever since supported any act of armed struggle overtly or covertly or provide any kind of help to any armed group. It is also a fact that from last 30 years, militancy related cases registered against me and my colleagues were not pursued by any government, and all governments from 1994, led by prime ministers like P. V. Narasimha Rao, H. D. Deve Gowda, I. K. Gujral, A. B. Vajpayee, Manmohan Singh to a large extent, honoured the pledge made by the Indian government in 1994 to us. Even through the first five years of the present government led by PM Narendra Modi there was no trial of militancy related cases against me and my colleagues. But suddenly from 2019, TADA court in Jammu started the trial of these 30-year-old militancy related cases which is actually against the spirit of the ceasefire pledge made in 1994.'

The government and their intelligence agencies needed him in the mid-90s. In 2022, the NIA asked for a death warrant, but the court conferred a life imprisonment.

Malik, in fact, lost his primacy many years before his arrest. The hero, perceived as Kashmir's liberator, ended up as one among many separatists. The JKLF too, was banned soon after a big blast in Pulwama in February 2019, which claimed the lives of 40 CRPF troopers.

The Pulwama attack redrew the security matrix and the political destiny of a state once called Jammu and Kashmir. The abrogation of Article 370 altered Jammu and Kashmir's history and geography, but more on that in another chapter.

Pulwama also altered Yasin Malik's reality. The man who was chosen as New Delhi's poster boy in 1994 and released on bail, is now back in Tihar.

He is now neither a separatist nor a street commander. His wife, Mushaal Hussein and daughter live in Pakistan, miles away from a man who was once a rebel with a cause.

Malik met Mushaal in 2005, while on a trip to Pakistan and the two married in 2009. Mushaal, born into a Kashmiri family served as a special advisor to Anwaar ul-Haq Kakar, who headed a caretaker government from August 2023 until the 2024 elections in Pakistan. She created a flutter, later the same year, when she wrote a letter to Rahul Gandhi, the leader of the Opposition, urging him to initiate a debate on her incarcerated husband, saying he could bring peace to Jammu and Kashmir.

Peace has multiple interpretations.

In conflict zones, the practitioners of 'peace' are sometimes led by the compulsions of the ground reality. Often, they are led by the ideological bent of the parties in power. The pursuit of peace has swung like a pendulum between the early '90s, when violence was at its peak, and the Narendra Modi era when Article 370, which gave Jammu and Kashmir its special status, was seen as the main impediment.

Yasin Malik was only one player on the chessboard.

I never sought a meeting with him after the evening I walked past his gunmen. I did bump into him once at a local journalist's office in Srinagar, but we did not exchange a single word. Silence can be eloquent.

Babri Masjid to Ram Mandir

We were suspected at every stop and seen as 'Hindus from India'. The common refrain at the time was, 'You are snooping around temples in an effort to defame us and portray us as Muslim fundamentalists.' Our mission was actually the opposite, and it was challenging in several ways.

The trees were barren, shorn of life and colour. The clouds over the Srinagar sky were dark and foreboding. I sat in my hotel room and looked out of the window. I ought to have been on a flight to Delhi but inclement weather ensured that I stay trapped in the unsettling serenity of Kashmir's winter.

The date: 6 December 1992.

Miles away from the surreal beauty of a wounded city, India's secular dream was dying. Thousands of volunteers, or kar sevaks, had gathered at Ayodhya following a clarion call from BJP leader L. K. Advani, who had told a restive army of followers that a 'symbolic kar seva' would be performed, to correct a 'historical wrong'.

On that fateful Sunday in December 1992, India changed in several ways. Overzealous, frenzied mobs carried all the equipment they needed to demolish the Babri Masjid, a sixteenth-century mosque that was claimed to be the birthplace of Lord Ram. That Sunday, the masjid became a focal point of conflict between Hindus and Muslims. The conflict was social, political, and legal. The politicians notched up the heat and ratcheted up the rhetoric. The promise of '*mandir yahin banayenge*' took deathly shape.

The equipment had already been stocked. Armed with sickles, trishuls, pickaxes, hammers, and ropes, the agitated kar sevaks behaved like men possessed. They tore down the Babri Masjid, dome by dome, pausing only to remove the idols of Ram which had mysteriously been placed beneath the central dome in 1949. The Babri Masjid complex was declared a disputed structure and no namaz was offered since then. The gates were secured with locks.

The locks were opened in 1986 during the tenure of Prime Minister Rajiv Gandhi. The politics of faith started soon after and Advani set off on a 10,000 kilometers rath yatra, that meandered its way from Southern India towards Ayodhya in Uttar Pradesh, in 1990. The objective was to liberate the 'birthplace of Ram'.

On 6 December 1992, there was no leader who invoked the law to stop the barbarism of the mob. Prime Minister P. V. Narasimha Rao failed, as did his home minister, S. B. Chavan, who, as I reported then, stayed ensconced in the puja room of his official residence in New Delhi. Home ministry officials told me then that they kept waiting for a call from him that never came. 'It was 36 hours before the 190 paramilitary companies posted in and around Faizabad moved to evacuate the kar sevaks. Only a few days earlier, Chavan had boasted that the "Rapid Action Force" could reach the spot within eight cracking minutes,' I wrote for *India Today*'s special issue, 'Nation's Shame'. The magazine came out just before the year ended. It was a sombre note to end the year with. It ended with the burial of India's secular dream.

I was able to return from Srinagar to file for the special issue – a collector's item that showcased how journalists can put their heads together to produce a profound piece of work. The issue also had a strong letter from Editor-in-Chief Aroon Purie.

> There come moments in history when a nation's soul is seared. For India, that moment came on the afternoon of December 6 when the Babri Masjid-Ram Janmabhoomi-disputed structure, call it what you will, was demolished. It exposed the fragile face of India's secular democracy. The true character of a person is often unveiled in times of crisis....
>
> So it is with countries. This one tragic event has revealed the shocking state of Indian society. It has held out a mirror to all of us, and all the world has looked on. The reflection is an ugly one. A society so hollow that a mockery is made of the highest court of the land, a government so weak that it cannot enforce the rule of law, and a social fabric so tenuous that it soaks itself in blood at the slightest provocation.

He wrote, without mincing his words.

There were more words, in the same letter. The words were prophetic and hair-raising. They're ringing true in 2025, and reproduce them, I must.

> The jackboot of fascism shows scant respect for the pillars of democracy and therefore the crushing of the press in Ayodhya was quite in character. It showed the sinister underbelly of this so-called religious movement. It is a matter of great concern that the radical fringes of every community, because they make the loudest noise and attract the maximum attention, falsely create the impression of representing the silent majority. While this majority, who by and large are more interested in peaceful coexistence and in improving the quality of their lives than in killing fellow citizens, become the unfortunate victims of extremism.
>
> This tolerant majority must find peaceful ways of making their voice heard above those of power-hungry leaders who play with our lives. I, for one, am hopeful because I believe that there is a kind of inevitable justice.
>
> History has shown that evil carries its own seeds of destruction. Brave men and women who stand against these forces of bigotry can hasten this day of justice. In my opinion, the religious fanaticism which has reared its head today will be defeated by the innate common sense and decency of our people.

Holding truth to power has undergone a sea-change since 1992. But in that year, journalism was courageous, fearless, and bipartisan; editors and owners were still aligned to being the watchdogs they're meant to be. I was amongst those encouraged by my editor to go out of the way to call a spade a spade, and call out hate and bigotry.

Soon after the Babri Masjid was demolished and smoke billowed in thick plumes, Advani, the charioteer who had lost control of his disciples, was not sure how to frame his response. He had led the rath yatra and announced a symbolic ceremony but the kar sevaks had been charged up. They were not paying heed to the announcements being made by Uma Bharti and others on the public address system, asking them to get off the domes of the masjid.

Advani vacillated between calling 6 December 1992, 'the saddest day in my life,' to also saying, 'None raised a voice when 40-odd temples were desecrated in Kashmir. Why these double standards?' In a two-part article published in *The Indian Express*, he wrote, 'It was the saddest day in my life. I have seldom felt as dejected and downcast as I felt on that day.' Yet, Advani, who was also the party president at the time, pointed to the 'desecration' and 'demolition' of temples in the Valley which had been virtually emptied of Kashmiri Pandits by then.

Whataboutery is not a new phenomenon. It had been politically honed and chiselled in the early '90s. A year before the demolition, Advani had said, 'Look at the deafening silence of all civil liberties organizations about Ayodhya. Why? Because it is an issue pertaining to the Hindu religion. If it was related to the Muslim religion, their response would have been different. All political parties which think it is their duty to defend the mosque, not one of them has spoken a word of criticism about the 55 temples broken in Kashmir. No one talks about it. Why these double standards?'

We decided to check out Advani's claims. Had temples been broken in Kashmir? Purie called me to his office one day, soon after the fires lit by the demolition of the Babri Masjid were still burning. Riots that followed the demolition had claimed around 2,000 lives. The death toll was spread over different states. From Uttar Pradesh to Gujarat, and from Maharashtra to Madhya Pradesh. India's soul had been seared.

'Go to the BJP office and ask them for a list of temples they claim have been desecrated,' Purie said. It was important to get the list from the BJP because the 'what about temples in Kashmir?' had become the most powerful counterattack weapon in the BJP's propaganda armoury.

It was a tactic used by the BJP to demonstrate that its crusade against 'pseudo-secularism' was not without foundation and that its opponents were hypocrites and anti-Hindu.

It was time to investigate if the BJP's counter-argument had any substance to it. Since I was already reporting the conflict in Kashmir, I was asked to travel back to the Valley and verify Advani's big claim.

I had to first get the list. Which temples were Advani and other BJP leaders talking about? Where were they located? When were they broken? Were these temples damaged at all?

An *India Today* investigation – backed by photographic

evidence – revealed that the BJP and its leaders had either been misled or were deliberately using the tactic of the Big Lie (if you repeat a gross untruth often enough, people begin to believe you), in order to score political gains. That the BJP was unsure of its facts became evident even before I reached Kashmir.

Obtaining a complete list from the BJP of the 'damaged' temples was an uphill task. While BJP leader Kedarnath Sahni provided a list of the temples that he said were damaged in 1986, party Vice President K. R. Malkani insisted that when they spoke of broken temples, they meant shrines damaged by 'Muslim fundamentalists' after 1989. Riots had broken out in the state in 1986. It was also the year the Centre dismissed the G. M. Shah government in Jammu and Kashmir. Despite the Congress party being the main player behind the midnight coup that ended in the ouster of the Farooq Abdullah government, Shah – married to Farooq's sister – became a liability. Politics aside, the riots took place in the backdrop of Shah wanting to construct a mosque inside Jammu's secretariat building and the opening of the locks of the Babri Masjid in Ayodhya.

Kashmir saw the first eruption of communal violence in 1986 when scores of homes and shops were burnt and looted, mostly in Anantnag, an hour's drive from Srinagar. It was in the midst of this frenzy, in which close to 350 houses were damaged, that the organized mobs also attacked and looted temples. Malkani referenced 1989 because that was the precise year when the insurgency saw a definitive upswing after the kidnapping of Rubaiya Sayeed and her subsequent release in exchange for militants.

Investigating the BJP's claims was not easy. The claims lay hidden in a complex web. The labyrinth had to be slowly and carefully negotiated.

What the saffron party omitted from mentioning, when they gave me the list, was an important fact: the temples that had been damaged in 1986 after large-scale riots, had been subsequently repaired.

Immediately after the riots, the damage was assessed and the temples reconstructed. And just as Muslim neighbours had given shelter to their Pandit friends during the riots, the two also joined hands in collectively rebuilding the shrines.

The BJP, however, chose to sidestep these facts and tried instead to justify the demolition of the Babri Masjid. There was a psychological dimension to this strategy: it reinforced in the 'Hindu' mind the idea that they were the continuing victims of Muslim tyranny; that, as in the past, Muslim 'invaders' were still destroying temples.

No one in the BJP, however, was able to give the exact number of temples damaged. While Sahni said 'hundreds have been destroyed,' Advani had mentioned two separate sets of figures: 55 at one point and 40 at another. The BJP's central office in Delhi gave a list of 46 temples said to have been damaged in 1986, but its Jammu office furnished a list of 82. Two years before the demolition of the Babri Masjid, a senior Rashtriya Swayamsevak Sangh (RSS) leader had given journalist B. G. Varghese a list of 62 temples which were burnt and damaged in Kashmir by terrorists in 1990.

Surprisingly, the 1986 list had names of the same temples. How is it possible that exactly the same temples were damaged both in 1986 and in 1990? The confusion about the dates and the temples on the lists raised doubts about the BJP's credibility on this issue. But even that paled into insignificance after Shipra Das, my photographer colleague, and I visited 23 temples which according to the list had either been burnt, damaged or desecrated.

After hitting the ground, and travelling from one temple to another, we found that except for two – Shailputri and Bhairav temples in Baramulla – the rest were all intact.

The more important ones, like the famous Kheer Bhawani Temple at Tulmulla village in Ganderbal, 25 kilometers from Srinagar, or the Dashnami Akhara, located at Srinagar's Badshah Chowk from where the annual yatra to the Amarnath Cave once started, were also safe even though the BJP would have liked us to believe that they were 'completely burnt'. The Amarnath Yatra is one of the most revered religious journeys undertaken by Hindu devotees every year as thousands of devotees set off on an arduous uphill journey to seek the blessings of Lord Shiva at the cave, where an ice lingam forms naturally.

Neither was the akhara gutted nor was Kheer Bhawani damaged by rocket attacks.

We found both temples being guarded by the Border Security Force (BSF), round the clock. In fact, most of the important temples were being protected. The BSF jawans said they would die but not let anyone damage Kheer Bhawani temple, where the Jeth Ashtami festival continued to take place even during troubled times. At this temple, local Muslims mingle with the Hindus in offering prayers. Considered by Kashmiri Pandits to be one of their holiest shrines, Muslims of the area also observed the custom of entering the temple only if they had not eaten meat.

Shipra and I kept slithering through Kashmir's snow-laden districts, moving from one temple to the next, ticking them off the list as we went along. It is important to remember that the insurgency was raging in the early '90s and it was not uncommon for the militants and the security forces to exchange fire.

In Srinagar, we visited the Dashnami Akhara and Ganpatyar temples that had seen crossfiring, but the priests of these temples believed that the attack was not on the temple but on the paramilitary forces. Mohan Lal, the priest at Ganpatyar told us that puja had continued uninterrupted in this 200-year-old Hanuman temple. The security picket located within the temple precincts had attracted fire twice, but the temple itself was not damaged.

The same was true for the akhara, where the godown of New Suraj Transporters, a company adjacent to the temple, caught fire during a shoot-out between the militants and the security forces. The temple, however, remained untouched, unharmed.

The pursuit for the truth through Kashmir's militant-infested districts was challenging. It was especially exacting because the Valley simmered with rage over the destruction of the Babri Masjid. The demolition in Ayodhya had deeply impacted India's only state with a Muslim majority population.

The locals looked at us with suspicion as we visited the temples. At each stop, we had to convince them – as they would gather around our car – that we were not there to defame them or paint them as members of 'Babar's army'.

We were mostly seen as 'Hindus from India', with the common refrain being, 'you are snooping around temples in an effort to defame us and portray us as Muslim fundamentalists'.

Our mission was actually the opposite, and it was challenging in several ways. We were out in the field in the month of January when Kashmir is in the harsh embrace of snow and temperatures plunge below sub-zero.

At one point, two pheran-clad militants waved their guns and asked us why we were checking out temples. After a sustained interrogation, they let us go, but only after my Kashmiri driver convinced them that I was a regular visitor and had been coming to the Valley since 1989.

We were relieved to be back in the comfort of the car but worse was still to come.

It came with a sudden burst of fire. We found ourselves trapped, as a hail of bullets came flying over our head at Anantnag's Raghunath Temple, about an hour's drive from Srinagar. It was an example of a temple being caught in an exchange of fire between the militants and the security forces.

It started when our car drew up at the Raghunath Temple. The shops opposite the temple were bustling and people peered out of homes atop the shops. Like with all our other stops, a crowd quickly gathered wanting to know what we were there for. Yet again, we had to explain our mission and tell them that we were undertaking a temple tour to check out the BJP's claims.

'This is a place of worship. Why will we harm it?' members of the crowd argued.

'Yes, that is what we have come to verify,' I said.

I requested the agitated crowd to let us go in. They agreed on the condition that two of them would accompany us to show us that the temple had in no way been harmed.

It seemed like a fair bargain to me but the BSF sentries guarding the temple refused. 'We cannot allow Muslims in,' they said. Soldiers spend long months away from home and remain on edge in an environment they perceive as hostile. Conflict forces men in uniform to take sides.

Shipra and I were standing at the entrance of the well-guarded temple. Even as we tried to negotiate our entry, the sound of bullets pierced the air. Before we knew it, the BSF guards pulled her and me in and flung us to the ground and shut the gate.

We crawled into the temple complex on all fours, waiting for the priest to come and talk to us. The sight of the trembling priest, who must have heard the gunshots, is a memory I have not been able to shake off.

I took out my pen and notebook and started scribbling. The priest did not want to be quoted by name, and I assured him that I was taking notes but would not identify him. He stayed largely confined to the temple complex, he told me and confirmed that the temple under his guard had not been damaged or desecrated.

He spent the better part of an hour talking to us, but the sound of bullets had clearly unnerved him. Suddenly, he asked me for my notebook. He insisted that I hand it over to him. I leaned across and gave it to him. I had no choice.

He yanked out the pages titled 'Raghunath Mandir' from my spiral notebook. His fingers worked fast and furious as he tore the pages to shreds to obliterate any trace of the fact that he had even had a conversation with me. 'I have to live here amongst the people,' he explained, adding, 'They might ask you once you step out.'

But how were we to step out? The local civilians, eager to showcase the temple to us, had not been allowed in. Would bullets fly again, once we left the temple complex? The BSF guards were sure we would be shot. '*Goli toh chalegi madam*,' a BSF jawan said with a ring of certainty. His finger was on the trigger. He was preparing for the eventuality of having to fire back.

It was Shipra's first trip to the Valley and the burden of responsibility weighed me down. What should I do, I kept asking myself. The dilemma was agonizing. Had luck run out on me? Was this how my journey through conflict would end? One bullet, well aimed, was all it would take.

I decided to step out of the temple. We had to. We couldn't make the temple our home. The risk had to be taken and getting back to Srinagar before dusk was imperative. The BSF sentries reminded me that we were leaving against their advice.

Holding Shipra by her hand, I walked out, my heart thudding, overtime. The hustle and bustle was gone. The shops had been shuttered and there was a deathly silence in the now deserted street.

What about my driver? Where was I going to find him? Was he safe?

A man gestured to us from a house atop one of the shops. 'Your car is at the police station next door,' he said. I walked gingerly, step by step, holding on to my photographer's hand, waiting for a bullet to hit us.

The agony ended a short walk later as we found our car and the driver at the police station. We raced back to Srinagar in near-silence. The encounter had been close… very close.

We ticked one more temple as 'safe', on the list given to us by the BJP.

During the course of that trip, we found that smaller temples, located in villages where militants took refuge, had not been harmed. The Kashmiri Pandits had migrated to Jammu and Delhi in large numbers after several from amongst their community were targeted and mercilessly killed.

By the time the Babri Masjid was demolished, the Pandit families had been forced to flee and become migrants in their own country. They were leading wretched lives in tented camps in Jammu.

Even in villages where only one of two Pandit families remained, the temples had not been singled out for wilful desecration. The Pandit families had become custodians of the temples and were encouraged by their Muslim neighbours to regularly offer prayers. In Dayalgam, for instance, a small village in district Anantnag, Maheshwar Nath's was the only Pandit family left. '*Gita ki kasam*, this temple has never been touched,' Nath said, as he opened the temple to show us that it was not damaged at all.

When challenged with this evidence, the BJP had ducked behind a question answered in Parliament by the then Congress minister of state for home, M. M. Jacob. On 3 March 1992, Jacob had stated that '38 places of worship' had been damaged between 1989 and 1991. Inquiries into the details of the unstarred question once again revealed that the BJP was conveniently building a myth around this figure too.

What no BJP leader was willing to reveal was that of the '38 places of worship' mentioned by Jacob, 16 were mosques and mosque-related properties. And just as mosques had been damaged in Muslim-dominated Kashmir, so too had 22 temples and dharmshalas.

The administration – and this is important – said that the damage was caused by crossfiring and not because there was any concerted attempt at targeting temples. There is evidence to support this view.

I was an eyewitness to one such 'caught in the crossfire' incident. In the August of 1991, I happened to be on the spot at Srinagar's Karfalli Mohalla soon after militants set fire to the Sharda Peeth Girls' Higher Secondary School. The blazing fire spread to the houses around, as also to the temple located nearby. Fire engines, however, were able to save the temple, which the BJP claimed had been destroyed after 6 December.

The evidence indicated that the temples were not demolished or desecrated by the 'Muslim militants' as claimed by the BJP, but in riot-like situations by bomb and rocket attacks.

That is why the figure included both temples and mosques. If temples had to be singled out, they could easily have been attacked in village after village, each abandoned by Pandits who fled for fear that they would be killed. In many places such as Lukh Bhawan in Anantnag, the Muslims were feeding the fish in the pond around which three temples stand. The Pandit families had left by then.

Sifting fact from fiction was not easy.

It is a fact that 52 temples were damaged in Kashmir in retaliation to the demolition of the Babri Masjid but what is critical to note is that the BJP had used every opportunity available to announce that temples had been destroyed, not after 6 December 1992, but three years EARLIER (*emphasis mine*). The propaganda was successful. Like Advani – who said, what about the temples in Kashmir – many from the majority community had started mouthing the same line.

The distorted message was a dangerous one: that the demolition of the Babri Masjid was justified because it was the righteous reaction to the damage to temples in Kashmir.

After my return to Delhi, one important aspect remained. 'Call Advani and seek his response,' my editor at *India Today*, Inderjit Badhwar said. He was right. The charioteer had to be confronted with our findings.

I called Advani's residence late in the evening. It was the era of landline phones, and he answered the call himself. When asked about what his party's stand would be if someone were to find that the BJP was lying and distorting the facts, he replied: 'I don't have a list nor do I know the exact number, which is why I always say "scores of temples". In some statements, I have given a figure of 40 but the number is not important. If it isn't 40, it'll be 38 or 39.'

Neither number was correct. Visits to temple after temple proved that it was the BJP's propaganda which needed to be demolished. 'The Big Lie can fool some of the people some of the time but not all of the people all of the time,' I had written in conclusion to the *India Today* article. Published in February 1993, the investigation raised a mini storm.

Apart from a whisper campaign within the office – of how we had photographed the temples from angles that concealed the damage – we also had a large group of protesting Kashmiri Pandits arrive at the stairwell of the *India Today* office in New Delhi's Connaught Place. This was soon after the magazine hit the stands.

Displaced from their homeland, with no sign of return in the foreseeable future, the group was agitated and demanded an audience with the editor.

I was on my way back from lunch and ran into the group being held at bay by the security guards. 'Ask Mr Baweja to meet us. We will tell him many truths,' they said to my face as I tried to calm them down. I understood where their anger was stemming from. Kashmir was no longer a place they could call home. I had spent time with several Pandit families in the tents they had been forced into, in Jammu. They were living miserable lives.

Since January 1990, when they first started migrating, only a few thousand Pandits now remain in the Valley. No party, not even the BJP, which shared power with Chief Minister Mehbooba Mufti has been able to create an environment for them to return. The Pandits gravitated to the BJP politically and still vote for the saffron party, but while it shared power with Mehbooba, the communal chasm between the regions of Jammu and Kashmir only widened.

The anger I encountered at the stairwell of the office encapsulated their torment. As journalists, however, we also had the responsibility of sifting the chaff from the wheat. That is what we had tried to do by 'demolishing' a dangerous lie.

Print journalism has its facets – anonymity is one of them. Not knowing they were speaking with the target of their discontent and ire, the agitated Pandits handed me a memorandum that I promised would reach the editor's desk.

Aroon Purie had already made his views known in his fortnightly letter, published in the same issue. He had not minced his words and boldly stated,

> Rumours have always been the bellows that fan communal conflagrations in this country. In today's surcharged atmosphere of religious mistrust, rumours serve to harden feelings of hatred. And those who use disinformation for political gain, benefit, unless they are exposed.
>
> The BJP's most effective argument against those who denounced the demolition on 6 December was that they were "pseudo-secularists" who shed crocodile

> tears over the destruction of the "disputed structure" while maintaining an unspeakable silence over the destruction of scores of Hindu temples in Kashmir over the past five years.... Today, with violence being fanned through rumour, dissembling, and fanatical distortions designed to appeal to people's insecurities in order to divide them, the Press, as never before, has the burden and responsibility to ferret out the truth and to debunk lies, no matter what their origin. As the nineteenth-century American thinker Thomas Cooper said: "Fraud and falsehood only dread examination. Truth invites it."

The truth also is that the forlorn Ayodhya sky, that billowed with smoke, set the country on a different political path. The destruction of the Babri Masjid was a seminal moment that altered our history and politics. The debris pointed to an indelible saffron imprint. It also pointed to the painful shift from secularism to communalism. Advani had already coined the 'pseudo-secularist' jibe to kickstart the Hindutva project, a project that continues today through brutal assaults that lynch and bulldoze.

The Ram Janmabhoomi movement which culminated in the destruction of the Babri Masjid and dealt a blow to India's secular core, gave a massive boost to the BJP's political fortunes. A party which had only two members in Parliament in 1984, won 120 Lok Sabha seats in 1991, a year after Advani started his chariot ride. He effectively mixed religion with politics and many a BJP stalwart benefitted from the intoxicating brew.

The party continued its political strides and stayed rooted to the idea of constructing a grand Ram Temple as a centrepiece of its strategy to keep the Hindu ranks together. '*Mandir wahin banayegen*,' the slogan that reflected naked religious militancy, was further strengthened after the courts awarded the 'disputed site' to the Hindu parties. In September 2010, three judges of the Allahabad High Court ruled that Hindus and Muslims share the disputed site. The court said that two-thirds of the 2.77-acre site belonged to Nirmohi Akhara sect and Ramlalla Virajman, the Hindu groups, and the rest to Uttar Pradesh's Sunni Central Waqf Board. A bench of the Supreme Court, however, suspended the ruling after an appeal from both sides.

The final legal die was cast on 9 November 2019. The Supreme Court paved the way for the construction of the Ram Temple. The judgement came as a formality. It also came with a cruel rider attached to it. The apex court called out the demolition of the Babri Masjid as an 'egregious violation of the rule of law,' but signed in favour of those who were responsible for tearing the masjid down.

No one was punished for that egregious violation even though the demolition was called an illegality. The mosque had been torn down in broad daylight and in the presence of an array of political stalwarts such as L. K. Advani, Murli Manohar Joshi, Vinay Katiyar, Uma Bharati, and 'Sadhvi' Ritambhara among others.

They were physically present when the kar sevaks climbed atop the domes. Some calls were made to the kar sevaks to stop, but that day, the slogan also was, '*Ek dhakka aur do, Babri Masjid tod do*.' They had stirred the communal pot and brought India to a boil. They had, in fact, changed the idea of India.

A year after the apex court bowed in the name of *aastha*, as an ode to the faith of the majority, Advani and all others were cleared of charges. No one was punished for the demolition. Twenty-eight years after the domes had been pulled down, no one – repeat no one – was handed out any punishment for rioting, for unlawful assembly, for promoting enmity between groups, or for conspiring. Lakhs of armed faithfuls had joined hands – egged on by senior leaders – and a CBI special court gave everyone a free pass.

Advani, who had in 1992, referred to the demolition as one of the 'saddest days in my life', found fresh words to celebrate his acquittal. 'I wholeheartedly welcome the judgement by the Special Court in the Babri Masjid Demolition Case. The judgement vindicates my personal and BJP's belief and commitment toward the Ram Janmabhoomi movement,' the charioteer was quoted as saying.

By 2020, when the acquittal was celebrated, Narendra Modi was well into his second term as prime minister. It was clear that a grand temple would be built, where the masjid once stood, in time for the 2024 general election.

Months ahead of the 30 September 2020 acquittal order, the government had established a 15-member Shree Ram Janmabhoomi Teerth Kshetra Trust. It was setup on 5 February 2020 to oversee the construction and management of the Ram Temple. Modi laid the foundation stone of the temple on 5 August 2020.

In its mind's eye, the BJP was building – literally – what it foresaw as its ticket to political success. It saw itself riding to power with an unbridled majority to shore up its already impressive numbers. Though a part of the National Democratic Alliance (NDA), the BJP was miles ahead of its allies after it notched 303 Lok Sabha seats on its own in 2019, and it was now in pursuit of a hat trick.

It came as no surprise when Modi announced the *pran pratistha* (consecration ceremony) of the Ram Temple. 22 January 2024 was the chosen date and he was the self-appointed inaugurator. The country seemed to be caught in a rhapsody of religious fervour. Ram was everywhere: on banners and hoardings, in WhatsApp messages, in political speeches, and in commercial advertisements.

I awakened, one day to a video advert from a jeweller displaying images of sculpted-in-silver Ram idols, in different shapes and sizes.

The video was set to the words of, '*Ram aayenge, toh angana sajuanga… Deep jala ke, Diwali mein manaunga… Mere janmo ke paap, saare dhul jayenge, Ram aayenge….*' (I will decorate my courtyard when Ram comes. I will celebrate by lighting diyas. My sins will be forgiven when Ram comes.)

Ram had arrived in style and in different forms. For some he was political, for others, deeply religious, and for many, very commercial, as the videos and thousands of banners, posters, and billboards testified. For the media, especially television, it was the perfect 'live telecast' moment. *Aaj Tak* and *India Today* television – owned by the same media group I had once worked with – had 'Ram aayenge' emblazoned on its broadcast vans. The media's over-powering saffron shift was self-advertised.

The resident welfare association in my neighbourhood delivered a photograph of the grand, brand-new temple to my doorstep. An accompanying fact sheet listed all the vitals of the temple at Ayodhya, India's 'Vatican city, the holiest site for Indians across the world'. The words in inverted commas are not mine. They're Sharad Sharma's, the spokesperson for the Vishwa Hindu Parishad (VHP).

The fact sheet had intricate details. The entry to the temple has 32 steps, 44 doors. The length of the temple (North to South) is 380 feet, its width 250 feet; its height, 161 feet.

The headline was the consecration ceremony overseen by Prime Minister Narendra Modi. He declared with great pride that he had been chosen by God to be the 'representative of all Indians' for the inauguration of the temple. The VHP, at the forefront of the Babri demolition, believed that the new temple would finally address the 'subjugation' and 'oppression' of Hindus over the last 500 years.

The BJP went full throttle into the 2024 general election, firm in the belief that the inauguration of the long-promised Ram Temple in Ayodhya would take them well beyond the majority mark of 272 seats. In 2014, the party went with the slogan of '*Ab ki baar, Modi sarkaar.*' In 2019, it was changed to, '*Abki baar 300 paar,*' and it hit 303 with bullet-precision.

But 2024's '*Abki baar, 400 paar,*' threw up a nasty surprise. Thirty-three years after the Babri demolition and four months after the *pran pratishta*, the BJP's tally stopped at an unpredicted 240 seats.

The ultimate irony came with the defeat of the BJP from Uttar Pradesh's Faizabad in whose fold Ayodhya lies. Leaders do not always pay heed to the lessons of history.

Jawaharlal Nehru, one of India's founding fathers, was the only prime minister who kept faith out of politics. Two such moments are well documented. His opposition to the mysterious appearance of Ram Lalla idols at the Babri Masjid in 1949 and his written advice to President Dr Rajendra Prasad to not attend the inauguration of the Somnath Temple in Gujarat in 1951. Dr Prasad, however, chose to make his presence felt.

Political intent does not always change the course of history, but it is recorded. It is documented in books and is forever remembered and recalled.

The 2024 political jolt did not stop the government and the National Council of Educational Research and Training (NCERT), mandated to educate students, from trying to rewrite history.

An updated Class 12 political science textbook has removed the name of the Babri Masjid and referred to it as a 'three dome structure'. The revised textbook has also reduced the section on Ayodhya from four to two pages, and erased multiple references pertaining to the mosque's demolition on 6 December 1992.

Ninety-seven-year-old Advani – who was awarded the highest civilian award, the Bharat Ratna, in 2024 – must, however, be an unhappy man. The man who pioneered the Ram Janmabhoomi movement and described the *pran pratishta* as a 'divine dream' is no longer a part of the political science textbook, which has also pruned sections on the Emergency imposed by Prime Minister Indira Gandhi.

Amongst the deleted sections relating to Ayodhya are portions that detailed Advani's rath yatra, the role of the kar sevaks in the demolition of the Babri Masjid, and the communal riots that followed. NCERT has also deleted the BJP's 'regret over the happenings in Ayodhya'. A. B. Vajpayee, another BJP stalwart had in an interview to NDTV said, 'We tried to protect that structure but could not. We are sorry for that.' He described the demolition as 'very unfortunate'.

There are other deletions. Each deletion points to the precise issues that the BJP's political masters are uncomfortable with. Images too, have not been spared. An image of a newspaper clipping with the headline, 'Babri Masjid demolished, Centre sacks Kalyan Govt' has been removed from a revised textbook. Former Prime Minister Vajpayee saying 'Ayodhya, BJP's worst miscalculation' in an interview soon after the demolition, has also been edited out. So has the fact that Kalyan Singh, the then chief minister of Uttar Pradesh had been convicted by the Supreme Court for failing to 'uphold the majesty of the law'.

In 2024, Dinesh Prasad Saklani, director, NCERT, espoused a reasoning for the controversial deletions. 'Why should we teach about riots in school textbooks? We want to create positive citizens, not violent and depressed individuals,' he said.

What Saklani and his masters in the government need to understand is that seminal events cannot be papered over; that history cannot be hidden. Today's students and India's young adults are not just bookworms. Textbooks are not their only source of information. Does the NCERT really want its future generations to grow up without a sense of history, no matter how violent or distressing? Do students not have the right to learn about how Mahatma Gandhi was killed and by whom? Do they not deserve to know about the excesses committed during the Emergency imposed by Indira Gandhi?

An earlier version of the textbook contained the sequence of events that began with the removal of the locks on the gates of the Babri Masjid in 1986 by the Rajiv Gandhi government. While earlier textbooks referenced Mir Baqi as the one who built it in the sixteenth century, the new textbook now omits the word, Babri.

The revised textbook focusses on the Supreme Court's decision to allow the construction of a Ram Temple. In a section titled, 'From Legal Proceedings to Amicable Acceptance', it refers to the November 2019, 5–0 verdict of the constitutional bench of the Supreme Court. 'The verdict allotted the disputed site to the Shri Ram Janmabhoomi Teertha Kshetra Trust for the construction of Ram temple and directed the concerned government to allot an appropriate site for the construction of a Mosque to the Sunni Central Waqf Board. In this way, democracy gives room for conflict resolution in a plural society like ours, upholding the inclusive spirit of the Constitution. This issue was resolved following the due process of law based on evidence such as archaeological excavations and historical records. The Supreme Court's decision was celebrated by the society at large. It is a classic example of consensus building on a sensitive issue that shows the maturity of democratic ethos,' the new textbook says.

This is a half-truth.

The textbook makes no mention of the fact that the same Supreme Court judgement had also called the demolition of the Babri Masjid an 'egregious criminal act'.

What the rewriters need to understand is that while history can be distorted, even prettified, it simply cannot be erased. Apart from one political science textbook, there are scores of books, periodicals, videos, and court judgements that add to history's narrative. These imprints cannot be erased and they shouldn't be.

The Babri Masjid was razed to the ground. That's a historical fact that can never be erased.

Azad Kashmir
Inside Pakistan Occupied Kashmir

Suddenly, I found myself surrounded by a group of men. In unison, they chanted, 'Indian dog go back, Indian dog go back... I found myself quaking with rage. How 'azad' was 'Azad Kashmir'?

Landing in Lahore is always exhilarating and so it was that evening in July 2005, when the wheels of the Air India flight from Delhi touched down at the Allama Iqbal International airport.

I was minutes away from exiting the airport when the lady at immigration stopped short of stamping my passport.

'Sir, Sirrr... Sirrrr...' she started screaming. Her voice was shrill and conveyed a certain urgency.

'What's the matter,' I asked her, but all she said was, 'Sir, Sirrr, Sirrrrr...'

Her decibel level kept going up as she screamed out for her boss.

Soon, a burly man sauntered across and the lady, whispering, pointed to the screen in front of her.

'Get to a side,' the man told me, pointing me to a corner.

He forced me to give him my baggage tags and as I protested and demanded to know what was happening, he screamed, saying, 'We don't talk to deportees. I am only talking to you because you are a *khatoon* [woman].'

I could not comprehend what was happening.

'We are putting you back on the Air India flight to Delhi. You are blacklisted. Wait in the corner till we retrieve your luggage.'

'But I have a valid visa,' I protested like a good, argumentative Indian.

My visa had been issued by Pakistan's deputy high commissioner (DHC), and I demanded that I be allowed to speak to him.

I looked at my mobile helplessly as Indian phones don't work in Pakistan.

'Now you want us to pay for an international call?' the Sir at immigration scowled.

'Please let me talk to your deputy high commissioner (DHC). Why would your mission grant me a visa if I was blacklisted,' I pleaded.

He reluctantly dialled the number I gave him and fortunately for me, the DHC answered the call. I quickly told him what was happening, and he asked me to hand the phone back to the immigration officer.

The officer's words – and tone – made it quite clear that I would soon be pushed back onto the Air India flight that was returning to Delhi.

'You are from the foreign service. I am from the interior [home] ministry. We decide,' he said. The power to allow foreign nationals in lay with Pakistan's spy agency, the ISI. The immigration officer wielded more power than the second most senior official in Pakistan's India mission.

'Sir' literally shoved me and my suitcase onto the waiting aircraft and the air hostesses, who had politely bid us goodbye half an hour earlier, were surprised to see me back on board. My co-passengers, who had witnessed my argument with the immigration staff whispered, 'deportee, deportee, deportee…'.

I was deported for an article I had written in 1994 when I got access to what Pakistan calls 'Azad Kashmir' and what India refers to as 'Pakistan occupied Kashmir' (POK).

I visited Pakistan several times since that article was published in 1994 and that fateful evening in July 2005. The name on the blacklist showed up so many years later simply because their immigration records had not been computerized up until then.

In May 1994, while on a visit to Islamabad, I got permission to visit Muzaffarabad, the capital of 'Azad Kashmir'.

It was not a place Indian journalists could drive to. Visas to Pakistan are always city-specific (India does the same for Pakistani citizens). A stamp for Islamabad does not mean you can cruise to Rawalpindi, Islamabad's twin city, even though the airport is within the municipal limits of Pindi.

The '90s were a turbulent decade. Militancy was at its peak in Kashmir and Pakistan was strident in keeping the issue alive at various global forums. At the time that I got permission to go to POK, Kashmir had been under the glare of international attention. US President Bill Clinton had lent his voice to the issue and made a statement saying he shared Pakistan's concerns over human rights violations by Indian troops.

'We have nothing to hide. Go to Azad Kashmir and visit the refugee camps,' an official at Islamabad's foreign office told me, while clearing me to visit Muzaffarabad.

I could not believe that an Indian journalist had actually been given the go-ahead to visit an 'out of bounds' area. Muzaffarabad was not even on the list of options provided by Pakistan's high commission in Delhi.

The morning after my visit to the foreign office, I was getting ready to go down to the hotel lobby to meet the officer assigned to accompany me to 'Azad' Kashmir. I soon found him knocking on my door.

'I am Mujahid Hussain Naqvi, director general publicity,' he said, introducing himself. 'You can roam around freely in Azad Kashmir and go wherever you like,' he added with the refrain that no one in POK could resist making: 'We are not like Indian-held Kashmir. We have nothing to hide.'

Joseph Goebbels was not the only one who had mastered the art of oratory and propaganda in Nazi Germany. Lies, oft repeated, don't always attain the legitimacy of truth. Goebbels are everywhere. They operate across geographical divides and are deeply entrenched in the political and global matrix.

We have nothing to hide, was just a line and Naqvi was trying to curtail my 'azadi'. Unlike the scores of unrestricted visits to Srinagar, Baramulla, and Anantnag on the Indian side of Kashmir, I could move in 'Azad Kashmir' only with prior permission.

'Sardar Qayyum [Sardar Abdul Qayyum Khan, the prime minister of POK], wants to ensure that you have no trouble,' Naqvi said, justifying his presence. Another minder from the Ministry of External Publicity was waiting in the lobby and even before I could reach Muzaffarabad, hordes of government officials had descended at the guest house where I had to stay.

A conducting officer has been posted at the door and a detailed minute to minute programme had already been prepared, according to which I had to spend a better part of the two days visiting an agriculture university, a library, and a radio station.

I had not come to POK to visit the agriculture university or their radio station. I am accustomed to pushing my limits and the programme was quickly changed, at my insistence. I fought and demanded that I be taken to the refugee camps.

We left for the Ambore refugee camp, a stop that most journalists have to make, for this is Pakistan's most publicized propaganda tool. It entails a meeting with the 'refugees' who have been hounded out of 'Indian-held Kashmir' by the security forces and who, if they are to be believed, have been mercilessly beaten by the security forces and their women molested.

The refugee camp had been readied for my arrival. Red sofas were laid out at one end of a tented pandal and I was asked to sit on a fancy armchair resembling one that newly-wedded couples would usually sit on, like VIPs on their very special day.

Even as I soaked in the environs, one refugee named Mir Mohammad Ali spoke about how he had been forced to leave the Valley after his wife and daughter were killed. Soon thereafter, an official of the Rehabilitation Cell started his presentation. Pointing to a numerical chart pasted on a blackboard he told me that there were 11 refugee camps housing 9,705 refugees. Prime Minister Qayyum Khan had told me the previous evening in Islamabad that the camps have 8,500 refugees.

About 100 male refugees were seated in rows under the huge pandal and, one by one, they got up to tell their tales of woe. Naqvi wanted to know which one of them had been the most brutally wounded and Bashir Ahmed got up to display the cigarette burn marks on his leg. A resident of Kupwara, he said, he had fled to POK after his brother had been knifed by Indian Army jawans.

'Do they want freedom or accession to Pakistan?' I asked, but even before the refugees had a chance to open their mouths, Naqvi butted in saying: 'Do you want to stay with India or with Pakistan?' His question was a clear distortion, for anyone with even the minimum knowledge of Kashmir would know that at the time, the slogan for 'azadi' was far more popular than the demand for accession.

These men had clearly been briefed and, ironically, while all of them said they were troubled by the Indian security forces because they had raised slogans of 'azadi' in Kashmir, in POK all of them said that they wanted to be part of Pakistan.

They had no choice. There is nothing else that they could have said in the face of the dozens of POK government officials. When one refugee innocently named National Conference President Farooq Abdullah as his leader – in reply to a question on who he thought could give them their freedom – Naqvi and the plain-clothed men pounced on him saying: 'That was earlier. What about now?' The visibly frightened refugee was too scared to reply.

It was only in short, whispered conversations that the refugees gathered the courage to say that they were unhappy. That they were neither allowed to move out of the camps nor permitted to take jobs as field labourers. They were unhappy back home too but, as one of them said, 'at least we were under our own roof. But now I don't know if I'll ever see my house again.'

The only way to get to the truth was to speak to the refugees alone, so I decided to get up from the special chair and walk towards some women who were squatting outside their tents, not far from the pandal that had been set up for my visit.

Naqvi offered to send someone with me but I reminded him that his prime minister had already assured me that I was free to walk anywhere without an escort. 'You have nothing to hide, right,' I said, and he reluctantly agreed. Sometimes, your gender works to your advantage, even if inadvertently.

I had barely walked 10 steps when a young, well-dressed man came up to me and asked if he could help. 'I'm fine,' I told him politely, walking ahead, but he came straight at me and blocked my path, his arms outstretched. 'You cannot go alone. You ask too many questions. The women will answer your questions in all innocence and we'll get into trouble. The guides will get into trouble.'

Guides? What guides? Earlier, all of them had denied having taken the help of guides to cross the LoC into POK. As I stared at the man blocking my path, two things became crystal clear: one, that they had a lot to hide and two, that plain-clothed intelligence men were freely mingling with the refugees. All through the argument, Naqvi maintained an eloquent silence.

Suddenly, I found myself surrounded by a group of men. In unison, they chanted, 'Indian dog go back, Indian dog, go back....'

I found myself quaking with rage. How 'azad' was 'Azad Kashmir'?

My trip was not playing to their script and I was not going to let it.

I refused to go to the agriculture university and reminded Naqvi that his boss, the prime minister, had assured me that I could travel freely and talk to whoever I liked. He tried to calm me down and insisted that we go back to the guest house to have some lunch.

I was in no mood to eat.

The slogans of 'Indian dog go back' kept playing in my mind. I knew these tactics were meant to intimidate me. But I was not going to retreat, not when it was becoming clear that the refugee camps were a propaganda tool.

After lunch, I insisted I be taken to a different refugee camp where I be given the freedom to speak to women.

'Else, please call Qayyum saab and let me talk to him because he clearly told me that there is nothing you have to hide,' I told Naqvi.

After a lot of confabulations, of which I was obviously not a part, we left for Bararkot, another refugee camp, 15 kilometers away.

The minute our cavalcade – longer than any prime minister's – drew up, the refugees came running with chairs. I reminded my minders that I plan to go into the tents alone. After whispering something to some of the refugees, Naqvi told me that I could go.

I visited Muzaffarabad while I was working with *India Today* magazine and its archives helped me source information for this chapter.

I sat next to two women and asked one, Haneefa, in her late 20s, where she had come from. 'Kupwara,' came the prompt reply. 'Where in Kupwara,' I asked and was stunned to hear her reply, '*Enna zulm hoya hehji, gaon da naa hi nahi yaad.*' (After all the torture, I have forgotten the name of the village.) Kupwara is a district on the LoC bordering India and Pakistan.

Not only was Haneefa speaking Punjabi, she was also saying she had forgotten the name of her own village. The reply to the next question was even more astounding. Why doesn't she speak her mother tongue Kashmiri? '*Enna zulm hoya hehji, bhasha thodi yaad rehndi heh.*' (After all the atrocities, I've forgotten how to speak Kashmiri.)

Rafaiza, sitting next to Haneefa, came up with the same answers. How did you get past the Indian Army and cross the border, I had asked. 'With Allah's help,' was all she was willing to say. 'Who came with you?' I asked next, to learn that she took three days to cross the border all by herself. And even before she could complete her reply, a man came and handed her a child almost three or four years old. 'Who is this?' I asked and surprisingly, she said he was her son.

But you said, you came alone, I reminded her and she quickly added, 'Yes, I was pregnant then.'

She claimed she crossed over from the Indian side of Kashmir into POK in 1993. I visited in 1994. How could her son have been three or four years old?

The propaganda lay stripped bare. The naked truth was staring me in the face. Haneefa and Rafaiza were definitely not genuine refugees. They were definitely not Kashmiri. It was now clear why I had been shunted out of the Ambore camp. It was apparent why I had been surrounded and called an 'Indian dog'.

The refugees had their own reasons for being a part of the propaganda parade. A one-time grant of ₹600 to ₹2,000, free tents with beddings, a subsistence allowance of ₹15 per person per day, and free schooling facilities were incentives enough for the poor local POK citizens to seek refuge in the tents.

There wasn't a moment that I was left alone, except at night when I bolted the door of my room at the guest house. I had carried some vodka with me and a drink would have helped calm my nerves but I refrained. The transparent liquid could have passed off as a glass of water if any of the minders outside had decided to knock on my door, but I was not up to it.

The day had ended well. I thought again about having a shot but decided against it. There were too many intelligence sleuths just outside the door.

The next morning, we had set off for Athmuqam, a border village about 100 kilometers from Muzaffarabad. Naqvi was escorting an Indian journalist and his brief included unfolding the second part of the government's propaganda strategy. Innocent civilians were being killed by indiscriminate firing by Indian forces from across the Line of Actual Control (LAC), Qayyum had told me in Islamabad. Seventeen people had been killed in Abbaspur – which lay en route to Athmuqam – and twice the number injured the previous day, he'd said.

Strangely, none of the newspapers had gone to town about it. I expressed my desire to meet the injured but one of the officials, who had been telling me how he had arranged to send ambulances there, came up with the lame excuse of, 'But they may have been moved to another hospital.'

You can see the destruction caused by Indian firing in Athmuqam, a tehsil of Neelum district in 'Azad' Kashmir, I was told, but a landslide prevented me from reaching there and this time it was the turn of the officials to feel disappointed. Newspapers had carried photographs of the dispensary and the school bearing bullet marks. They had been displayed to local journalists.

We stopped instead at Chaliana village and various villagers testified that they often had to move to higher reaches because of 'excessive firing'. Part of the Pakistani claim was right. There had been an exchange of fire between troops in 1990 and 1991 in which one villager, Fakir Ullah, was killed and another girl, Mariam's leg was hit by a bullet. But as another villager said: 'For the last two years, the firing has been restricted picket-to-picket.' And as soon as my escorts heard the Chaliana residents talking of 'azadi' for both Kashmirs, I was once again politely reminded that we were getting late.

My minders were schooled to push for Kashmir's secession to Pakistan. The slogan for independence did not suit their narrative. The local population was putty in the hands of the army and the ISI.

Unlike Srinagar's striking beauty, Muzaffarabad was a one-horse town, backward and primitive. There was nothing in the name of tourism. 'Azad Kashmir' was an island of neglect and the roads that were being built were used for troop deployment rather than for infrastructure enhancement.

The only thing common to both Kashmirs – was the fervour that the slogans for independence generated. Large posters claiming 'Kashmir Banega Pakistan', were everywhere – atop homes, painted on shops, and emblazoned on walls.

Muzaffarabad district was, in fact, amongst the most backward districts in the subcontinent before Partition, and the lack of economic progress was visible. Large parts of the rural landscape had scant facilities for health or education.

Though 'Azad Kashmir' had a government and Qayyum was its prime minister, it was the domain of the Pakistan Army and promoting jihad its main agenda.

I was used as a vehicle to propagate their message – or so they thought – and they had made various presentations with facts and figures in an attempt to call out the human rights violations being perpetrated in 'Indian held Kashmir', often referred to as the 'most militarized zone' on earth.

The POK government, I was told, also gave financial help to what they rather strangely called the 'affectees'. Surprisingly, however, they were not very good at their homework, for during the presentation at Ambore the chart clearly said that there were 24,375 'affectees' and when I had asked for a detailed break-up of the affected, killed and injured, the figures totalled 13,196. The officials, of course, had no answer to why there was a discrepancy when both sets of figures were being provided by the same government department – the Rehabilitation Cell.

Rehabilitating either the refugees or the affected people, however, did not seem to be the main concern of the POK government. They were schooled to be Goebbels and propaganda is what they had tried to serve as their main dish.

Sardar Abdul Qayyum Khan, prime minister of POK, ever willing to meet Indian journalists was liberal with his time. He had always maintained that his government provided moral, financial, and political sustenance to Kashmir-based militants, but on that trip, he made a marked departure from his stand in his interview to me, for *India Today* magazine. In a startling admission, he conceded that Pakistan was training terrorists and also allowing them to cross the LoC into the Indian side of Kashmir.

It is well known that the deep state operates these camps and even provides cover fire to help them cross the LoC. The terror infrastructure exists even today. What was important was the fact that the POK PM was coming on record with the damning admission.

Q India is convinced you run training camps here [in POK].

A There are no camps as such but training may be there. Azad Kashmir has 1.5 lakh retired soldiers. There are officers of all ranks.

Q You mean these officers are imparting training to the militants within their homes?

A Of course, why not! We place no restriction on that.

Q So the trained militants are allowed to cross the LoC?

A We consider Indian-held Kashmir a part of our territory. It is no secret that militants keep coming and going. According to the UN resolutions, there is no restriction on the movement of Kashmiris from one side to another.

Q What about Afghans? They are not Kashmiris.

A They may be a trickle. The government is very strict about foreigners.

Q Do you also have safe houses on the line of control?

A The Americans and Britons have searched all over and not found any. People can live anywhere, so why make conspicuous safe houses on the border?

Q What else do you do to help the militants?

A We can't do much because of the heavy army presence.

We fire on built-in pickets. The Indian Army, however, has stepped up unprovoked firing. We don't return the fire because we consider Kashmiris to be our own citizens.

Q **But Kashmiris are disillusioned with Pakistan.**

A Pakistan raised very high expectations in Geneva. I wasn't in favour of the resolution because Kashmir is not a human rights problem, but a political problem. I think both governments were stupid in raising victory slogans because after all that, the Kashmiris are still left with zero option.

Q **Surely you are aware that most Kashmiris favour independence rather than accession to Pakistan?**

A Independence will open up a Pandora's box and nobody can go back to 1947. The third option has been projected by the West, partly innocently and partly deliberately. Only accession can provide a lasting solution.

Q **What about the Simla Accord?**

A It is completely redundant. It exists only because the US talks about it, otherwise it has been violated by both India and Pakistan. If we put more emphasis on the Simla Accord, the Pakistan Parliament might one day just throw it out. Either the Kashmiris give in and accept a fait accompli or the issue has to be resolved.

Q **Fed up with continued militancy, the Kashmiris might just resign themselves to living with India.**

A I don't think that stage has come. To the contrary, it may come to a saturation point. India is contemplating hot pursuit into Azad Kashmir and, given the hatred, the dangers of a war can only increase.

Q You say Kashmiris are unhappy with India. What about those in POK? They are not very happy with Pakistan either.

A People in the subcontinent grumble a lot. Here, too, they grumble but it's mostly because they haven't been able to pick up jobs. As far as freedom is concerned, it is a great advantage for those living in Azad Kashmir.

As soon as my report and interview were published in *India Today* magazine, editor-in-chief, Aroon Purie received a letter from Pakistan's Delhi-based high commissioner. I had violated my visa and the trust that had been reposed in me, he wrote.

Purie had no problems or regrets with the article. He thought it was a brave piece of work, accomplished under grave circumstances.

Unknown to us, I had been blacklisted.

The bureaucracies in both India and Pakistan work in identical ways. Helpful contacts usually bail you out of corners; especially when regimes change.

When I went to Muzaffarabad in 1994, Benazir Bhutto was in power. Much to my surprise, in 1998, I received a personal invitation from Mushahid Hussain, a powerful minister in Nawaz Sharif's government, to visit 'Azad Kashmir'.

Hussain was a close aide of Sharif and the minister in-charge of information. The Sharif government was celebrating 50 years of the United Nations resolution of 1948 which ruled that the question of the accession of

Jammu and Kashmir be decided 'through the democratic and fair method of a fair and impartial plebiscite'. Hussain was hosting a conclave in Muzaffarabad to focus global attention on this resolution.

Hussain had invited international media and it was important, from his perspective, to also have an Indian journalist at the conclave.

Who would give up the chance to visit 'Azad Kashmir' again? It was, and continues to be out of bound for Indians, and the invite was all too tempting.

I had to fight my way through a maze of lies in 1994. The second trip would be easier, I had mistakenly thought. I was going to be amidst foreign journalists and Hussain himself would be present.

In Islamabad, I was introduced as 'the only Indian' and welcomed into 'free and liberated Kashmir'. Hussain, whom I had got to know, was his charming self, instructing his staff to look after me. 'Make sure she goes to the Line of Control (LoC) to see the damage the Indian Army has wrought on poor civilians and their homes,' he had said.

That was a privilege indeed. To be allowed first into Muzaffarabad, the capital of 'Azad' Kashmir, and then to be taken to the forward areas along the LoC which had seen incessant firing in recent months between the two nations and heavy civilian casualties. 'If you go to the Line of Control, make sure she goes with you,' Hussain reiterated to Javed Akhtar, director of information, shortly before we left Islamabad.

The seminar was only beginning on the afternoon of 13 August, the day the UN resolution on Kashmir was adopted, and we had the entire morning for a trip to the border. However, as the evening wore on, Akhtar expressed reservations about the trip, saying it was not part of the schedule.

At dinner, Martin Sugarman, a fellow journalist from the US, had stunned me by asking if he would see me at 7.30 the next morning.

'The trip is not on,' I had informed him confidently as I returned to the hotel and joined two other colleagues from London for a cup of green tea.

The British journalists weren't sure about the next day's programme either. So I called Akhtar. 'There is no visit to the border,' he was categorical, but Sugarman's words, asking if he'd see me in the hotel lobby at 7.30 the next morning, kept coming back to me. 'Why don't one of you call Akhtar? He may be saying one thing to me because I'm an Indian,' I requested my friends from London, feeling guilty that I was suspecting my hosts. One of them spoke to Akhtar, and he confirmed the next day's visit to the border.

Akhtar had lied to me.

I set an alarm for the morning and was down in the lobby by 7.20, where Akhtar was eating breakfast with the other journalists. I was angry because he had misled me and said that he was only coordinating the seminar.

I contributed to a number of red faces in the Information Department when I told one of them, that I would have understood if I had been told straight away that there was a problem with an Indian visiting the LoC. But being lied to, was a problem.

I dug my heels in. I was a part of the foreign media delegation and saw no reason why I was being singled out for my Indian nationality.

The departure to the border was delayed as they didn't know how to handle me or the situation. Finally, an hour later, we were asked to get into the coaches. Like the others, I walked towards the bus, only to be stopped at the door. 'Your name is not on the list,' I was firmly told. My reply was simple: 'That is your problem, not mine.' I got into the bus and said they could throw me out if they wanted to.

'Let the rest go. We'll get special permission for you. There's been a miscommunication,' I was told but I stuck my ground. I had been invited as a journalist and was not out on a picnic.

'Why don't you understand that there is tension between the two countries,' one of the journalists said, angry that they were all held up because of me. I told them plainly they ought to be standing up for a colleague, and the hosts should have thought through their invitation to me.

Instead of standing in solidarity, other foreign journalists had asked me to get off the bus. Quite angry by then, I had screamed, 'You might think it is a crime to be an Indian, I don't.'

I had demanded that Akhtar come and face me. He was busy making telephone calls, certain by then that I was not going to give in. Sure enough, a little later Akhtar came out saying I could go. So what was the point in trying to keep me out? If being an Indian was a disqualification, why had they invited me at all?

Mushahid Hussain had been kind enough to invite me and I was not going to let anyone humiliate me. Pakistan often maintained that India unfairly accused them of being 'neurotic' about Kashmir. If anything, it was they who had displayed their obsession.

A huge dose of neurosis is what I had unwittingly let myself in for at a place they so deceptively call 'Azad' Kashmir. It was clearly the army's domain; their stomping ground. A minister had the liberty of inviting me but an Indian journalist being allowed into the border areas was not a political call.

Whether it was Brigadier Khalid Nawaz who had briefed us before we left for Chakoti, a village on the LoC, or Lieutenant General (Retd) Majid Malik, minister in-charge of Kashmir affairs, the paranoia was self-evident. India, according to Brigadier Nawaz, was deliberately supplying inadequate food and medicine to the Valley in order to weaken the armed uprising.

Accusing India of deliberately shelling civilians, Malik had asserted that the Indian Army had not been able to hit a single Pakistani military post. 'We consider Kashmiris as our brothers and so we don't target civilian areas. Only three civilians have been accidentally injured,' he told the audience comprising members of the local and foreign media.

I had gone prepared for propaganda. What I had not bargained for was the level of neurosis. According to Malik, 'a frustrated Indian Army was killing Pakistani civilians because it had not been able to quell the spontaneous uprising in Kashmir.' In Chakoti, the same views echoed among the people as we were taken around the village where shops lay in a heap of rubble. Frightened locals said the shelling was worse than during the 1971 Indo-Pak war.

What about their own rights? Do they have the freedom to speak freely?

They did not answer. They could not answer.

There were too many minders around me, watching my movements, hanging on to every word I uttered.

'Breathe free, madam, for the three days that you are here. This is liberated Kashmir,' one of them had said with a sardonic smile on his face.

I soon realized how liberated 'Azad' Kashmir was when I stepped into my room that night, for a brief reprieve from the 'neurosis' that had enveloped the seminar. As soon as I had entered the room, the hotel intercom, placed on the bedside, started buzzing. *Must be Mushahid Hussain*, I had thought to myself. I had been waiting to meet him, to complain about the morning.

The caller introduced himself as Jamil. He needed to speak to me urgently, he said.

'What about? Who are you?' I asked.

'I can't tell you on the phone,' he said.

I told him he could meet me downstairs at the conference room or in the dining hall.

'There are too many intelligence people around. Can I come to your room?'

No, I had said, and he again wanted to know if I was alone. 'None of your business,' was my terse reply, as I put the phone down.

No one approached me at the restaurant where we all went for dinner.

Well past midnight 'Jamil' called again.

'Can I come to your room? Are you alone?'

I disconnected and asked for a meeting with Hussain.

I faced pure harassment and no one had the power to do that other than the ISI. They were the only ones 'azad' in their Kashmir.

Jamil called me every five minutes, and I had to finally place the receiver off the hook.

The next morning, Hussain apologized for what had happened, and I told him quite clearly that I would have returned to Islamabad if it were not for him. It was not probably in Hussain's hands because the caller was obviously using an internal line and his aim was to harass me.

I began to wonder if the 'neurosis' was enveloping me too. At the conference, speaker after speaker had spoken about how Kashmiris were being subjugated by Indian troops. When an invitee, Professor Ainslie Embree, a member of the US-based Kashmir Study Group, asked if the UN resolutions had lost their allure, I had waited in anticipation for what the seminar hosts would say. 'You don't know enough,' he was told, in a tone that implied that he should shut up.

A lot has changed in the India-Pakistan equation.

During the tenure of Prime Minister Narasimha Rao, Parliament passed a unanimous resolution in 1994, to 'retake' POK. The demand is regularly articulated by senior ministers of the Narendra Modi government and by the RSS, the ideological fountainhead of the BJP. After the cessation of hostilities in May 2025 following the Pahalgam attack, the Government of India reiterated that the only conversation it would have with Pakistan would be on terrorism and the 'return of POK'.

There has been no official dialogue between the two nuclear neighbours since the Pulwama attack in 2019. The relationship went cold after the audacious 26/11 attack in Mumbai in 2008, and further deteriorated after the revocation of Article 370 in August 2019.

'Terrorism and talks cannot go hand in hand,' is India's official position. That position is now seeing a more belligerent articulation. '*Ghar mein ghus ke maaregein*,' (We will enter your home and kill you) is the common political refrain.

Pakistan downgraded ties with India after the Modi government abrogated Article 370 that bestowed a special status to Jammu and Kashmir. Imran Khan, the then prime minister of Pakistan withdrew the country's high commissioner from New Delhi, after the revocation of Article 370.

In Muzaffarabad, local citizens are protesting a denial of their fundamental rights. In Srinagar and the rest of the Valley, a sullen silence envelopes an alienated population that once took to the streets regularly. Both cities are a stark contrast to their earlier avatars. Muzaffarabad, subjugated by the deep state has risen in protest. Srinagar, the capital of protests now lives in fear of being at the receiving end of laws liberally used to quell signs of dissent.

India sees Jammu and Kashmir as an inalienable part of its territory and Pakistan often likens it to Gaza and rakes up the UN resolutions.

For now, the slogans of azadi have died down in the union territory of Jammu and Kashmir. Instead, its residents took to the streets after the Pahalgam attack singed their soil and their soul. They came out against the killings of tourists and the message, 'Not in our name' was a clear change from the time in the early '90s when slogans of azadi rent the air.

In POK, protests have intensified over rising prices of food and fuel. A ₹23 billion subsidy announced by Pakistani Prime Minister Shehbaz Sharif has failed to quell the protests.

Both sides of Kashmir bear testimony to how their lives and livelihood are upended, each time tensions between India and Pakistan soar.

The 'azad' Kashmir that I visited twice is perhaps worth revisiting again, but that is one place Pakistan will now not allow an Indian to tread.

The Masters of Muridke

'Welcome to the headquarters of the Lashkar-e-Taiba. Would you like to spend the night here... You are in an educational complex and the Jamaat-ud-Dawa is a charitable organization, but you are from India so it will take you time to change your mind.'

Two weeks after 10 gun-wielding terrorists brought India's financial capital to its knees in November 2008, I woke up to a message from my editor, Tarun Tejpal.

'Apply for a visa to Pakistan,' read the message from *Tehelka* magazine's editor.

He's lost it, I thought to myself, rubbing my eyes.

Twenty-one-year-old Ajmal Kasab, one of the 10 terrorists who came to Mumbai via the high seas had been caught alive and had told interrogators how he had trained at the Lashkar-e-Taiba (LeT) headquarters in Muridke, a bustling town on the outskirts of Lahore.

Who in their right mind would allow an Indian journalist

into Pakistan when it was becoming increasingly clear that the bloody strike, referred to as 26/11, had ISI written all over it? Kasab had revealed names of Pakistani intelligence and army officials. The spectacular strikes could not have been carried out without assistance from the Pakistani deep state.

Always willing to take risks, I messaged the Minister Press at Pakistan's high commission in Delhi. To my utter shock – and amazement – I was granted a visa. Was Pakistan allowing an Indian journalist in because they had just bloodied India's nose?

In office, that day, Tarun asked me what stories we could possibly report from Pakistan.

'There is only one story,' I told him.

I was clear that I had to find a way of getting into the Lashkar headquarters. 'But it is risky. What if I am deported? What if I am held hostage?' I asked Tarun.

'That will be an even bigger story,' he said, laughing.

Mumbai was still on edge. The 72-hour-long siege had ended and the dead had been counted but the investigation was still ongoing. Kasab, who was chosen to attack the Chhatrapati Shivaji Terminus (CST), had used his Kalashnikov to deadly effect. He was captured alive late on the night of 26 November, when a group of policemen were asked to put up blockades on the road at Girgaon Chowpatty. Mumbai was shaking to the sound of bullets and bombs when the police spotted a suspicious-looking Skoda. Kasab was in this vehicle and realizing that he would not make it past the barricades, raised his hands, gesturing that he was willing to surrender. Minutes before that, his accomplice Abu Ismail Khan had opened fire and injured some policemen. Ismail was grievously injured in retaliatory fire by the police.

Tukaram Omble, armed with nothing but a lathi, walked towards the Skoda. Kasab, who had misled the police by raising his hands, whipped out a weapon and opened fire. Omble was injured and later succumbed, but not before overpowering Kasab.

Details about Kasab soon started trickling in.

He was from Pakistan's Faridkot and one of five children of a poor vendor. He had tried to eke out a living as a helper with a caterer but gave that up quickly. Along with a friend, he carried out a few armed robberies and soon signed up to join the Lashkar. Terrorist organizations recruit their cadets openly, putting up posters on village walls and distributing pamphlets at major markets. Jihad is sold as a direct ride to *jannat*. There is also the lure of money: recruits are promised that their families will be well looked after financially.

Within 24 hours of his arrest, Kasab told his interrogators, 'We wanted to acquire weapons, but it was not easy. We filled up forms and joined the organization where we were given weapons and training. We went through an induction training in Muridke for 21 days. The trainers were very strict and everything from namaz to lunch to dinner happened with clockwork precision. After the completion of the first phase, we were taken to a small village in Mansehra where we were given initial training of handling AKs. We were also given lectures on Islam. We were told that our religion was in danger and Muslims were being killed everywhere. That was when we decided we would not go back to robbery but would continue with the Lashkar.'

Muridke figured for a second time in his interrogation and that is where I wanted to be. I kept soaking in the details, calling my contacts in the intelligence agencies, to find out more about how the audacious attack had been planned and executed. Kasab was revealing more.

'I went home in between and returned to participate in a training camp at a hilly area in POK. Here we were trained to handle explosives, mortars, and rocket launchers. At the end of the three months training, 32 of us were selected by Zaki-ur-Rehman Lakhvi [called Chacha in LeT circles] for waging jihad. Sixteen were sent for some operation, the details of which I don't know. Of the remaining 16, three escaped and the rest of us were sent to a training camp in Muridke. Here we were trained to operate GPS instruments and to navigate boats. We were conditioned to sail on the high seas. We were taught how to swim,' Kasab was telling his interrogators.

The 10 terrorists who set sail from Karachi, shifted to a fishing trawler named MV Kuber. They hijacked the vessel on 23 November and forced its captain, Amar Singh Solanki to take them towards Mumbai. The last stretch to reach Badhwar Park in South Mumbai's Colaba area was completed on an inflated dinghy. Late in the evening on 26 November, 10 merchants of death hit land, secured their backpacks full of arms and ammunition, split into pairs and headed for different locations. The targets included the busy CST, the iconic Taj Mahal Palace Hotel, Oberoi's Trident Hotel, and the Nariman House.

Kasab paired with Ismail Khan, the leader of the group, and wreaked havoc at CST, firing indiscriminately, killing over 37 and injuring over 100. The CCTV cameras at the station had captured him wielding the deadly weapon with which he had sprayed death and felled innocents.

The baby-faced, diminutive but indoctrinated terrorist was on the front page of newspapers.

26/11 remains India's worst terror attack. The three-day-long siege in Mumbai claimed 166 lives – including of foreign nationals – and injured and maimed scores. Kasab, who gave details of his interactions with the Lashkar founder, Hafiz Saeed, pointed the needle firmly in Pakistan's direction. Each aspect of the strike had been thoroughly thought through. The terrorists even came with the red thread tied to their wrists, in a feeble attempt at pointing the needle in a different religious direction.

I had been to Pakistan several times, but this visit was amongst the most challenging, second only to the two visits I had made to what Pakistan calls 'Azad Kashmir' and what India claims is Pakistan occupied Kashmir (POK).

As I packed my bags to catch a flight to Lahore, I dialled the headquarters of the Lashkar-e-Taiba.

No Indian journalist had been allowed into the sprawling complex on the outskirts of Lahore, but that gate was the one I desperately wanted to breach. Would that be possible two weeks after an attack that world capitals were studying and examining? Foreign nationals including six US citizens had been killed.

Publicity is vital oxygen for terror groups but Abdullah Muntazir, information secretary of LeT, based in Lahore, was not taking calls from an Indian number even though he was the person in charge of speaking to the international media. He had already guided a group of foreign journalists through the complex, a few days before I got my visa, to make the point that the complex at Muridke was actually a charitable organization. The LeT was operating under the charitable alias, Jamaat-ud-Dawa (JuD). No Indian journalist was part of that entourage, though two Indian correspondents were based in Pakistan at the time.

Was I being unreasonable in thinking that the Lashkar – which by then had changed its name to Jamaat-ud-Dawa – would open its gates to an 'enemy' journalist? After reaching Lahore, I called Muntazir from a local number but again hit a dead end. He would not take calls.

I kept trying and held my breath when he finally answered and I introduced myself.

'What's your name again?' he asked.

'Shammy Baweja,' I replied. I did not say Harinder, a name Pakistanis have always had problems pronouncing. My email and social media profiles are all based on my pet name, a fetish most Punjabi families have adhered to for long.

Unknown to me, Muntazir was Googling Shammy Baweja.

'There is no such byline,' he said.

'Try Harinder Baweja,' I urged, giving him the spelling.

'You have already lied. How do I trust you; you are an Indian after all,' he said, castigating me.

'Let me see. I don't know if we can allow an Indian into Muridke,' he said, hanging up.

I was at a dead end.

The next day I went to have lunch with a powerful former minister in the Nawaz Sharif government. I had met him several times over the years and mentioned that I wanted to visit the LeT headquarters. I was surprised when he said: 'I'll try and help out. They owe me one. They have often called for help when their associates have been picked up by the police.' The former minister was like a friend I had made in Pakistan and I was pleased with his offer of help.

The nexus between the state and non-state actors was clear. A former minister was conceding the connection. He picked up his phone and called someone. Even before I finished lunch with him, a group of men were waiting in the anteroom.

Before he ushered the men in, he asked me, 'Do you want to go to Muridke or do you want to interview Hafiz Saeed? Choose one, both will be difficult.'

It was a tough choice. Hafiz Saeed, who had painted himself as a pious professor, would only deny his involvement in the Mumbai attacks, I thought to myself.

What should I do? I had to take a quick decision. Till yesterday, Muntazir was not answering my calls and here I was, being offered access to the headquarters and its founder.

'I would like to go to the Lashkar headquarter,' I told my minister host. He took me to the room next to the dining hall where we had just had lunch. In the anteroom, he introduced me to Muntazir, who had not been answering my calls and to Khalid Waleed, the son-in-law of Hafiz Saeed.

The same Muntazir who had refused to take my calls was to soon guide me through the headquarters. 'We can't say no to you,' the group had told the former minister.

We fixed a time for the next morning. When I asked them about the logistics, Muntazir was acerbic: 'You want us to hire a car for you? Please book a cab. We will pick you up from the hotel gate,' he said. He was not happy with the task at hand but could not refuse the minister.

I had a sleepless night. Would they keep the appointment? Would they honour the commitment they had made to the minister? Apprehensions often cloud a journalist's mind and deadlines hang forever, like the sword of Damocles.

The next morning, I, an Indian journalist, was following several cars belonging to the Lashkar, or the 'Army of the pure' as they like to call themselves, to Muridke. Several armed men stood guard at the gates of a 'charitable organization'. It was not a complex you could just drive into. It was a fortress, but Khalid Waleed, Hafiz Saeed's son-in-law had full access to it.

'Welcome to the headquarters of the Lashkar-e-Taiba,' said Muntazir, looking me straight in the eye and continuing with, 'You are in an educational complex and the Jamaat-ud-Dawa is a charitable organization, but you are from India so it will take you time to change your mind.'

I was within the precincts of a complex where Kasab said he had been trained. The name may have been changed to Jamaat-ud-Dawa but it was known worldwide to be the headquarters of the LeT. I could barely hold my breath.

The guided tour took me through a neatly laid out 60-bed hospital, schools for boys and girls, a madrasa, a mosque, an extravagantly large swimming pool, and a guest house. The hospital beds were empty. There were no doctors or nurses in sight. The white hospital sheets looked unused. I saw a few uniformed school children; young girls with white scarves covering their heads.

I did not go there thinking I'd see firing ranges or target shooting in progress, but the tour itself was surreal. As I walked through the neatly trimmed lawns, passing the hostel, mosque, and the hospital, the conversation was dotted with words such as terrorism, Lashkar, and in my case, Kashmir.

Even though the gates were opened to dispel the impression of Muridke being the training camp that 'India has made it out to be', the conversation between me, Muntazir, and Waleed was not about the school syllabus but solely about how India was the enemy.

Muntazir and Waleed did not deny the fact that Kasab was 'schooled' in Muridke.

'So, did Kasab study here, in Muridke?' I asked, pointedly.

'Even if he did, we are not responsible for what any one of our students does after passing out.'

The student was caught on CCTV causing mayhem and came to be known as the 'butcher of Mumbai'.

'Do you support the Lashkar-e-Taiba?'

'We used to,' replied Muntazir.

'You used to?'

'Yes, we were like-minded but the group was banned after Indian propaganda, following the attack on its Parliament, which was done by the Jaish and not the LeT. We used to provide logistical help to the Lashkar, collect funds for them, and look after their publicity.'

'Did you also provide them arms?'

'They must have bought weapons with the money we gave them. They were obviously not using the money to buy flowers for the Indian Army.'

Muntazir was never short of sarcasm. He ticked me off when my dupatta accidentally slipped off my head. I pulled it back up and continued.

'Do you consider India an enemy?'

'Without a doubt.'

'Your Amir, Hafiz Saeed, has given calls for jihad….'

'He supports the freedom movement in Kashmir. We think it is right. It is ridiculous to call him a terrorist. Even when a thorn pricks India, the whole world stands up.'

'Pervez Musharraf, the former president was in negotiations with India on Kashmir….'

'Who is Musharraf to speak about Kashmir….'

'Does the ISI support you?'

Muntazir just laughed.

'Would you like to spend the night here?'

'No, thank you. I have another appointment.'

I left wondering if Kasab had learnt to swim in the gigantic pool I saw within the precincts of the Lashkar headquarters. I was also amazed with Muntazir's denigration of Musharraf. They were a power unto themselves, answerable to seniors in the ISI or the army. Former chiefs didn't matter.

My next appointment was with Nawaz Sharif, the former prime minister of Pakistan. He had been thrown out in a bloodless coup in 1999, soon after the Kargil war, and had returned to Lahore in 2007, after spending over seven years in exile in Saudi Arabia.

I had first met Sharif in 1998, soon after India and Pakistan brought their nuclear bombs out of the basement. 'India is now a nuclear weapon state,' Prime Minister Vajpayee had announced to the world on 11 May 1998. India had conducted five underground nuclear tests in Pokhran. The country went into chest-thumping mode and a triumphant BJP tried to cover itself in glory.

A ballistic Pakistan rose in collective unison and pressurized Prime Minister Nawaz Sharif to do the same. Either you, or the bomb, was what Sharif was being told by the hour, as the Pakistani media went into a frenzy, demanding that their government match India's nuclear status. 'Give India a befitting reply,' was the popular slogan.

I was allowed into Pakistan at the time and it was clear that the visa had been granted because Pakistan would be forced to test. The country wanted Indian journalists to be on their soil to report the 'historic moment' it went nuclear. The day I got a call from Pakistan High Commission telling me that my visa had been granted, I was sure that Pakistan would soon go ahead and test.

The mood at every street corner was clear: test or be damned. Former prime minister Benazir Bhutto went to the extent of throwing bangles on stage at well-attended rallies to suggest that Prime Minister Sharif better start wearing them.

Public pressure was mounting. District-level surveys conducted by the Urdu press showed that people in the towns and villages were overwhelmingly in favour of going nuclear. A divide along the lines of 'Islamic Pakistan' and 'Hindu India' was also created by the indignation that followed Indian Home Minister L. K. Advani's statement warning Pakistan against continuing its proxy war in Kashmir. Nisar Ali Khan, a senior minister in Pakistan's cabinet had summed it up for me when he said: 'Advani's statement turned the screw.'

Pakistan tested its nuclear bombs on 28 May 1998 at Ras Koh hills in Chagai in Balochistan. It was Pakistan's turn to erupt in collective triumphalism. India had tested three on 11 May and two more on 13 May. Pakistan responded with five on 28 May.

Indian journalists were given rare access by the Pakistani government and Prime Minister Sharif agreed to meet me for an interview. That was my first meeting with him. He was measured in his tone and his responses.

'Pressures were mounting by the hour and by the minute after the Indian detonations. Politicians in Pakistan also started saying we should give India a matching response without any further loss of time. There is no doubt that there was immense international pressure not to test, but the balance of power in the region had been violently tilted. I wanted to test the world response before testing our nuclear capabilities.

I was not keen on giving a tit for tat response. Pakistan has had the capability for the past 15 to 20 years but I never felt the need to test it unless India again tested it after 24 years. Whatever we did was dictated by our national interests which no sovereign country can compromise. Finally, I think we took the right decision,' Sharif told me in the interview that was published in *India Today.*

As we ended the interview and I prepared to leave, I was stumped by what Sharif said next. I am still not sure whether he was serious or said it in jest. 'India is not a safe place. Why don't you take Pakistani citizenship… I will help you,' he said, leaving me totally taken aback.

'No, thank you. I am a very happy Indian,' I told him, and left.

The next morning, his office delivered photographs of our interview. He had autographed them using silver ink. They remain a part of my collection and lie amidst a stack of other photographs taken at different conflict zones.

History has not been kind in inking Sharif's political journey. He, ironically, was the one who would soon have to leave not just the prime minister's office but his country as well. Sharif has the dubious distinction of not completing his elected term even once – like his predecessors and successors – despite being sworn-in thrice. He contested the elections in Pakistan in 2024. He returned from self-exile in London, after former cricket captain and founder of Pakistan Tehreek-i-Insaf, Imran Khan was barred from being a part of the electoral fray. Sharif is now the patron, the political elder to his brother Shehbaz Sharif who is Pakistan's prime minister.

A little over a year after bringing nuclear parity between India and Pakistan, Sharif was deposed in a coup by President Pervez Musharraf on 12 October 1999. The coup took place less than three months after Musharraf's misadventure in the high mountains of Kargil and an imprisoned Sharif was soon on his way to Saudi Arabia for a long period of self-exile. The Saudis negotiated an exile deal that helped Sharif escape being imprisoned in Pakistan.

My second meeting with Sharif took place after his return from exile, in 2008. I drove straight from Muridke to Raiwind Palace, his ostentatious farmhouse spread over 1,700 acres on the outskirts of Lahore. He greeted me warmly and asked me how my trip to Pakistan was going?

I told him I was coming straight from Muridke and he looked surprised. 'They let you in?' he asked incredulously and proceeded to talk about the 26/11 attacks.

Sharif told me he had been glued to the news, as he watched the terror strike on live television, much like the rest of the world.

He wanted to know everything about Karambir Kang, the general manager of the Taj Hotel who had lost his wife and two sons, as he tried to save his guests.

'My heart goes out to the general manager,' Sharif said, adding, 'If you ever get a chance, please give him my regards and tell him he's a brave man.'

Kang's story has been told and retold. He was out for a meeting when staff members called him frantically asking him to rush back to the hotel. He realized the hotel was under attack as soon as he returned. His first question was, 'How many terrorists are there?'

The chaos was evident from the replies he got. Some said, 2, others said, 4, 6, 10. All along, he could hear bullets being fired. Hotel guests were stuck in restaurants, in the conference hall, and their rooms. As he and his staff advised guests to leave from the rear exits, he also made a call to his wife, Neeti and asked her to hide somewhere safe. 'Keep Uday and Samar close to you,' he said, referring to his sons who were 12 and 5 years old. He promised to come to their aid as soon as he got a chance and turned his attention to his staff and guests.

The Taj is where Karambir, whose name means a person of brave deeds, had met Neeti when he was 23 years old, and 17 years later, it was the same Taj where he lost her and both their sons. The sixth floor, where he and his family lived, had been set on fire by the terrorists. He couldn't bear to look at their bodies.

Kang became the face Sharif saw 26/11 through. For India – the government and its citizens – Kasab and Hafiz Saeed were the standout primers, one an indoctrinated, gun-wielding terrorist and the other, a model motivator who had tried to paint himself as a pious professor.

On my return from Pakistan, it was more than evident that Hafiz Saeed, the Lashkar supremo was the mastermind of the Mumbai attack. The Indian government shared dossier after dossier with Pakistan and Hafiz Saeed was placed under 'house arrest', a move aimed at satisfying the international community.

While I did not take up the offer of interviewing Saeed while in Lahore, I did call his lawyer A. K. Dogar after he was put under 'house arrest'.

The conversation with his lawyer, once again, was surreal.

Q You're representing a man the Indian government thinks is the mastermind of 26/11...

A If Karl Marx is the mastermind of all socialists, then Hafiz Saeed is a mastermind. He is a masterly religious scholar who runs 140 schools all over Pakistan.

Q But Hafiz Saeed openly calls for jihad.

A I have read books about Mahatma Gandhi...

Q Are you comparing Hafiz Saeed to the Mahatma?

A I can't dare to do that. Muslims have a different point of view. We don't go by Jesus Christ's principle of turning the other cheek.

Q Hafiz Saeed is well known as the founder of Lashkar-e-Taiba, which was behind the Mumbai attacks...

A The Indian government has not a shred of evidence, no tangible proof that Hafiz Saeed was in any way connected to the Mumbai attacks. Jihad is a word that means struggle, even if it is done through monetary assistance and charity work. All over the world, there is a feeling that Muslims are terrorists...

Q Let's talk specifics. Ajmal Kasab, the lone terrorist captured alive has testified to the role of your client.

A My dear lady, such evidence will not even be admissible in an Indian court of law. Any statement made by an accused is not credible evidence....

I also called Khalid Waleed, Saeed's son-in-law, who did not let me off his sight for all the time that I had spent in Muridke. India has presented evidence of Hafiz Saeed's involvement in the Mumbai terror attacks, I told him.

'The Lashkar does not respect the LoC. They are working towards the accession of Kashmir to Pakistan. We help with propaganda, money and arms,' he said, dropping the pretence that the Jamaat-ud-Dawa was a charitable organization.

I then said, 'India believes Hafiz Saeed, your father-in-law is the mastermind of 26/11.'

'It is nothing but Indian propaganda,' he said in chaste Punjabi – a language that always opens doors for Indian journalists – adding, '*Bazurgan nu badnaam kita hai India ne* (India is besmirching the reputation of the old man). The Indian Home Minister [P. Chidambaram] asking for Saeed saab to be investigated and sent to Mumbai for trial is like Pakistan asking that Narendra Modi be brought here because he masterminded the killings of so many Muslims in Gujarat.'

I reminded him that Modi had been through the process of law.

Several trips to Pakistan helped me build sources and contacts. *India Today* was a well-known and respected magazine and ministers always made time. Interestingly, my gender never came in the way. Pakistan's independent media had several women journalists at senior positions. Making contacts was made easier because I spoke Punjabi and that helped open several doors. Nawaz Sharif always spoke to me in Punjabi – switching to English – only when the tape recorder was put on.

In 2011, when I was with the English news channel *Headlines Today,* I sought Nawaz Sharif's help to gain access to Muridke once again. I visited the Lashkar headquarter for a second time with the help of a former prime minister. His staff took two days to tie up the visit, probably because the visit to Muridke entails a sign-off from the ISI. The linkages were clear once again. They were staring me in the face. The Sharifs, a powerful political force in Pakistan's Punjab, always kept the LeT on their right side. They knew that the terror outfit had the support and sanction of the deep state – the army and the ISI.

The LeT – or the JuD – were also indispensable for the Sharifs. They had a wide network of supporters and while they exported terror to India, they also did charitable work on the ground that helped them spread their net far and wide. When a devastating earthquake struck Pakistan in 2015, killing close to 300 and damaging over 25,000 homes, the JuD assisted the military in providing relief and rehabilitation.

JuD's freedom to operate despite US and UN sanctions spotlights Pakistan's reluctance to reign-in terror outfits that are willing to train and send their jihadis into India. The Sharifs – all political forces, in fact – know that organizations like the LeT are the deep state's assets. The JuD publicly disavows its involvement in terror activities, but the world knows that it is only a front for the Lashkar.

There was a marked difference between my visit to Muridke in 2008 and my second foray into the sprawling complex in 2011. Under huge international pressure following the 26/11 attacks in Mumbai, the government led by the Pakistan People's Party (PPP) took over the Jamaat headquarters and appointed a chief administrator. The takeover was supervised by the local bureaucracy and police.

The fact that this was a charade, a mere move aimed at sending a message to the international community, was clear to me when I reached the gates of the headquarters for a second time in three years. The gates were still locked and secured by Hafiz Saeed's men. I saw the same schools and hospital – which had not a single patient or a single doctor in sight. The most important reminder for me was the fact that I was once again being escorted by Waleed, Saeed's son-in-law. He got the gates opened in a jiffy and the government's propaganda that it had taken control, lay stripped bare, before my eyes. I saw the government-appointed chief administrator salute Waleed. There was no doubt who the real administrator was.

Covering conflict is perilous. It is also heady. It also leads to a deep understanding of how states work and in the case of Pakistan, I was a first-hand witness of how non-state actors like Waleed work and how valuable they are to their masters in the ISI and the army. The two are intertwined.

Covering the aftermath of the Mumbai attacks came with other valuable insights. I was with *Hindustan Times* in 2013, when we worked on a special package detailing the progress – or rather the lack of it – in bringing the perpetrators of 26/11 to justice.

Ajmal Kasab had been hanged in full secrecy on 21 November 2012 at Yerwada prison, Pune, where he was buried, but Pakistan was refusing to cooperate on investigating the evidence provided by India in at least six different dossiers. Chidambaram had driven himself hoarse saying the evidence lay in Pakistani soil but Hafiz Saeed was not a man any Pakistani prime minister could touch.

Even the US was not willing to walk the talk despite Saeed's provocative speeches that directly targeted America. The US administration even placed a $10 million bounty for information on the professor of terror but did little else. It needed Pakistan's support in its own global war against terror, announced soon after the 9/11 attacks, when jihadi pilots flew straight into New York's iconic twin towers, changing Manhattan's skyline – and the world – forever.

For the 2013 special project for *Hindustan Times*, I reached out to former ISI chief, Lt. Gen. Hamid Gul, an advisor to Saeed who had often shared the stage with him. Former R&AW chief A. S. Dulat described Gul once as 'the most dangerous and infamous ISI chief in Indian eyes'. I met Gul on almost all my trips to Pakistan. The retired generals and spies there were approachable and friendly; always keen to add to the narrative of Kashmir, which had been internationalized at various fora. Meeting him helped me garner a better understanding of how the deep state worked. Due to our long association, perhaps, he agreed to help secure a telephonic interview with Saeed.

Gul assured me that he had spoken to Saeed and gave me his landline number. I was asked to send a questionnaire, which I diligently did. 'Just call and ask for him and he will come on the line,' Gul said.

A few days after I had sent the questionnaire, I was told, 'Saeed [saab] will not be talking to you. You have clearly sat in the R&AW headquarters to frame your questions.'

The pious professor who had no problems openly threatening India with 'more Mumbais' was too scared to take on a few direct questions from an Indian journalist. '*Ek Mumbai kya hota hai...*,' he had said at a rally.

He had no time for questions directed from India but was a familiar face on Pakistani television screens. I had often watched his televized interviews, including during my trip to Muridke. At first sight, he passed off as a cleric, a scholarly-looking man, an elder seldom seen without a walking stick in his hand and a cap on his head.

His is not a face that draws easy attention, but his views did. Each time this 'pious' man addressed a congregation, he could hold a crowd spellbound. The powerful orator was clear-headed about his interpretation of the Quran and believed that killing is 'every pious man's obligation' and the destruction of non-Islamic forces a duty assigned by Allah, the almighty.

In fact, he functioned as an improvised explosive device (IED) in the hands of his mentors in the establishment. His hatred for India – also openly echoed by his son-in-law during our tour of Muridke – stems from reasons personal and religious. His 'cause' for revenge is linked to his past – 30 members of his family were murdered during Partition when his father, an ordinary landlord, moved from Simla to Pakistani Punjab's Sargodha district. Talha Saeed, his son is believed to be the LeT's second in command. He tried entering Pakistan's Parliament from Lahore in the election held in February 2024, but suffered defeat at the hands of Imran Khan's candidate. Two years prior, India's home ministry designated Talha as a terrorist under the Unlawful Activities (Prevention) Act (UAPA). A ministry statement said, 'Hafiz Talha Saeed has been actively involved in recruitment, fund collection, planning and executing attacks by LeT in India and Indian interests in Afghanistan. Hafiz Talha Saeed has been actively visiting various LeT centres across Pakistan and during his sermons propagating for jihad against India, Israel, United States of America, and Indian interests in other Western countries.'

Hafiz Saeed – under whose shadow his son grew – was brought up learning the Quran. He pursued religious studies in Saudi Arabia, from where he obtained a master's in Islamic studies. The professor, who speaks only Urdu and chaste Punjabi, taught Islamic Studies at the University of Engineering and Technology in Lahore. He also taught and preached jihad. In several speeches, he can be heard saying, 'Allah has ordained every Muslim to fight until His rule is established. We have no option but to follow Allah's order. The blow struck by jihad does not come from man, it comes from Allah.'

Allah's man is now in jail, sentenced concurrently for 31 years. He was sentenced – ironically for terror funding charges by Pakistan's Counter Terrorism Department – and not because of the inscrutable linkages to the 10 terrorists who were trained under his command and helped across the high seas from Karachi to Mumbai. America never went ahead to apprehend the man against whom it had announced a large bounty.

I was still with *Hindustan Times* in 2018, 10 years after the Mumbai attacks. This time, I put in a request – well in advance – for an interview with Kenneth I. Juster, the US Ambassador to India.

Justice had still not been done and the conspirators who planned the 26/11 attack were still free. They had the azadi to openly propagate jihad and make virulent anti-India and anti-America speeches.

Ambassador Juster had agreed to do the interview. I was repeatedly assured by his office and they even asked for a questionnaire in advance. Sending advance questions is a practise most journalists dislike because the replies are often rehearsed, and they just take away from the spontaneity of an interview. Only in very special circumstances do we agree to sending questions.

I was banking on the Juster interview for the '10 years after 26/11' special issue.

At the very last minute, a very apologetic employee from the US embassy called to tell me that the interview would not take place.

'Why?' I asked incredulously, when all along I had been assured that only the time had to be allocated.

The answer stunned me. The US ambassador did not want to answer the question of why his government had not executed the $10 million bounty it had announced in 2012 for Saeed.

Saeed continued to be a free man. His movements were known. He was visible everywhere. At rallies and television studios.

India's most wanted terrorist was not America's terrorist. Doval had made the same point in the context of Dawood Ibrahim. In the interview he gave me after retiring as Director IB, he had said, 'Certainly, if Dawood Ibrahim was Osama bin Laden, then probably, with the same evidence, much more would have happened. That's the reality. That's how the entire game is played in the international community.'

A few months after I returned from Muridke in 2008, I learnt that I had been put on Pakistan's blacklist for a second time.

Covering Pakistan was exhilarating even though Indian journalists are followed bumper-to-bumper from the minute they land and are constantly trailed. The experience is discomfiting. The sleuths in safari suits would perch themselves on a sofa in the hotel – usually facing the elevator – trying to hide their faces behind a newspaper. They'd jump up immediately and kick-start their motorcycles and follow you, every step of the way. The thought of having been escorted by the Lashkar and being tracked by the ISI is a thought that brings an occasional smile. The journey through conflict zones and conflict situations is not easy.

There was no way I could have entered the Lashkar headquarters without the ISI's clearance. Blacklisting me was just the intelligence agency's way of saying it did not like what I wrote. The truth is seldom convenient for covert agencies, especially powerful ones like Pakistan's. They control their own prime ministers and guide the powerful jihadi network, alike.

In India, agencies like the IB and the R&AW deny access to make their displeasure known. In one case, again related to crucial information pertaining to 26/11, an IB officer who had become a good contact just refused to take calls. He was unhappy with an article that had exposed a slip on their part. A few months before the Mumbai attacks, S. M. Sahai, a senior officer posted as IG (Crime), in Jammu and Kashmir had informed the IB of a stellar covert operation in which he and his team had provided Indian SIM cards to the LeT. Sahai had put together a team that managed to infiltrate the ranks of the LeT.

Planting your own men into terror organizations is a long, arduous, and extremely dangerous job. One amongst Sahai's team was a man called Mukhtar Ahmed. He had, earlier, spent a few years in Kolkata, where he drove an auto rickshaw, after his brother was killed by militants in Kashmir.

He joined the Jammu and Kashmir police force as a follower – the lowest rank in the police cadre – for a paltry sum of ₹1,500 a month. But Mukhtar had the appetite for dangerous missions and threw himself – as part of a plan – into a cell in a police station where a hard-core terrorist was lodged. Slowly but surely, Mukhtar built contacts within the LeT, after his cellmate shared a mobile number with him. The number was soon put on a tracking list.

No spy thrillers that encase covert operations – in books or movies – can match the operation that this team carried out. The imprisoned terrorist was desperate to leak the news that he had been caught, so his comrades could flee to safer hideouts. Bit by bit, month by month, Mukhtar gained the confidence of the LeT operatives on both sides of the LoC. His cellmate was an important import and his trust led him to several others. Step by step, he entrenched himself in the ranks of the terror outfit, who, in turn, started believing that he was one of their own.

Then, one day, came the demand for SIM cards for an attack on 'Watan-e-Hind'. Chillingly, the demand was made by Zaki-ur-Rehman Lakhvi, aka 'Chacha', also the Lashkar's military commander. Mukhtar, by now apparently had managed to win over the trust of Saeed's top confidantes.

The question that confronted Sahai and his team next was: How do they procure the SIM cards and send them to Pakistan? Mukhtar went back to Kolkata where he once worked, to buy multiple cards. In the meanwhile, Sahai's team established contact with a Kashmiri militant, code-named 'Kesar', who had already crossed into Pakistan and was ready to return and be a part of the police force. Kesar was a good – rather, safe choice – mainly because he was a part of the inner circle of the Pakistan-based terror organization.

This part of the covert operation has never been revealed before. It is definitely not a part of any archival domain. It is unlikely to be a part of official files either, for such sensitive operations are seldom put down in black and white. I sourced it from conversations with several officials of the police and intelligence agencies.

The team arranged for Kesar to cross the LoC into Uri, a district on the Indian side of Kashmir. Since the Indian Army keeps a sharp eye on border infiltration and has orders to shoot to kill, seniors within the organization were requested to allow the operative to cross over.

Upon his return, a passport was issued in his name, and the next step was to get a visa. This was a relatively easier task than infiltrating the ranks of the terror organization that was planning a big attack. Why else would they ask for Indian SIM cards?

The visa application was submitted with a written request from hard-line separatist, Syed Ali Shah Geelani, well-known for his calls for Kashmir's merger with Pakistan, as also for his infamous calendars wherein he exhorted Kashmir's youth to take to the streets in protest. Geelani's calendars kicked in at all times: when a militant was killed; when innocents became victims of gun battles between the security forces and the terrorists. Calls for curfew were even issued by Geelani on dates commemorating the anniversary of the United Nation's resolution on Kashmir.

Sahai's team was confident that Kesar's visa would be issued. It was well known within official circles that applications recommended by Geelani were processed within a day by the Pakistan High Commission.

Mukhtar was back from Kolkata with the SIM cards and Kesar had a valid visa. The SIM cards were stitched into the pages of a diary and handed over to Kesar, who crossed the land border at Wagah, to return to his comrades, whose trust he already had. Indian officials at Wagah were told to let Kesar pass.

The SIM cards were now in Lakhvi's custody. They had been personally delivered by Kesar. 26/11 had been planned to the last detail.

It was time for Sahai to write a note marked 'Top Secret' and provide details of the mobile numbers that had been sent across the border to the LeT. It was clear to Sahai that the SIM cards would surface in India but he wasn't sure about when or where. Sending the note was important because the numbers could not have been monitored out of Jammu and Kashmir. The state police could only request service providers who operated within their domain. In this case, the SIMs had been procured from Kolkata.

Sahai sent the 'Top Secret' memo to Arun Chaudhary, the Srinagar-based joint director of the IB with a copy to Kuldeep Khoda, director general, Jammu and Kashmir Police.

It was now the job of the IB to keep a close watch, on where and how the SIM cards were going to be used. One thing was clear: the phone numbers would be put to use in India. That was the only reason the LeT had sourced them.

At least three of the over 30 SIM cards, used during the serial attacks in Mumbai, were in the possession of Kasab and his nine compatriots who had alighted at Colaba's Badhwar Park. It is entirely possible that the terrorists activated their numbers after reaching Badhwar Park, the urban fishing village in South Bombay, from where they unleashed terror on the city. Shockingly, these numbers had not been placed on tracking, despite credible information lying in the hands of those who were supposed to act on it. It was only on the night of 26/11, once the terror strikes were well under way that the IB was reminded of the 'Top Secret' memo.

Soon, the Anti-Terror Squad (ATS) – who had lost their chief, Hemant Karkare and two other officers, Ashok Kamte and Vijay Salaskar – began recording the conversations between the terrorists and their handlers in Pakistan. The IB was also listening in, in their own control room. By the time the IB officials called the ATS office at about 1 a.m. to tell them, the mayhem in Mumbai had begun.

Several agencies including R&AW had enough intercepts that had warned of a strike in Mumbai but the different agencies sharing information were not joining the dots. This, despite the fact that Taj Mahal Palace Hotel was specifically mentioned as a potential target in the intercepts.

Four days after the deadly attack, Prime Minister Manmohan Singh's government quickly changed the home minister, replacing Shivraj Patil with P. Chidambaram. In an interview to *The Indian Express*, in January 2009, Chidambaram rightly said, 'You will not get an invitation card which says you are cordially invited to come and witness a sea side incursion into India.' He was angry and was using sarcasm to drive home the point about the importance of analyzing intelligence and being ahead of the enemy.

Journalism, as I've practised it, is not meant to suit anyone's narrative. It must always be an honest attempt at digging facts, chronicling the truth, adding perspective and providing a deeper understanding of how the powerful operate. The powerful can be from within the system or outside of it. The LeT remains a powerful non-state actor.

No one from the LeT has been prosecuted for the Mumbai attacks. Quite to the contrary, Lakhvi or Chacha, the top LeT commander – second only to Hafiz Saeed – who was initially arrested by Pakistan for masterminding the 26/11 attacks, fathered a child while being held on terror charges at the high-security Adiala jail in Rawalpindi.

Abu Jundal, a 26/11 plotter who was with Lakhvi, monitoring the attack on live television, told intelligence officials that Lakhvi's youngest wife was allowed to visit him in jail, despite him being on trial. While at *Hindustan Times*, I had reported the news of Lakhvi fathering the child. Jundal, an Indian had been tracked, arrested and deported to India from Saudi Arabia in April 2012. Jundal told Indian interrogators that Lakhvi shared this information with him when he called on him in Adiala jail to tell him that he had got married.

Pakistani-American terrorist David Coleman Headley, who had made several trips to Mumbai, to videograph the potential targets like the Taj Mahal Palace Hotel, had also told the National Investigation Agency (NIA) team – that went to Chicago to interrogate him – that Lieutenant General Shuja Pasha, ISI chief, had visited Lakhvi in jail.

'The American government too shared intelligence with India that Lakhvi had access to a mobile phone in jail and that he continued to run the Lashkar's operations from prison,' I had written for *Hindustan Times* in November 2012.

Lakhvi's current whereabouts are unknown. He was never brought to justice for being one of the masterminds of 26/11. The only solace India can draw is that the UN rejected a petition by Hafiz Saeed asking it to remove him from the list of sanctioned terrorists, twice.

The 2019 report of an ombudsman – endorsed by the UN Sanctions Committee was categorical. Saeed's 'argument of dissociation with LeT was not credible,' the report concluded, adding, 'He [Saeed] will continue as a listed individual.'

His benefactors in the Pakistan establishment came to his aid by refusing to grant a visa to enable the ombudsman from travelling to Lahore to interview Saeed.

The pious professor remains a terrorist in the eyes of the world. So does the JuD. It is not the charitable organization it likes to portray itself to be. The United Nations doesn't think so – it remains proscribed.

Postscript: India could point a firm finger in Pakistan's direction because it was able to record conversations between the 10 terrorists and their handlers in Pakistan. Mukhtar, who should have been awarded for his gallantry, was instead arrested and jailed for criminal conspiracy and for having links with militants. Intelligence agencies don't like being outed. In this case, the police had dared and succeeded in penetrating the ranks of the organization that wreaked havoc in Mumbai. Mukhtar was eventually released and all charges dropped. By then he had spent an agonizing three months in jail. No one pins medals on the chests of undercover agents who risk their lives in the national interest.

No medal was pinned but the Modi government gave the defence forces the freedom to strike at the terror infrastructure in Pakistan, after the killings of tourists in Pahalgam. Unlike the surgical strikes after Uri and Pulwama, India's air defence aimed their missiles to strike the headquarters of the LeT at Muridke and the JeM in Bahawalpur. Visuals of the damaged headquarters in Muridke reminded me of my two trips there. Out of sheer curiosity, I dialled Waleed, Hafiz Saeed's son-in-law's number several times. Each time, a recorded message said, 'The number you are trying to reach has been powered off.' Operation Sindoor hit nine targets. For the first time, Indian defence forces targeted the heart of Pakistan's Punjab which is also the heart of its army domain. The uneasy question that remains unanswered is simply this: Has Operation Sindoor also powered off the terror that Pakistan exports into India?

Azadi, Unrest and a Furious Uprising

'Why is India occupying our land?'
'Why do men in uniform, who are not even from Kashmir, walk into our homes and demand proof of our identification? We want azadi from oppression...'
'How can you fire bullets at our young boys... each one of us is Burhan... the Indian forces have automatic weapons but they are so scared even of our mobile phones, they have cut off all connectivity.'

On one of my visits to Srinagar in 1990, I thought I was being kidnapped. I was on my way to meet Jagmohan, the governor of Jammu and Kashmir at the Raj Bhawan, and the drive entailed an isolated stretch. The stretch was so long, I wasn't sure where I was being taken. Apprehensions clouded my mind. I was new to the battlefield of Kashmir.

I was trying to understand the reasons why the Valley had erupted in anger. Why were thousands taking to the streets every day, raising slogans and marching to the United Nation's headquarters, which still exists in Srinagar.

My meeting with Jagmohan did not help. When militancy exploded in 1990, Jagmohan was reinstated to bring Kashmir back from the brink. He had been governor of Jammu and Kashmir earlier as well, from 1984 to 1989. His second tenure, however, lasted just five months. By the time he was removed by Prime Minister V. P. Singh, two important dates stood out for the sheer violence they had unleashed.

The first relates to the infamous Gawkadal massacre on 21 January 1990 when paramilitary forces lost their nerve and opened fire at a procession that was protesting random searches of their homes. What stands out as one of the worst massacres in the Valley, over 50 people were killed on that one day. Many died of multiple gunshot wounds while several drowned because they jumped into the Jhelum to dodge bullets.

Kadal means bridge in Kashmiri. On 21 January 1990, when the slogan for azadi was responded to with bullets, Jagmohan – who should have acted as the 'bridge' between his people and the men in uniform – decided to stay quiet.

Two days before the Gawkadal massacre, the Valley had been virtually emptied of Kashmiri Pandits who left in the dead of night on 19 January, commemorated each year as 'holocaust day'. Announcements had been made from several mosques, openly threatening the Pandits to leave the Valley. They loaded their belongings into trucks and drove in the direction of Jammu, using the cover of darkness as their protective shield. The mass exodus was triggered by the gunning down of prominent members of the minority community. On 14 September 1989, Tika Lal Taploo was shot dead by masked assailants. Other high-profile killings of a judge and the director of Doordarshan spread complete terror.

The second massacre during Jagmohan's controversial short tenure came in May. It was triggered soon after the chief priest, Mirwaiz Maulvi Farooq, a respected but controversial figure, was shot dead at his home on 21 May 1990. In death, he was conferred the status of a 'martyr'.

The security forces made their second big mistake when they opened fire at the large procession that was a part of the Mirwaiz's final journey. The government, led by Governor Jagmohan, claimed that the CRPF opened their guns in retaliation, after coming under fire from amongst the thousands who were a part of the procession.

I was in Srinagar that day as the bullets flew. Ironically, bullets also hit the already dead Mirwaiz and also killed another 60, mostly women and children. I remember escaping through by-lanes choking with teargas smoke.

Srinagar was on the boil and the ground situation was highly explosive. Jagmohan ordered an inquiry, but by then, Jammu and Kashmir had become a communal tinderbox. The governor was as worshipped by the Kashmiri Pandits as he was reviled by the Kashmiri Muslims.

Jagmohan was recalled by the V. P. Singh government soon after, but militancy had taken firm root in the Valley. Apart from the JKLF, other pro-Pakistan terror outfits like the Hizbul Mujahideen were aiding the insurgency.

If I've singled out the two massacres, it is because they became important milestones in the very long history of human rights violations. Until then, Kashmiris were agitating about how they were politically oppressed and how they had been deceived into believing that they would be given a chance to choose whether they wanted to stay with India or not.

Pick a calendar that spans decades and there will be several years, several dates, several phases that mark the twists and turns that Kashmir has endured. Each date and year have contributed to the deep sense of betrayal and alienation that have fuelled Kashmir's long and bloody tryst with violence.

Let's look at some key dates.

Maharaja Hari Singh signed the Instrument of Accession to make Jammu and Kashmir a part of the Indian Union on 26 October 1947.

Four days before that, thousands of Pakistani 'tribesmen' invaded Kashmir. The local population came out in the thousands to defend their land from the 'tribesmen' who had the clear backing of the Pakistani army. The army, headquartered in Rawalpindi, has not stopped meddling in Kashmir since 1947 but New Delhi, too, hasn't stopped treating Kashmir as a piece of real estate.

Many books have been written on the history of Jammu and Kashmir. This chapter, however, is an attempt at understanding the state's journey through conflict. Why did the same Kashmiris – who fought the invading Pakistani tribesmen in 1947 – then lend support to terrorists? Delhi's meddling certainly did not help. In fact, it sowed the seeds of betrayal.

The betrayal was evident from the manner in which Sheikh Abdullah was jailed, first by Jawaharlal Nehru and then by his daughter, Indira Gandhi. In August 1953, Nehru got Sheikh – also referred to as the 'Lion of Kashmir' – jailed on charges of conspiring against India's sovereignty. Sheikh Abdullah stayed in jail for nearly 22 years till an agreement, the Indira–Sheikh Accord, was signed between the two in 1975.

The accord lasted barely two years. Indira Gandhi dealt a fresh blow by getting the Congress to withdraw its support to Sheikh's government in the state. She resented the fact that the Sheikh stayed committed to not merging his party with the Congress.

Politics kept muddying the Kashmiri waters. Discontentment with New Delhi set in and people began to lose faith in the credibility of democratic processes. Farooq Abdullah, the Sheikh's eldest son, who had a convincing victory in the 1983 election was stabbed in the back by his brother-in-law, G. M. Shah. With the help of the Congress MLAs – ably guided by the Indira Gandhi government at the Centre – Shah split the National Conference and went on to dethrone Farooq. Jagmohan was the governor in Jammu and Kashmir at the time.

In 1987, Farooq was back in the electoral contest. The National Conference and the Congress fought the elections together, after Farooq and Rajiv Gandhi came to power following the assassination of his mother, Indira Gandhi in 1984. The 1987 election, another year that can be marked on the calendar, was marred with allegations of large-scale rigging.

Politics doesn't just make for strange bedfellows. In conflict zones, it creates havoc and fuels insurgencies that are difficult to contain.

1987, thus, is the year that can be identified for when the seeds of insurgency were sown. Candidates of the Muslim United Front were denied victories in what was seen as a brazenly rigged election. One of the candidates who lost was Syed Salahuddin. He decided to cross the LoC into Pakistan and train himself on how to use the Kalashnikov. Hundreds followed him, each a byproduct of mistrust sown by politicians in the Valley and New Delhi.

New Delhi and Srinagar had muddied the waters, and Pakistan was waiting for the opportunity to avenge the loss of Kashmir. As the country's only Muslim-majority state, Jammu and Kashmir was seen as 'India's crown' to showcase its secular credentials.

The credentials took a hit soon after the 1987 election, credited to be the final straw that soon manifested itself into a full-blown insurgency. Yasin Malik, who also crossed the LoC for training, was Salahuddin's poll manager in 1987. All through the counting process, Salahuddin was way ahead of Ghulam Mohuddin Shah, the National Conference's candidate, in a direct contest for Amira Kadal, a seat in the heart of Srinagar. A dejected Shah had in fact left the counting centre but was called back and declared the winner by a margin of about 4,000 votes.

The political victory led to disenchantment and thus began the process of alienation. Unknown to Farooq Abdullah, who was sworn-in as the chief minister, this was the time when government employees, too, were crossing the LoC.

The insurgency burst out in the open in 1989 with the kidnapping of Rubaiya Sayeed and the subsequent capitulation by the V. P. Singh government and his home minister, Mufti Mohammad Sayeed. By then Salahuddin had become the head of the deadly terror outfit, the Hizbul Mujahideen and Yasin Malik, the chief of the JKLF.

I got the chance to interview Farooq Abdullah for *India Today* magazine and pose some direct questions regarding the rigging. He took them straight on. I reproduce a few excerpts:

Q How do you plan to tackle the militants who are dead set against you?

A Why are they against me?

Q Because they think you rigged an election and you headed an administration that was corrupt.

A (*Raising his voice*) Are those people not corrupt? Are those militants not raping my mothers and my sisters and taking money from them? Are they not, at this time, building homes, beyond their capacities? Are they not raping government land? (*Screaming by now*) Who are you calling corrupt? Rigged election, my foot. I don't believe it. Why did they not go to the Election Commission and complain?

Q Because they had lost faith in the system.

A Then they have no faith in themselves and have no right to be there.

Q You seriously believe the election was not rigged?

A You accept all other elections as unrigged. All of you make the '87 election out to be the turning point. It is India that is responsible for what has happened in Kashmir and not Farooq Abdullah. They betrayed my father in '53. They betrayed my father in '75. They betrayed me in '84. They are responsible, not Farooq Abdullah.

Farooq left for London in 1990, soon after Jagmohan returned to Srinagar as the state governor. I asked him why he had left and true to style, Farooq thundered, 'I did not leave. I was made to leave otherwise I would have met the same fate as Mirwaiz Farooq and they would have buried me. I am not ready for burial as yet. I will bury others before I go.'

Violence became a daily feature in the '90s and the Indian Army found itself trying to understand the reasons for why the Kalashnikov was becoming so popular. Why were the youth choosing to wield guns? Why were they willing to risk their lives to go to Pakistan for training?

The findings were contained in a unique study conducted by a team of professional psychologists and psychiatrists from the Indian Army. Conceived by Brigadier Arjun Ray, the Brigadier General Staff (BGS) to Corps Commander Lieutenant General S. Padmanabhan of the 15 Corps headquartered in Srinagar, the study sought to probe the mind of the militant.

Conducted on militants who were in custody and also willing to be put through the psychological examination, the tests found that the average Kashmiri militant was driven more by economic and political frustration and less by Islamic fundamentalism. No less startling was the revelation that the battle for independence was fuelled not so much by any ideological zest as it was by a deep-seated desire for revenge against the perceived 'tormentors' and 'oppressors'. The men in uniform were viewed as the 'tormentors' and the politicians as 'oppressors'.

Brigadier Ray had told me in 1994, when the study was conducted that while they knew the names of various gangs and their modus operandi, they 'wanted to find out the motivating factors'.

Ray, who went on to author a book *Kashmir Diary: Psychology of Militancy* in 1997, used the study to probe the mind of the militants.

Through the study the army was able to understand why Ahmad Ganai, only 19 years old and in jail, felt no remorse or regret for having chosen the path of violence. Ganai revealed why two years after his return from Pakistan – indoctrinated, trained, and armed – he had no doubt that he did the right thing by picking up the gun. He had spent seven months in jail when he was psychologically screened and all he could think of was returning, not to his family, but back to the militant fold.

Like his friends and peers, he found the gun emotionally and financially gratifying. He also said that the weapon vested him with power and gave him relief from 'oppression'. And quite unlike the foreign mercenaries who, fired by Islam, called themselves 'holy warriors', the study concluded that religion was not high on the list of motivating factors for the local militants, unlike in the '90s.

The findings, revealed that, as in the case of Ganai, for others too, the gun had become a potent weapon to fight the system which, they felt, had left them frustrated. 'Most of them talked about corruption, the rich having got richer and they having been denied their dues,' Lieutenant Colonel D. Saldanha, the psychiatrist at Srinagar's Base Hospital, who put 31 captured militants through the psychological tests, had told me.

Many of them were drawn by the improved lifestyle of their militant 'friends'. This was also how they chose to join one group over another – not for ideological reasons but because their peers were in a particular gang.

For most militants, the gun had become the midwife of progress, a tool for gaining wealth and acquiring power over people.

The study revealed a clear pattern. Ninety-five percent of the 31 militants were not even matriculates. Only six of them had held jobs before they opted for militancy and most of them came from large families where they were one of four to eight children.

'Ridden with a feeling of being underprivileged, the gun had become the compensation mechanism for them,' Saldanha had analysed. I was still with *India Today* magazine and the findings, which explored the motivation and the mentality of the militants, were published in December 1994.

Frustration with the political system, economic backwardness, and a feeling of oppression were motivating factors for even the better-known militants who climbed the hierarchy. Javed Mir, a plumber by profession, went on to become the publicity chief of JKLF and later, its commander-in-chief. Before the advent of the gun, Javed was known as Javed 'Nalka', a reference to his plumbing profession.

Not all youth who chose to become militants became public figures. The lesser-known ones, however, wielded great clout in their respective areas of operation. Most militants went on to become 'area commanders' and earned more than they ever would have in their traditional vocations as agricultural workers or shopkeepers. However, they were not only being funded by Pakistan but were also in the business of extorting money.

While the army understood the reasons for their initiation into the militant fold, what it found disturbing were the levels of motivation, indoctrination, and the sheer ruthlessness they saw amongst the militants. Hardened by violence and criminal activity, 22 of the 31 militants indicated that militancy had become a profession they were pursuing with zeal.

None seemed afraid of dying. Three amongst the 31 had suffered serious gunshot wounds in encounters with the security forces but still said they would like to return to the militant fold.

While 30 percent of the militants interviewed said they had voluntarily taken to the gun, the rest revealed that though they were initially not inclined, they later became active participants.

Apart from one captured militant, named Farooq Ahmed Dar, who wanted to give up militancy so he could return to his wife and one-year-old son, family ties did not seem to tug at the heartstrings of the 12 others who were married. Of the militants who were single, none showed a desire to raise families of their own.

My notes from that time has another quote from

Lieutenant Colonel Saldanha, which reads, 'They found more emotional bonding within the militant gangs rather than in their families.' Even the married ones – because of the level of brutalization through violence – indicated that, given a chance, they would go back to being gun-toting militants.

Evident in the psychological test was the deep sense of alienation which was sustaining the movement in Kashmir. For unlike in Punjab where the common man gradually withdrew their support for the militants after their abject surrender during Operation Black Thunder, an operation which also revealed how they had desecrated the Golden Temple, the Kashmiris nursed a deep sense of betrayal.

Given the choice between militants and the security forces, they have, over the years, made their choice clear. They have sided with the former, even though he also alienates them, but is better than the force in olive green which remains the 'tormentor'.

Brigadier Ray, who published *Kashmir Diary: Psychology of Militancy* after he had become a Major General, wrote, and I quote, 'Militants are not criminals or psychopaths or men with twisted minds. They are unquestionably genuine, normal and straight people, as normal as the neighbour next door, the vegetable seller, the policeman on the beat, the banker, the soldier, the bureaucrat, the salesman. The only difference is that militants have a psyche and logic of their own. This is borne out by the fact that Kashmiri militants even in captivity are not found distressed. Only 3.22 percent show symptoms of mental anxiety.'

Irrespective of which group they belonged to, those trained in Pakistan turned out to be more hard-core. They were ruthless mercenaries in comparison to those who had been locally trained. The only difference was that while the pro-Pakistan militants considered violence as the only alternative, those who were a part of the JKLF spoke of a political process and a solution.

The same army which tried to probe the mind of the militant through the psychological testing, then went on to engage surrendered militants to take the battle straight into the ranks of the Hizbul Mujahideen. After Jagmohan's dismissal as the governor, following the catastrophic fallout of the Mirwaiz's killing in May 1990, Jammu and Kashmir stayed under the shadow of the gun. Militants would openly mock New Delhi and dare them to hold an election. I remember coffins being openly placed at street corners. The message was clear: Anyone who dared to vote would be killed.

The surrendered militants, deployed by the army struck deadly blows and helped the security forces retrieve some ground. They were as mercenary as their counterparts in the Hizbul Mujahideen. They helped pave the way for the 1996 election, the first since the infamous 1987 polls which lit the fire that engulfed the state.

Farooq Abdullah returned to power in 1996 and made attempts at securing a political solution. In June 2000, he tried to force New Delhi's hand by passing a resolution for greater autonomy in the assembly. A. B. Vajpayee was the prime minister then, and though he had endeared himself to the Kashmiris by his famed policy he outlined as

'*Insaniyat, Jamhuriyat, Kashmiriyat,*' (within the realm of humanity) the autonomy resolution was rejected.

Kashmiris had witnessed a litany of broken promises. Decision makers in New Delhi, across party lines, were content when the Valley went through phases of near normalcy. The degree of normalcy was measured by the number of tourists thronging the Valley and through voter turnout at elections.

But the semblance of normalcy had to crack. An entire generation had grown up under the shadow of the gun. The Valley resembled a military garrison, and the Kashmiris resented that they were suspects in the eyes of the uniformed personnel. Like the militants surveyed in 1994, many amongst the new generation saw no hope. Rage and resentment had been building up.

The breaking point came in May 2010. Farooq's son, Omar Abdullah was at the helm and was left to deal with the fallout of a fake encounter that hit too close to the Kashmiri bone.

The Valley erupted in collective anger after news broke that the army had picked up three young men on the promise of finding them jobs. However, they passed the three off as militants trying to infiltrate into India from Pakistan. The killings took place in North Kashmir's Machil. There was a public outcry after photographs of the alleged militants were released. The families of Shehzad Khan (27), Shafi Lone (19), and Riyaz Lone (20) were adamant: their sons were not militants, nor connected with militancy. Were they killed to buttress the army unit's performance? There was a time when battalions were rewarded for the number of militants they killed and arrested. They were also rewarded for the number of terrorists and arms they captured.

The encounter had indeed been staged and the agitation that followed was intense. The crowds that took to the streets only grew in numbers. The protests were not limited to areas around Nadihal village from where the three men had been taken.

Over the years, reporters covering Kashmir have come to realize – and understand – that protestors persist on the streets when their anger is genuine; when they know that the 'encounters' are cold-blooded murders. The same was visible in 2000, when the army passed off five Kashmiris as foreign mercenaries in what is now infamously known as the Pathribal encounter. The army claimed the slain men were responsible for shooting 36 Sikhs five days before, on 20 March 2000, in the incident now known as the Chittisinghpora massacre. The bodies of the five had even been burnt so they could not be identified.

The sheer fury of the protestors had forced then Chief Minister Farooq Abdullah to exhume the bodies. DNA tests had established that the five were neither infiltrators nor mercenaries but innocent Kashmiris. The CBI pinned the blame on the officers of 7 Rashtriya Rifles. In the end, justice was not served – and this often lies at the heart of why the conflict continues to fester. The army conducted a court martial but gave its officers a clean chit in 2014, saying, 'The evidence recorded could not establish a prima facie case against any of the accused persons.'

Unlike Farooq, his son Omar Abdullah, was not able to deal with the angry protestors in 2010. Farooq had stood by the graves of the Pathribal boys as their bodies were being exhumed, but Omar crawled into a shell as his state witnessed one of the worst phases of violence. Over a hundred protesting youth were killed by the security forces.

Slogan-shouting, stone pelting boys and girls took over the streets of the Valley but the chief minister was nowhere to be seen. Edgy personnel of the CRPF and the local police responded to stones with bullets and the death count kept mounting as innocent civilians were killed, one after the other.

At the time I was working with *Headlines Today*. I was on the streets of Srinagar with my cameraman when we came across a visibly upset CRPF jawan who had seen his colleagues being injured by the protestors pelting stones. He started crying, 'They will kill us. Our officers have left us on the streets to die. I have parents and a wife at home. For how long will we continue being hit?'

His words drove home the divide between the street and the security forces. Variant truths often coexist in conflict zones. I made sure to call the office in Delhi and request them to use the video but blur the jawan's face. I did not want him to lose his job.

If he felt like he had become cannon fodder, it is because he and his comrades were being used as human shields by the politicians who were only willing to look at the complexities of the insurgency as a military problem. But solutions seldom flow from the barrel of a gun.

Omar Abdullah conceded this a few years later, in November 2014, when in an interview with me for *Hindustan Times*, he said, 'The 2010 summer agitation haunts me… I made my mistakes at that time. I hunkered down and went into a shell and tried to deal with a law and order problem as a law and order problem. My colleagues also disappeared. I should have dealt with it politically.'

While in Srinagar, when innocent after innocent was being killed, I requested for an appointment with Omar. 'Don't you have blood on your hands?' is the question I wanted to ask the chief minister but, while he agreed to meet me in his office, he refused to be drawn into an interview.

He sat by the window of his office in Srinagar's secretariat, looking grim and helpless. Normally an easy man to converse with, he was in no mood to talk but finally asked me a question: 'What do you think I should do?'

The answer was simple and obvious: You have to step out and assuage your people. You have to visit the injured and go to homes that have lost young ones.

The same evening, news came in of Omar having gone to Srinagar's hospital to meet with the injured, but he had made a fatal mistake. He took a helicopter instead of driving or walking down streets where his people were being killed.

I know he will not mind me revealing our conversation, for in a tweet in December 2012 – two-and-a-half years later – he wrote, 'I made the mistake of not being seen or heard in 2010 summer.' Omar is amongst the very few willing to concede to mistakes.

The ferocity of the street subsided only after Prime Minister Manmohan Singh's government at the Centre set up a team of three interlocutors led by senior journalist and former *Times of India* editor, Dileep Padgaonkar. The other two members included academician Prof Radha Kumar and former Central Information Commissioner M. M. Ansari. They were empowered to hold a sustained dialogue with all stakeholders in the state. The committee made several bold recommendations, including removing the word 'temporary' from the heading of Article 370 and a reappraisal of the same Article's erosion over the years. The committee also asked for a review of the Armed Forces Special Powers Act (AFSPA) and for the release of 'stone pelters' and political prisoners against whom there were no serious charges. None of these came up for any discussion. The protests had abated, and a semblance of normalcy was back. New Delhi was back to doing what it does best: Count the number of tourists who had started thronging the Valley. In 2011, after the interlocutors submitted their report, the BJP saw red. It condemned the report, saying, 'The recommendation to make Article 370 a permanent provision of the Constitution will lead to dangerous consequences with the prospect of the integration of Jammu and Kashmir with the rest of India becoming bleak.'

The tragedy of Kashmir lies in the fact that the windows of opportunity have never been pursued with political zeal by New Delhi. Many interlocutors have been appointed but their suggestions have seldom been actioned. The Narendra Modi government also appointed former IB director,

Dineshwar Sharma, as its interlocutor in 2017, at the time when the BJP was in alliance with People's Democratic Party (PDP). It paid heed to Sharma's recommendation of granting an amnesty scheme for stone pelters who were first-time offenders, but that was the only concession it made. Sharma worked hard to get a passport for the son of Afzal Guru, hanged for the attack on Parliament in 2001, but the Centre did not relent. Guru's hanging in 2013 had alienated the Kashmiris further because it was done in complete secrecy and without the mandated last meeting with the family that all prisoners on death row are accorded. Sharma's argument that Afzal's son, Ghalib be allowed to go to Turkey, where he had secured a medical scholarship fell on deaf ears. 'I will do anything that can bring happiness and satisfaction to any young person, including Afzal Guru's son,' Sharma had told me, but his efforts didn't yield dividends.

New Delhi has always prevaricated. The one exception, perhaps, was Vajpayee. He pursued peace seriously and even initiated a dialogue with the separatists and with members of the Hizbul Mujahideen. The efforts, however, never stood the test of time. They did not pass like a baton, from one government to the next. Each prime minister has had their own ideas and ideologies guiding them. Interlocutors were appointed – even authorized – to hold talks with 'all stakeholders' but New Delhi, the ultimate stakeholder seldom walked the talk.

Omar summed it up well, when in another interview with me in 2014, he said, 'We keep waiting for the ideal time and realize it has slipped us by. We had an ideal opportunity when we were dealing with Pervez Musharraf at the height of his power and we kept wondering if we could trust him and we let that go by. We had several opportunities in the Valley from time to time that we didn't take advantage of. You cannot wait for the last gun to fall silent, to engage with J&K politically. It is important to tell the state that you don't just engage with it when there is a problem on the street. You only engage them when there is trouble and when the trouble goes away, you feel there's no need for a solution. You have had several Government of India ministers accept that J&K has a unique distinction in the Indian Constitution and needs to be dealt within that framework, so why shy away? Delhi needs to incentivize peace, and we don't do that.'

Omar's National Conference lost power in 2014 and Jammu and Kashmir saw a disastrous alliance take shape between the BJP and PDP. Mehbooba Mufti, the feisty street fighter who built the PDP, had in all her election meetings, implored the people to defy the boycott call issued by the separatists. 'Vote in large numbers,' she would say, because 'it was important to keep the BJP from opening its account in the Valley.' The election results once again reflected the wedge between the two regions of Jammu and Kashmir.

Mehbooba's father, Mufti Mohammad Sayeed was convinced that he needed to be the bridge between the two ideologically different regions of Jammu and Kashmir. He recognized that the two parties were like 'North Pole and South Pole', but he went ahead, despite his daughter's opposition, to finalize an alliance that saw him being sworn in as the chief minister in March 2015.

The rage of 2010 had deep consequences that changed the ground reality. The PDP–BJP alliance that gave the saffron party its first shot at being in power in Jammu and Kashmir, was seen as a deep betrayal and added to the complexities, especially in the PDP's stronghold of South Kashmir. The electorate had responded to Mehbooba's call. They voted to keep the BJP at bay. They perceived the BJP's commitment to the abrogation of Article 370 – which guaranteed the state its special status – as a threat to their identity. The Kashmiris have forever lived with the fear – they still do – of a demographic change that will alter the reality of Jammu and Kashmir being the only Muslim-majority state.

The BJP agreed to maintain the status quo on Article 370, in the agenda for alliance worked out by the two coalition partners. It was their first shot at being in power in the state and agreed also to review the AFSPA, which gave the forces a quantum of immunity. The act empowers the army to shoot and kill in disturbed areas and can be prosecuted only after sanction from the central government.

When he took over the reins of the troubled state, Mufti kept appealing for Narendra Modi, who became prime minister in 2014, to re-model himself as another Vajpayee in his dealings with Kashmir. Former prime minister Vajpayee was the one BJP leader the Valley had warmed up to, after he had spoken of '*Insaniyat, Jamhuriyat, Kashmiriyat*'.

Mufti knew he was risking a gamble by allying with the BJP. The alliance was seen as a deep betrayal and the youth started scripting a new reality, a disturbing one.

2015 soon became another watershed year. It gave birth to a new wave of militancy, very different from the one that had been put under the psychological lens in 1994.

This new set of militants announced their arrival on social media. Leading a very young brigade of gun-toting militia, was 15-year-old Burhan Wani, who went on to become a household name. Unafraid of showing his face, he put up a post of himself holding a gun, on Facebook. Burhan looked like the boy next door – an antithesis of the masked terrorists of the '90s.

Why did the young student and the son of a headmaster decide to give up the comfort of a classroom and disappear into the mountains in South Kashmir's Tral? What made him into a cult figure? Why were many other students leaving home and disappearing into the same mountains?

I spent several days in different villages of South Kashmir, looking for answers. The ground under Kashmir's feet was slipping. Sixty percent of the Valley's population was below the age of 30 and Burhan had become a role model.

Why? That was a question that needed answers.

My first stop was at the home of Naseer Ahmed Pandit, a young Jammu and Kashmir Police constable. During the 2014 elections, he had gone out of his way to offer cups of tea to paramilitary forces that fanned out across villages to provide security to polling staff.

He was usually the first to cast his vote and during contentious India-Pakistan matches, he stood out for being amongst the few who cheered for India.

Yet, one day, Pandit disappeared and took his service weapon with him. His father realized that his son had joined the ranks of terrorists after a press release, issued by the Hizbul Mujahideen, claimed him as a trophy. The policeman had metamorphosed into a militant.

Pandit's father Ghulam Rasool described his son as a social worker and a crusader against drug peddlers. He was at pains to fathom why the 29-year-old, who loved his police uniform, disappeared into the high mountains. Rasool never heard from his son after he reinvented himself into a terrorist. He'd seen him though – posing in pictures that went viral on social media.

The ground reality in Kashmir was changing. I recorded the change in detail in a piece I wrote for *Hindustan Times* in 2015, a few months after Mufti had been sworn-in as the chief minister.

For the first time since the insurgency took firm root in 1989, the number of locals joining militancy overtook the number of foreign terrorists. In 2015, north Kashmir had 66 local and 44 foreign terrorists. In the PDP stronghold of South Kashmir, locals outnumbered foreign terrorists. The police records pegged the number of locals at 109, and foreign terrorists stood at a mere seven. The new local recruits, pertinently, also included the educated.

Among the homes I visited was that of 21-year-old Zakir Rashid Bhat, a Chandigarh-based civil engineering student. Zakir had come home to Noorpura village, Pulwama, for a brief vacation with his friends in 2015. The young student even took them to the snow-clad picture towns of

Gulmarg and Pahalgam, but while his friends went back to Chandigarh, Zakir never returned.

His father, Abdul Rashid Bhat, a senior engineer working with the state government, woke up to a note that said, 'Don't try and look for me. Jihad is the only way forward. It is the only way to deal with the atrocities faced by Kashmiris.'

Rashid had heaved a sigh of relief when his youngest son Zakir had got admission in an engineering college. The older son was a practising doctor while his daughter had a master's degree in botany.

The insurgency had not touched the family until the unrest of 2010, when stone pelting became the new form of protest to call out human rights violations. Zakir was amongst those who had joined fellow Kashmiris to protest.

Young Zakir, remembered in Noorpura as a boy who loved zipping his Yamaha motorcycle at high speed, finally joined the ranks of the Hizbul Mujahideen and soon became part of a video that showed his transformation. A boy fond of clothes and chocolates grew into a new role in which he could be seen sporting a long beard and caressing an automatic weapon.

Zakir joined the ranks of Burhan Wani, the young Robin Hood-like figure who had become a role model for Kashmiri youth. He clearly inspired many to follow in his footsteps – to disappear into the mountains – only to emerge transformed, on Facebook.

Burhan dropped out of class 10 and literally knocked on the doors of the Hizbul Mujahideen at the young age of 15 after his older brother Khalid was beaten up by security forces. Burhan, who once wanted to become a doctor, dropped out of school and echoed several themes in his recorded videos which instantly went viral on social media. He spoke about injustice and about 'oppression'.

Burhan had vowed to avenge the beating he and his brother Khalid got from the security forces, who had stopped them while they were out for a motorcycle ride. According to Muzaffar Wani, the father, members of the police's special operations group (SOG) asked them to fetch a pack of cigarettes. Once they delivered the pack, the SOG personnel pounced on them and thrashed the two brothers. This, according to the father, left a deep impact on Burhan, who eventually decided that he had to push back against what he perceived as injustice and oppression.

The word 'oppression' had been used by the captured militants who undertook the psychological tests too. In an uncanny similarity, some of the new-age militants who were appearing on Facebook had, according to several police officials, canvassed for the PDP in the 2014 election.

Burhan and his comrades had grown up in the Valley and never knew the meaning of normalcy. They grew up to violence; they grew up in a militarized zone. They also grew up watching elected leaders going back on promises.

The alliance between the PDP and the BJP was a turning point. Burhan's brother, Khalid, was killed in a controversial firing incident. Khalid's death on 13 April was the first casualty at the hands of security forces in Jammu and Kashmir since Chief Minister Mufti Mohammad Sayeed took over. By then, Burhan had already disappeared into Tral's high mountains and dense forests.

I asked Lieutenant General Satish Dua, Corps Commander, 15 Corps, why Kashmiri youth were choosing the path of violence once again. Why were local militants outnumbering the exports from Pakistan? The corps commander is the senior most army officer in Jammu and Kashmir, and also the head of the Unified Command comprising the local police and other paramilitary forces operating on the ground.

'The new strategy is to recruit locals and give them rudimentary training in the hinterland because the adversary [Pakistan] is not able to push terrorists across the line of control,' Dua had explained in the interview published in *Hindustan Times*. He was worried about how active the new demographic bulge was on social media.

'They make their names and faces known and their outreach is wide,' said Dua, implying that social media had become a fertile recruitment ground. He also talked about shrinking job avenues being a cause for concern. Other officials I met underlined how social media posts were affecting the psychology of Kashmiri youth who spent hours watching videos uploaded by young local militants.

'Their only role models are militants with guns like Burhan. We haven't been able to provide them with alternative role models,' another official told me.

There was another crucial factor. Former chief minister and National Conference patron, Farooq Abdullah articulated it well, when he said, 'Everyone is feeling choked because the political system has failed to deliver. The youth are looking at the nation very carefully and because they are educated, they first become militant in their minds.' Farooq also pointed directly at how the beef debate and the cow protection movement were dividing the nation and affecting Kashmiri youth. Mohammad Ikhlaq, lynched in Uttar Pradesh's Dadri on 28 September 2015 on mere suspicion of consuming beef had become a household name in Kashmir. So had Zahid Ahmed, a young Kashmiri trucker who was attacked and killed in Udhampur in October 2015, again on the suspicion that he was transporting beef.

Omar Abdullah blamed the uptake in locals joining militancy on the alliance between the PDP and the BJP in Kashmir. 'The PDP with its slogan of self-rule filled a gap that existed between the National Conference and the separatists but after they tied up with the ultra-nationalist BJP, the space has shrunk even more for the youngsters who have gravitated towards militancy,' he told me, for the same article I wrote for *Hindustan Times*.

In several villages across South Kashmir, people expressed their reservations about the alliance and were apprehensive about the dilution of Article 370, which guaranteed the state special powers.

The ground under Kashmir's feet was indeed slipping. An officer pointed to a survey conducted by the local police that showed how neighbourhood mosques were becoming congregation points in which maulvis were holding animated discussions on the threat to Islam and Kashmiriyat.

The trip to South Kashmir would have been incomplete without a visit to the home of Burhan Wani, the new local 'hero', who continued to fire the imagination of the youth.

Interviewing his father, Muzaffar Wani was a surreal experience. He was not just proud that Burhan had become a rallying point, he was openly supportive of him. Radicalization had become a new reality and was staring me in the face.

A conversation with him, in his village home in Sharifabad, a 90-minute drive from Srinagar, was also published in the same *Hindustan Times* article.

Q So, what is the main motto of Burhan and young boys like him?

A Freedom from India. It's not only his motto but everybody's. Even mine.... Look at the current incident of beef ban where a truck driver was lynched in Jammu only because he was a Kashmiri, a Muslim. This has happened so many times before also. Beef is halal for us [Muslims], we sacrifice it, and they have banned it.

Q But isn't it hard to win against the might of Indian Army?

A Yes, it's very hard. Everyone knows it. It is a hard task, but a Muslim has his faith in God. He knows if he dies in the path of God, he goes to God. In our religion, whosoever dies because of the oppression from India, or by an Indian bullet, doesn't die. He goes from this world to the other world (as promised in the Quran); there will be no disease in that world, no oppression. This is what our Islam says. That's why Muslims don't fear that. We prefer dying with honour rather than living a life of shame under oppression.

Q You know Burhan will be killed one day.... That is the outcome of the path he has chosen.

A Yes, I do get a bit disturbed, but our Islam says that God, Quran and the Prophet are bigger than anything, even bigger and more important than our sons. It's not the other way round. If our God is not happy with us, then we don't need our sons. Our God should be happy with us even if my son's or my sacrifice is needed for that.

Here was a father, who was prepared to receive his young son's body. He was not the only father willing to sacrifice sons.

Muzaffar Wani's words rang true the very next day. Two new-age militants were killed in an encounter and thousands joined the funeral procession. For someone who has tracked Kashmir since 1989, this was disturbing. The common Kashmiri had stopped bothering about militant deaths after the mid-90s.

But now they clearly felt politically choked. It also pointed to a high degree of radicalization, as echoed by Muzaffar Wani.

Chief Minister Mufti Mohammad Sayeed understood the sentiment but was constrained by his alliance with the BJP. He did concede to me that bullets could not be used to contain protests. 'We have to fight it politically. You may imprison Burhan, but you cannot imprison his mind,' he told me over breakfast. He wanted Mehbooba to join us and asked his granddaughter, Iltija Mufti, to call her. She did not come. Perhaps she was aware that she would find it hard to defend an alliance she clearly did not want to be a part of.

The Muftis – both father and daughter – knew that the problem was essentially political. The one concession they had been able to get from the BJP was the promise that the abrogation of Article 370, be put on the back burner.

The fear of the special status being withdrawn was a hot topic of discussion. Hemmed in by bunkers, curfews and frequent internet bans, people were desperately searching for dignity and justice. The tragedy, however, was that neither Srinagar nor New Delhi was wising up to the new reality. Neither looked beyond security perspectives.

Mufti Sayeed died at the age of 79, while in office in 2016. Mehbooba prevaricated for three months before agreeing to don the mantle and become the first woman chief minister of Jammu and Kashmir. Her alliance with the BJP, the same party she asked her constituents not to vote for, 'so they couldn't open their account in the Valley', was besieged by her own conscience.

She was hit hard when in July 2016, Burhan Wani was killed in an encounter in South Kashmir's Anantnag. There are varied versions of the encounter. According to some police officials, the intelligence information that led the security forces to village Bamdoora on 8 July, was aimed at other militants and that Burhan's presence in the hideout in Bamdoora was not mentioned. Security officials I spoke to believed that Burhan was not the intended target. In the end, that didn't matter. What mattered was the sheer fury of the protests that followed.

The young Facebook warrior had recruited at least a hundred young men. He wasn't just another militant. He had become a symbol of resistance eulogized by the ordinary Kashmiri.

His death spurred further rage. If the summer of 2010 was a period of deep unrest, 2016 was an uprising. Angry youth took over the streets and kept the Valley on the boil for over four months. Security forces responded with pellets and bullets and the death toll kept rising, crossing the figure of 116 killed in 2010.

The Valley slipped into a vortex of violence within the fraction of a few minutes. As soon as news of Burhan's killing started spreading, all roads led to Sharifabad, the village where I'd met his father, Muzaffar Wani. Thousands started walking in that direction, despite the restrictions.

My colleague at *Hindustan Times*, Toufiq Rashid, and I tried to drive to Pulwama, a hotbed of militancy in South Kashmir, to gauge the mood of the street. Entering South Kashmir was not easy. Going towards Sharifabad where the Wanis lived, was impossible. All the roads had been blocked.

We were stopped on the outskirts of Srinagar by a small group of men. They were not interested in speaking to the media. They pulled our driver out and started beating him and ticked off Toufiq, a local Kashmiri, because her head was only 80 percent covered.

We took a different route into Pulwama to find its streets littered with stones. There were no signs of life. Offices were shut, shops were closed, and there were no vehicles on the streets. The sharp, urgent hoot of ambulances were the only sound that broke the silence of the journey. The protestors had taken over the streets and were pelting stones at police stations, paramilitary, and army camps.

While in Pulwama, we met a family that had just buried their young son. He was out watching the streets on fire and had been hit by pellets. In the half an hour that we spent there, we were bombarded with angry questions.

'Why is India occupying our land?'

'Why do men in uniform, who are not even from Kashmir, walk into our homes and demand proof of our identification? We want azadi from oppression....'

'How can you fire bullets at our young boys... each one of us is Burhan... the Indian forces have automatic weapons, but they are so scared even of our mobile phones, they have cut off all connectivity.'

'Tell Mehbooba Mufti to come and visit us. We want to ask her why she asked for our votes and then tied up with the BJP....'

The great divide between the leaders and their people was as visible in 2016 as it was in 2010. It would not be wrong to say that 2016 was a consequence of 2010. Not paying heed to the interlocutors' report had come at a cost.

The writing was on the wall. Successive governments had forcefully crushed mass agitations. Each time the Valley erupted, the Centre flew in additional troops. The same was done in 2016, as hospital beds filled with the injured and by those blinded by pellet fire.

Mehbooba, the chief minister, made the same mistake as Omar had in 2010. Instead of engaging with her people, she retreated into a shell after Burhan Wani was killed.

There was no political interface between the enraged protestors and the men in uniform who drew their ire. This time, they did not just pelt stones, they also set police stations on fire and snatched weapons from the forces.

Senior officials of the local police, the army, and the paramilitary took immediate stock after reports trickled in that their men had opened fire against the protesters. The information they were receiving was worrying: the intensity of the mob was greater than it was in 2010, and their numbers larger. They were better prepared to deal with teargas attacks and had covered their faces with wet towels. Hopelessly outnumbered in many places, security personnel were in a state of nervous tension and as a result some had opened fire on the protestors.

The security forces were injured too. I remember meeting Nitin Kate, a CRPF jawan who was admitted in Srinagar's army hospital, after a splinter pierced his abdomen. He and his colleagues had tried to push back a large crowd for over three hours before being hit by a grenade. He had been serving in the Valley since 2009, and his training stood him in good stead. 'Did you open fire?' I asked him. His reply spoke volumes. 'If I had opened fire, I would have gone to jail. We have orders not to fire. Yes, I can hold a gun to my own head, but I cannot fire at a crowd. Even human rights bodies don't think of us. They don't think we have rights.'

The civilian deaths, however, were a testimony to the fact that not all men in uniform were as disciplined as Nitin Kate. The deaths, on both sides of the divide, showed, as one officer put it: '...we are used as human shields. If the politicians had done their job, we would not have blood on our hands.'

My trip to Kashmir during the uprising in 2016 would have been incomplete, without another visit to Sharifabad. I wanted to speak to Muzaffar Wani, who had advocated jihad. Going back to Burhan's village was not easy. It was a 90-minute drive from Srinagar and the only way of making it past groups of angry stone pelters was to leave at 4.30 in the morning.

My photographer Waseem Andrabi and I stole our way out of Srinagar when it was still dark and made it to Sharifabad without being stopped. Muzaffar Wani had just offered his first prayer of the day. He recognized me immediately and quietly walked me to his son's grave. I reminded him of our last conversation and asked him if he had changed his mind. I also asked him if he was willing to lead the movement as some media reports were suggesting. 'I have sacrificed two sons. It is now the turn of others to step in,' he said. Advocating jihad and lowering the bodies of two sons into graves had taken its toll.

Waseem and I were on our way back – and looking forward to breakfast in Srinagar – when our car slowed down and came to a halt. One of the injured protestors had died in hospital and his body had just been brought back to a village outside Srinagar. Enraged protestors placed his body on the road and blocked the highway.

The protestors would not let us move. We took a U-turn, in the hope of finding an alternate route, when a group of angry young men, stones in hand, flagged our car down. 'Don't stop,' I told the driver, and as he pressed the accelerator, the men ran behind us, pelting stones. 'We won't return alive today,' Waseem said, fear visible on his face.

I'd seen a board signalling an army unit and told my driver to take us in that direction. I quickly called Lieutenant General Dua's office for help. The corps commander radioed the local commander in Tral, where we were stuck, and we entered the security of the cantonment just in time.

The clock showed 9 a.m.

The local commander was kind enough to offer two rooms to us. As we sat there, wondering how we'd ever make it back to Srinagar, the internal phone in the room rang.

'Good morning, Ma'am. I just wanted to enquire who the other two gentlemen with you are. Are they local Kashmiris?' he asked.

'One is my photographer colleague and the other a driver, who is under my care, since I have hired him,' I replied.

He called back again after about half an hour and said, 'Ma'am, you can stay but the other two are security risks. They'll study the layout of our unit and come back tomorrow to pelt stones at us.'

I could not believe what I was hearing. Is this how great the divide was? Wasn't the army deployed in aid of the civilian population? Were two bona fide Kashmiris, accompanying a journalist, a threat to their safety?

How were they ever going to bridge the gap and earn the trust of the population?

I dug my heels in and said they would leave when I could. Fortuitously, mobile connectivity was restored for a few hours, and I made several calls to my contacts in the security establishment, asking them how we could get back to Srinagar. The army camp where we were stranded advised us not to move until midnight, when the enraged mob returned home for some rest.

At about five in the evening, a police officer called me saying one of their convoys was on its way back and we could be a part of it, if we wanted to come back to Srinagar.

We quickly joined the convoy. The protestors, who saw us as our car passed, raised slogans calling us traitors. My Kashmiri companions were terrified.

What if they've made a video?

What if they identify us and come after us?

What if they upload the video on social media?

What if?

Kashmir had sunk into a political abyss and was swirling in troubled waters.

Mehbooba Mufti cut a sorry figure in 2016 when her own bastion of South Kashmir exploded in anger.

My mind travelled back to 2014, when I'd accompanied her on an election campaign. Driving through the picturesque countryside in South Kashmir, where she was campaigning, she was clear about one thing. 'There is no question of allying with the BJP. We have nothing in common,' she had told me as she hopped in and out of the car. Each time she got out, she made sure to wear shades. 'Why do you wear dark glasses?' I asked incredulously, wondering why she would not want eye contact with her constituents. 'The people throw toffees, and I've escaped being hurt,' I remember her saying.

The toffees had turned into stones. The once-gutsy woman politician, always quick to be with the families of those who lost their loved ones, had the political instinct to steer the party to electoral victory on more than one occasion, but her instinct failed her when it came to sharing power with the BJP.

The once-grounded politician had so completely withdrawn into a shell, after pellet wounds became the new leitmotif, she did not even heed political advice from within the party to consider walking out of the alliance with the BJP. The feisty street fighter had swiftly moved from being a soft separatist to being what many in Kashmir called an ultranationalist.

The 'ultranationalist' braved insults and humiliation at the hands of her alliance partner who contradicted and questioned her on every move. She was berated for calling for a dialogue with the separatists and with Pakistan, and the only time she had her way was after the outrage over the rape of a minor Muslim girl in Kathua. The battered body of the eight-year-old girl, who went missing in the new year of 2018, was found three weeks later. According to investigators, the child was confined to a local temple for several days and given sedatives to keep her unconscious. The chargesheet alleged that she was 'raped for days, tortured and then finally murdered.'

The PDP–BJP alliance was rocked after the shocking crime made headlines. Equally shocking was the support the accused got from within the ranks of the BJP. Two cabinet ministers – Lal Singh, in charge of the forests portfolio and Chander Prakash who held the industries and commerce portfolio – joined protests organized by the Hindu Ekta Manch, in favour of the accused, who included a retired government employee.

That was the one time Mehbooba secured the resignations of two BJP ministers. The resignations only widened the chasm between the two regions Mufti Mohammad Sayeed had thought he could bridge.

In the end, her allies beat Mehbooba in the political game. The BJP pulled the plug on the alliance when she least expected it. They made a political move in the hope of salvaging themselves in Jammu from where they had won 25 seats. Mehbooba had no option but to tender her resignation in June 2018. She had the option of not taking on the mantle of chief ministership after her father's death, but did not.

I got the opportunity of asking her why she didn't. In answer to a question I posed while representing *Hindustan Times*, she said, 'My father had a political vision not only for Jammu and Kashmir but also for the country. He put everything at stake, including his credibility, while aligning with the BJP, only with the intention to secure what we already had – our special status – and to find a peaceful and dignified solution to the Kashmir problem. He was of the firm opinion that the resolution of Kashmir issue would not only end the bloodshed in the state but would also be in the interest of the country, nationally as well as internationally. So even though I have never been a great fan of the BJP, I could not walk away from his decision.'

The BJP had no problem in walking away from her and the alliance. It had other plans for Jammu and Kashmir.

Another stunning blow was in the offing. But before I describe the blow that changed Jammu and Kashmir's destiny, I must document how the army, which once tried to study the mind of the militant, transgressed to form a militia of its own. I had the militia point their guns at our car. I was one of three occupants. Each one of us had an AK-47 pointed at us.

The Indian Army's Rogue Army

Rafi's voice still had us spellbound when our driver suddenly braked, and Meraj and I were jolted out of the mesmerizing lyrics of a song that had been once composed as an ode to Kashmir's paradisical beauty.

Deewana hua badal, saavan ki ghata chhayee,
Yeh dekh ke dil jhooma, lee pyaar ne angdaai...

The melodious voice of Mohammad Rafi wafted through the cassette player in the car as we made our way back to Srinagar, from Hajan. We sang along and tried to soak in the beauty of the Valley – the undulating fields, the little rivulets, the apple and walnut orchards, and the luminous skies.

Kashmir ki Kali starring Sharmila Tagore and Shammi Kapoor became an instant hit when it was released in 1964. The Valley was picture perfect when, 'Deewana hua badal', the famous song was shot. It was still enchanting.

Photographer and friend, Meraj Ud Din and I were driving back and humming the lyrics, after a rather dangerous assignment we had undertaken in 1995. Kashmir's beauty was still mesmerizing, but grief and suffering had singed its soul.

Violence had overtaken every district, every colony. The insurgency had enveloped a once-beauteous state in a tight embrace of untold misery and grief. The need to race back to Srinagar before the sun disappeared behind the mighty mountains was a stark reminder of the ground reality.

Meraj and I had travelled to Hajan, a town 50 kilometers north of Srinagar, to meet Mohammad Yusuf Parray alias Kuka Parray, a legendary and infamous gunman, who had been persuaded by intelligence agencies to become the leader of the army's rogue army.

Few dared to go to Hajan in the mid-90s. It was the sole domain of Parray, the chief of the Ikhwan-ul-Muslimeen. The Muslimeen was a militant group with a difference. Like other secessionist groups, it was also in the fray for Kashmir's 'independence'. Unlike them, however, Parray and his men were fighting for Kashmir's 'liberation' – not from India, but from the pro-Pakistan Hizbul Mujahideen and the Jamaat-e-Islami. In Parray, New Delhi and the Indian Army had found a useful ally.

However, in the process of recruiting Parray as an ally, the waters had been muddied further. The ordinary Kashmiri was now trapped between three sets of guns: the militants, the security forces, and the Ikhwanis, or renegades, as Parray's men were called.

Territories had been divided by brutal use of force. Hajan was firmly in Parray's control and he and his rogue army – comprising surrendered militants – had managed to shoot its way through about 40 kilometers towards the outskirts of Srinagar, the capital city.

A fortnight before we travelled to Hajan, there was a fierce shoot-out between the Muslimeen and the pro-Amanullah Khan faction of the JKLF. Parray had been empowered, and he was aiming his guns at the JKLF and the Hizbul Mujahideen in particular.

When militancy first took root in 1989, Parray was a JKLF activist, having undergone training in Pakistan. He surrendered – like several others did – because he felt that his masters in the ISI were paying more attention to the Hizbul Mujahideen.

Conflict is murky. It is a cat and mouse game played amongst internal agencies and against external spies who are masters of the same craft.

Surrendering is not easy. It can entail a long jail term. It is, however, the perfect time, for spy masters to step in and co-opt militants who have already been trained to wield weapons and terrorize.

Parray was quickly snapped up by the IB and introduced to the army generals heading the counter-insurgency grid in the Kashmir Valley. He was promised men and ammunition and given a free run.

Soon, Parray embarked on his new role as a 'government sponsored militant'. He was invaluable to his mentors for the damage he was causing to the Hizbul Mujahideen, which had gained in strength and numbers.

I still remember the trip to Hajan. It stood out for several reasons and the memories remain etched. It was perhaps the only place in the Valley where the landscape was not dotted with security bunkers. The army did not need to patrol Parray's domain. It was also the only place where militants strutted around openly, unafraid of being arrested or killed. They were there in large numbers that day too, their AK-47s slung casually across their shoulders. Hajan also stood out because it was the only time I saw children play cricket with gunmen. This was a different haven where the setting sun didn't send people scurrying into the safety of their homes.

Meraj and I had managed to interview Parray and as we made our way back, we got a good taste of how exactly the attrition between the Ikhwanis and the Pakistan-sponsored terrorists was playing out on the ground.

Aisi to meri taqdir na thi…
Tumsaa jo koi mehboob mile…
Dil aaj khushi se paagal hai…
Aye jaan-e-wafaa tum khub mile…

Rafi's voice still had us spellbound when our driver suddenly braked and Meraj and I were jolted out of the passionate lyrics of a song that had been composed as an ode to Kashmir's paradisical beauty.

Our musical journey had come to a frightening halt. We found four gunmen, one at each window of our car. Before I could comprehend what was happening, the gunmen thrust open the driver's door and dragged him out, by his collar. I could see the fear in Meraj's face as a gunman asked him for his name.

Are you Meraj?

Is your name Meraj?

Are you Zafar Meraj, he demanded to know and started dragging him out too…

'Wait, wait,' I found myself screaming.

'If you are taking them, then I'm coming too,' I yelled. 'Either all three of us go, or none goes,' I said, opening my side of the door.

Fortuitously, the AK-47 wielding gunman who was training his weapon at my window, seemed to be the leader of the pack.

Who are you?

What are you doing here?

Where are you coming from?

The questions were aimed like bullets.

That day, I dealt with one of the most difficult questions of my journey through conflict.

Where was I, I asked myself.

Were we still in Parray's territory or had we crossed into the Hizbul Mujahideen's domain?

We were definitely on the outskirts of Srinagar, but I was not sure which outfit the gunmen belonged to or whose territory we had been stopped in. I was lucky that the gunmen were willing to have a conversation, perhaps, because of my gender.

The answer to the question of 'Where are you coming from' was a difficult one to answer.

I only had a few seconds to answer his questions.

Truth was our only weapon.

'We are journalists,' I said, fishing out my *India Today*

identity card. We are on our way back from an interview with Kuka Parray.

The four then went into a huddle and had a chat amongst themselves, and I found myself breathing again. They let us off saying, 'You can go, but make sure you send Zafar Meraj. Tell him we will be waiting for him.'

Meraj Ud Din, who was singing the loudest had fallen deathly silent. We knew we had been through a life-or-death situation. The rest of the journey was completed in utter silence. Meraj hugged his wife the minute we reached his home and narrated the details of our encounter. His wife gave me a warm embrace that evening.

We were extremely lucky that the members of the militia had spoken on their walkie talkies, to perhaps check whether we had actually interviewed their chief. We were also fortunate that neither of the four was a trigger-happy hothead. There were already reported stories of how the renegades had been killing, looting and raping, and how their masters in the army would just turn a blind eye. For the army, the renegades were an indispensable force for the sheer scale of damage they were inflicting on the Hizbul with lethal precision.

We had no doubt that the gunmen who were dragging Meraj and the driver out of the car, were Parray's men. They were looking for Zafar Meraj, a prominent Srinagar-based journalist and editor, not to be confused with my colleague and friend Meraj, the photographer.

Parray had been writing threatening letters to editors of leading Urdu and English newspapers published from Srinagar. He was free to issue threats and he was angry that the publications had not been carrying press releases issued by them. Zafar Meraj, then reporting for *Zee TV*, was amongst the journalists who Parray thought was way too defiant.

Soon after returning from Hajan, we met Zafar Meraj and narrated our experience to him. 'Be careful, he is asking about you,' we told him. In his wisdom, he decided to go and meet Parray. On his way back, he was pulled out of the car, shot multiple times and left for dead.

A bullet-ridden Zafar lay bleeding at the same place that we had been ambushed just a fortnight earlier. He somehow managed to stop a truck whose driver was only willing to drop him to Srinagar. Once in the city, still bleeding, Zafar finally took an auto rickshaw to reach the Shri Maharaja Hari Singh Hospital. The attack sent a shiver through the spines of the local media.

Zafar was lucky to survive the brutal attack. He was airlifted to Delhi's All India Institute of Medical Sciences (AIIMS), where he underwent two surgeries. He recovered slowly and stayed in Delhi for a few months. Srinagar was not a city he could return to in a hurry.

'There is little difference between the editors and the Hizbul Mujahideen. Journalists are writing posters and pamphlets for them,' Parray, the folk-singer-turned militant had told me. In his heydays, he was known more for his fight against the dreaded Hizbul Mujahideen than for the music he once used to compose for Radio Kashmir.

Sponsoring Parray was an expensive gamble. The security architecture needed him to pave the way for the 1996 elections, which he himself contested as an independent and won. But before he took oath in the hallowed precincts of the assembly, he had transgressed his brief and gone unchecked. Each time he went beyond the grasp of law, killing innocents who he thought were Hizbul's informers, the army turned a blind eye.

His masters were focussed on the mercenary and the damage he was inflicting on Hizbul.

Parray and his band survived, not just on the Indian Army's largesse, but on extortions and loot. He ran an illegal trade in timber and his men would fell precious walnut trees, right under the nose of the district administration and the security forces. The environmental destruction was not a problem that worried his mentors.

In his interview with me, he admitted to his transgressions with a sense of bravado that came from the fact that his supporters comprised many from amongst senior policemen, paramilitary, and military officers. Sitting on a Kashmiri rug, surrounded by armed members of his militia, he had no qualms in answering questions I kept throwing at him. The interview was published in *India Today* magazine in December 1995.

Q You are being called a government-sponsored militant.

A This is only propaganda. This is the Hizbul's only weapon, to spread false stories about me.

Q But you yourself say that your fight is against Pakistan and the Hizbul.

A Yes, that is true. We will fight anyone who abuses the Kashmiris. It is a state where Pandits and Muslims were living happily and peacefully until the Pakistanis and their agents moved in. It is because of this that we decided to get the people to raise their voices against them while we ourselves decided to raise our guns.

Q **You're very different from the usual Kashmiri militant, for you are actually fighting the battle on behalf of the security forces.**

A If our actions turn out to be in the government's favour, what can we do? Initially our fight was also against India, but that is a chapter we have forgotten about.

Q **So, you are an Indian agent?**

A How am I an agent? I am also fighting for independence.

Q **Why is it that your group has not suffered a single casualty at the hands of the security forces?**

A There have been several instances.

Q **Can you cite a single one?**

A I can't remember offhand.

Q **But you remember all the instances relating to the Hizbul.**

A Yes. We've killed about 125 of them and forced hundreds of them to flee for their lives. And we will continue to kill them.

Q **You agree that your fight is exactly the same as the government's.**

A I told you, it is no fault of ours if our actions end up in India's favour.

Q **So how can you say that your fight is also for independence?**

A Independence doesn't always mean freedom from India. It can also mean freedom from Pakistan. We want to liberate the Kashmiris from the agents of Pakistan. From liars like [SAS] Geelani, Abdul Ghani Lone, and Shabir Shah [all members of the Hurriyat Conference comprising separatist voices]. Shah was the one who said that he wants to see the Pandits return to their homes in the Valley. But what has he done about it? They are Indian agents because they are taking money from both Pakistan and India.

Q **Yon don't mind being used by the army. You are said to be taking money from them.**

A This is all propaganda. But yes, our fight is not against India as much as it is against the Hizbul and Pakistan.

Q **If the government offers you money, will you accept?**

A We have ways of raising funds and don't need to take it from the government.

Q **There is a charge that you are felling trees to raise funds.**

A I don't tell lies. Yes, I do cut trees. Or how else am I going to get the money to support my cadre? It costs ₹4,000 to ₹5,000 per month to maintain each man and I have 6,000 of them. We are not getting money from Pakistan. If I am cutting trees, so what? For every tree that I cut, you can plant another one. But what about the innocents who are being killed. Can you return them to their families?

I had no doubt about where his power came from. One afternoon, while I sat in the headquarters of the 15 Corps, the senior most military establishment in the Valley, the wait stretched far too long. The officers were busy in a meeting with Javed Shah, another prominent Ikhwani, who like Parray had trained in Pakistan and then chosen to be a part of the pro-government militia. Ironically, Shah was a policeman who gave up his job to cross the LoC for training in Pakistan.

The army was playing with fire in the hope of taking the battle straight into the Hizbul's bastion.

Instead of rehabilitating those who chose to surrender, the government decided to use them as counter-insurgents. This only added another layer to the complex web of violence in the Valley.

In the '90s, when violence was at its peak, different agencies of the government competed against each other. Under pressure to notch up the number of 'kills', the army, the BSF, and the police's special operations group (SOG), ran a dangerous race to collate the numbers of terrorists they'd killed or lured into surrendering. Units were awarded based on numbers.

Counter-insurgency is a complex exercise. It is extremely murky.

Mistakes – and the sense of competition – not only led to human rights violations; they also reflected on how crucial resources were wasted in the pursuit of tentative peace.

There were several instances when BSF personnel surrounded villages on being tipped off about militants being holed up there, only to run into Parray's men. I remember a BSF official telling me, 'Each time we surrounded them, they would lay down their arms and say their fight is not against us. That's when we realized that they were Parray's men. And on a few occasions when we picked them up, we were inundated with calls requesting that they be let off.'

Parray had the protection of the state and was unfazed about being a part of Kashmir's complex chessboard. He had carefully crafted an image for himself and revelled in the fear he had managed to create amongst the ranks of the pro-Pakistani militants. Hajan was the only area in which he was revered. He held a darbar in his domain once a week, where he doled out money to the poor and to the families who suffered at the hands of the Hizbul.

With Parray at the forefront, the security forces began making inroads into areas which had hitherto been in the control of the militants. He brought large swathes of Baramulla and Anantnag under his jurisdiction and started moving into the capital city of Srinagar. Officers boasted about how Parray had taken effective control of the capital's hospital, the SKIMS (Soura) Medical Institute, in particular. The Institute was amongst hospitals which had earlier been raided several times. The militants (the real ones) were confident that hospitals would not come under the scanner and were being used as hideouts. Weapons were kept in cupboards marked for drugs.

Parray's reputation of being a mercenary spread instant fear. Doctors and nurses at Soura reported to work on time for fear of reprisals from the Muslimeen. For the same reason, newspapers started publishing statements issued by the outfit. They'd got the message after four local journalists were kidnapped in August 1995 and let off only after the group's message had sunk in: their viewpoint should find space in the newspaper columns.

Parray had changed the contours of the militant movement in Kashmir and made himself a force to reckon with, even though he was reviled by the local population. His men had the license to kill, to loot, and to extort.

For militants, tired of being on the run, Parray's party became the perfect refuge. When a few surrendered their weapons to him and sought his protection, the government sweetened the policy on how it would deal with those who were willing to lay down arms.

Militants were assured that once they turned themselves in, they would not be harassed. They were also promised that they would be allowed to stay with their families and paid ₹5,000 for every Kalashnikov handed over. A monthly dole of ₹1,500 was also packaged in.

The announcement, in 1995 met with initial success. According to records, within a month, 111 militants surrendered with their weapons in August; the number rose to 213 in September. But figures soon fell to just 17 in November and 34 in December. The decline highlighted the limitations of the surrender policy.

Surrendering came with its own dangers. I had the opportunity of meeting a large group in North Kashmir's Bandipora, where they opened up only after I requested an Indian Army personnel, who had given me access, to talk to them alone.

The policy, in fact, was fraught with risk; made riskier by the competitive streak between security forces. The surrendered militants slowly started disclosing their problems, often in hushed whispers, afraid that they would be targeted if their minders heard them.

I remember meeting Abdul Majid, a former Hizbul militant who had surrendered to the police a year earlier. He said his family was being constantly harassed by the group he had weaned himself away from. They wanted the family to cough up ₹1 lakh for the Kalashnikov that he had surrendered. Then there was Mohammad Ashraf Lone, a former section commander of the Hizbul, who had surrendered mainly because of pressure from his wife and mother.

Lone was bitter. Like him, many of the surrendered militants felt that they were better off as 'real militants'. After surrendering, they had no source of livelihood and were afraid of leaving their homes. They feared they would be killed. The popular sentiment still favoured the insurgents and as Lone said, they were often taunted by their own extended families. 'They ask me what I've earned by surrendering?'

The only consolation for Lone and the others like him was that they could spend time with their families and children. They had to, however, return to the safety of the army camp before nightfall.

The surrender policy only heightened the enmity between the various security agencies – mainly the BSF and the army. Numbers mattered and both were trying to notch higher tallies.

Most of the surrendered militants I had been given access to, had suffered at the hands of the BSF. Salim Javed, one amongst the group I met, displayed his injuries. His crime? He had surrendered to the army and not the BSF. I was shocked when one of them said, 'The BSF officials tell us to pick up the gun once again and then surrender it to them.' The intense rivalry was undermining the counter-insurgency operations.

I remember returning to Delhi and narrating my Bandipora experience to a senior bureaucrat in the home ministry. 'Don't write about this. This is anti-national,' he said. The irony was inescapable. The prime players in the conflict zone were acting against the national interest. A journalist was only holding the mirror.

Violence begets violence. Both Javed Shah and Kuka Parray were killed within a fortnight of each other in 2003. Parray died unmourned after militants opened fire on his car while he was on his way to Hajan, his own bastion, to inaugurate a cricket match. Deputy Prime Minister L. K. Advani described his death as a setback to the process of restoring peace in Jammu and Kashmir. His comments only cemented the fact that he was a government stooge. Javed Shah was gunned down in an attack on a hotel in the heart of Srinagar. His killing took place on a day when Prime Minister Vajpayee was in the city for a meeting.

Before they died, Parray and Shah had paved the way for the 1996 election. I was a witness to how Parray – with the help of his mean army – managed to drive people to voting booths.

The security forces credited the Ikhwanis for creating the ground for the 1996 election. Farooq Abdullah, who had left Srinagar for London in the early '90s, returned to win the state for himself and his party, the National Conference. He even shared the stage with Parray.

Parray had outlived his utility before he was gunned down by the Hizbul Mujahideen in 2003. So reviled was he by fellow Kashmiris – for his extrajudicial methods of killing, looting, and plundering – his family was forced to bury him in their backyard. There was no space for him in the village graveyard.

His son, Imtiyaz Parray, is now a member of Jammu and Kashmir Apni Party, created in the aftermath of the abrogation of Article 370 in August 2019. Imtiyaz constantly battles the tag of being an Ikhwani, a word that still conjures fear and loathing in the Valley. He feels his father was never given the credit he deserves. The common Kashmiri – at the receiving end of the Ikhwan's excesses – rue the fact that Parray and his men were never brought to justice.

In conflict zones, contrary realities co-exist.

The only time they were officially painted as villains was during the 2002 assembly election when chief election commissioner, James Lyngdoh, was unwilling to allow the private militia to patrol the streets. The Ikhwanis were allowed to vote, but on the condition that they leave their arms at home. The men who had terrorized the population and forced them to queue up outside polling booths in 1996, were curtailed by Lyngdoh's respect for the law.

The Ikhwan lost its firepower after Kuka Parray's violent death in 2003. The rogue army soon became a forgotten army. They had outgrown the role for which they had been birthed. Some from amongst the ranks went back to the militant fold.

They did so because the choices were unpalatable. The local population hated them, and the state did not deliver on the promise of absorbing them into the security fold.

Imtiyaz believes his father should have been awarded with a medal for flying India's flag in the Valley, at a time when no one was willing to look at New Delhi.

No one, however, pins medals on the chests of a rogue army. Imtiyaz is perhaps aware of this grim reality. He often speaks of how the political battle in Kashmir can be won, not through the bullet, but through the force of the ballot.

He can try and carve a political destiny for himself but never completely sever himself from the past. His father's tombstone in the backyard of the Parray home will always be a reminder of Kashmir's tumultuous past and still uncertain future.

An Article of Faith and a Great 'Betrayal'

The tectonic shift was difficult to absorb. The Centre had not only hollowed out Article 370, it had also reaped the ultimate humiliation of cleaving one of the most empowered states – which had joined the Union of India in 1947 under special guarantees – into two union territories. 'The crown of India' had been sliced.

An unprecedented advisory was issued on 2 August 2019. Signed by Shaleen Kabra, principal secretary, Home Department, the order asked all tourists and Amarnath yatris to leave the Kashmir Valley immediately.

Earlier in the day, Jammu and Kashmir's DG of Police and the corps commander held a press conference where they warned of a specific threat to the yatris who undertake an annual pilgrimage to the holy cave.

The government made sure all non-Kashmiris left the Valley in special flights and buses. Additional troops had been flown in and there was a sense of fear and foreboding. A leaked advisory, issued by the Indian Railways, had talked about stocking up for four to five months.

Kashmiris, who had nowhere to go, flooded the markets and started buying bulk provisions.

What was the Narendra Modi government planning to do? Modi had been sworn in as the prime minister on 30 May 2019, for the second time. He had led his party to a grand victory and garnered more seats than the BJP had got in 2014.

On 26 February 2019, a few months before the general elections, Modi had demonstrated his prowess and taken political ownership of a second surgical strike. The Indian Air Force was used to target the Jaish-e-Mohammed's training facility in Balakot in Pakistan after the killing of 40 CRPF troopers in a suicide attack in South Kashmir's Pulwama.

Questions kept swirling and gave way to several rumours, which had started before Kabra's advisory. Why had the Amarnath Yatra been suspended? Why were additional troops being flown in?

Was the Modi government planning to abrogate Article 370, which gave Jammu and Kashmir its special status? Would it do away with 35-A, a provision that safeguarded land rights for the residents of the state and defined its permanent residents? Would the government carve Jammu out and make it a separate union territory?

It was apparent that a major change was in the offing. If there was a specific threat to the Amarnath Yatra, why were tourists in other parts of the Valley being hurled into buses, taxis, and flights? The turbulence that followed the killing of militant poster boy Burhan Wani had passed and the Valley had limped back to a semblance of normalcy. Why the need for more jackboots?

The Abdullahs – Farooq and Omar – called on Modi to find out what was being planned. Accompanied by an MP from Anantnag, Hasnain Masoodi, the three National Conference leaders met the prime minister in New Delhi on 1 August 2019. The details of the meeting have never fully been revealed. However, in an article published a year later in *The Indian Express*, Omar indicated, that he left the meeting with 'a completely different impression about what was going to unfold.'

What came next was unimaginable. As the shadows lengthened over the state on the night intervening 4 and 5 August in 2019, concertina wires were being rolled out and troops deployed to the left and to the right. National Security Advisor A. K. Doval visited the Valley to monitor the preparedness. Without spelling out the details, he had indicated to several senior officials within the security grid that something 'big' was in the offing. The IB was asked to prepare a list of people who had the potential of leading protests. Since a complete internet clampdown had been planned, a list of select IP addresses was sent to the service providers to ensure that the police, intelligence, and other agencies don't suffer the rough end of the shutdown.

On the night of 4 August 2019 – the day before the 'big' announcement – social media posts indicated that internet connections were being snapped. Mehbooba Mufti, former chief minister, warned that there would not be a single Kashmiri willing to carry the Indian flag if the state's special status was altered.

Even as she was being called out for being 'seditious', more reports of restrictions started pouring in. I sat glued to my phone, refreshing my Twitter feed. Omar and Mehbooba still had their internet connections and were able to communicate and tell the world that they were being put under house arrest, as padlocks were placed on their homes.

Earlier in the day, the National Conference had held a party meeting and no one except Mubarak Gul, former Speaker, could predict what was going to happen in Parliament on 5 August. 'Gul was the only one who said, New Delhi will go the whole hog. They will abrogate Article 370, do away with 35-A and even split the state,' Omar revealed when I met him years later to research this book.

Aga Ruhullah Mehdi, three-time MLA and MP from Srinagar too, confirmed what Gul had said. 'We all laughed,' he told me, remembering that meeting. None of them thought that the Modi government would undo 70 years of history in one fell swoop. 'We stood up against terrorists and the separatists but the country we supported, betrayed us. I will continue to speak up in Parliament. I have not been elected just for *bijli*, *sadak*, and *paani*. I will continue to point to the depth of the wound we suffered in 2019,' he said.

On the morning of 5 August 2019, Omar had lost his internet connection but could still watch television. He watched the proceedings of Parliament as Union Minister for Home Affairs, Amit Shah, moved a resolution to alter Kashmir's history and geography. Like all Kashmiris,

Omar felt betrayed. He and his father had, earlier in the week, also called on the then governor, Satya Pal Malik, to ask if Delhi was contemplating a change to the state's special status.

Omar recalled his meeting with Malik with great clarity, when I met him in November 2024. 'The governor was sitting in his office in Raj Bhawan with the flag of India behind him. He said there would be no threat to Article 370. Special status *ko koi khatra nahi hai*. It was a barefaced lie,' he told me.

He was shocked by what he was watching on television. Did he despair? Was he depressed? 'I was just shocked. I'm not given to despair. I was worried about how it would play out for me and the party.'

He picked up the landline to call his family and colleagues and realized there was no connection. The telephone exchange and all mobile towers had been switched off. The Valley had been totally cut off from the rest of the world. 'My colleagues and I had exchanged landline numbers and foolishly thought we would be able to talk to each other,' he recalled.

New Delhi did not trust the Kashmiris. Parents were cut off from their married children, who lived in different parts of the city. There was no way to communicate. Mobiles and landline phones were pieces of dead equipment. Everyone felt like they had been imprisoned within their homes. A collective silence overtook the Valley.

The tectonic shift was difficult to absorb. The Centre had not only hollowed out Article 370, it had also reaped the ultimate humiliation of cleaving one of the most empowered states – which had joined the Union of India in 1947 under special guarantees – into two union territories. The state of Jammu and Kashmir no longer existed. In its place, there was a Union Territory of Jammu and Kashmir and a Union Territory of Ladakh. The crown of India had been sliced.

There has never been any justification for why the state was bifurcated. In India's independent history, union territories have been upgraded into full-fledged states; never has a state been downgraded and dismembered.

The Kashmiris view this as a deep wound that was inflicted on them. They did not expect balm from the Modi government. They were angry that their own leaders, the PDP in particular, had tied up with the BJP who had repeatedly promised – in all its manifestoes – that it would repeal Article 370. The only time it put the promise on the back burner was in 2014, when it shared power with Mufti Mohammad Sayeed.

Mehbooba remains the last chief minister of the erstwhile state. It was placed under Governor's rule after the BJP withdrew from the alliance in June 2018. Politicians often go against their instinct and pay a price. Why did she agree to be an ally of the BJP, I asked her, in an interview for *Hindustan Times* in January 2021. I also asked her how the revocation of the special status had impacted her personally and if she felt more Kashmiri than Indian, a sentiment that many in the Valley voiced.

The questions were not easy to answer.

The answers contained the hurt she and her constituents were feeling. '5 August was a black day in the history of our country. It destroyed the trust that people of Jammu and Kashmir had placed while choosing to be a part of this country. People like me who believed in the Constitution of this country too felt cheated. It was disturbing, and quite humiliating to see our special status robbed.... It has been a very difficult and traumatic experience, swinging from one extreme to another [between feeling more Kashmiri than Indian]. But my politics has revolved around my father's ideology, and I am sure he would never ever have given up on the idea of India.'

Her father died while he was still the chief minister. She knew how angry and betrayed the people in her own bastion of South Kashmir felt. Only a handful came to their hometown of Bijbehara for Mufti Sayeed's last rites. The unpopular alliance had deepened resentment against New Delhi but few imagined what was still in store. They were stunned by the announcement in Parliament that fateful day – on 5 August 2019.

Home Minister Amit Shah, who worked like a silent sleuth, before tabling the resolution, promised a 'Naya Kashmir' and an end to bloodshed. The few who were privy to what was going to unfold on 5 August, were concerned about protestors taking to the streets and casualties. They had discussed the possibility of local police deserting the ranks. Every minute point had been dissected.

Before the concertina wires were rolled out to curtail the movement of its own citizens, the security apparatus had picked up thousands of youths – or over ground workers (OGW), an acronym unique to Kashmir. When security officials talk about OGWs, they are referring to those sympathetic to militants; to unarmed informers who pass on information to those wielding guns against the state. OGWs were flown to jails outside the Valley. Mainstream leaders and separatists were placed under house arrest, and Section 144, which prohibits the assembly of more than four people, was imposed.

There was no space for dissent. There was no room for protests. There was no freedom to even walk. Edgy soldiers stood at every corner. The Kashmiris had simply been invisibilized. None of them knew what was happening in the lane behind their home. They were going to be subjected to what turned out to be one of the longest curfews in one of the most militarized zones in the world. It lasted for nearly a year.

Even as Jammu, Ladakh, and the rest of the country celebrated the abrogation of Article 370, the common Kashmiri bore the brunt of what many called a 'brutal coup'. It was bloodless but it was deathly. Banks were soon short of money, pharmacies of critical drugs, and the elderly, who needed access to hospitals, were stopped at every corner by paramilitary soldiers who had thrown a security blanket around Srinagar and the rest of the Valley.

On the afternoon of 5 August, Omar was driven to his father, Farooq Abdullah's home for lunch. Farooq had organized this through a police contact. That evening, after returning to his residence, Omar went down to the basement of his home, where he had a gym, when one of his staffers announced that a team had come to pick him up. He was going to be moved and locked up at the Hari

Niwas guest house, a picturesque property nestled in the hills overlooking Srinagar's Dal Lake.

'I packed for ten days,' he told me. His logic was, he'd either be released by Eid, which was only a few days later, or at the very least by 15 August when Independence Day is celebrated. Before moving to the guest house, he briefly stopped at his father's house and said, 'I'm off. I am now a guest of the state.' He forgot, momentarily, that Jammu and Kashmir was no longer a state.

When he reached the Hari Niwas guest house – where the Congress' Ghulam Nabi Azad had stayed when he served as the state's chief minister from 2006 to 2008 – Mehbooba Mufti was already there. Omar was given one instruction which he was told was sacrosanct. At no cost could he contact her. 'Your paths should not cross,' he was told in no uncertain terms.

The new reality was surreal. Two former chief ministers were under detention in the same guest house, situated in a picturesque locale, but were forbidden from coming face to face. The ultimate irony, as Omar revealed, was that the same security guards who were on duty at his home, for his protection, were now his jailers. The same security guards were now rummaging through his cupboard, where he was being held. They were also ripping open the box in which food cooked at home was being brought to Hari Niwas.

Omar worked out a schedule for himself, to keep his sanity. He had his phone, but it was a piece of deadwood. The only thing he could do with it was take photographs. He fixed a daily routine for himself and that included what time he would wake up, exactly what time he would eat his meals, which order he would read the newspapers in, for how long he would walk and what time he'd switch the lights off for the night. The only regular visitor was a doctor, who came daily, to check his blood pressure. Occasionally, his younger sister, Safia Abdullah Khan, was allowed to visit.

A few kilometers away, Farooq was under detention in his own house. He was an elected member of the Lok Sabha, but on the day that his state was dispossessed and disempowered, the former chief minister, who had always saluted the Indian flag, found himself being treated like a criminal. Amit Shah denied that Farooq had been detained. That is when Farooq managed to steal a few minutes with the media. Appearing before the cameras, he said, 'How do you think one would feel when your body is carved.... They [the Modi government] have divided regions, will they divide hearts too? Will they divide Hindus and Muslims? I thought my India was for all, for everyone who believes in secular, unity....'

Farooq was soon booked under the Public Safety Act (PSA) for 'disturbing public order'. It marked a disturbing new trend. This was the first time that the PSA, used against terrorists, separatists or stone-throwers, was used on a mainstream politician. The law was being invoked to detain an MP and three-time chief minister. He came under the purview of a law that allows an imprisonment of two years without trial. A man who had unfailingly and unflinchingly stood for India, a man who had often called out Pakistan for exporting terror, soon found himself being called an enemy of the state.

A few years later, I asked him how the detention had changed him. 'I found solace in the Quran,' he told me. Farooq, his family confirmed, took to religion and offered prayers five times a day. He'd spend long hours sitting in the lawns of his home, watching drones fly overhead. He also had conversations with his daughter, Safia, who was deeply embittered by how her community had been humiliated. Farooq's grandchildren asked questions he never thought he would ever have to answer. 'Is this the India you want us to be with?' they wanted to know.

At great personal risk, Farooq had always tried to be the bridge between Srinagar and New Delhi. In 2019, the BJP did not want his voice heard. They had no qualms in locking and silencing the 81-year-old politician. I can – and have – criticized him for being flamboyant, for being insensitive and for playing golf when his state was burning, but the draconian PSA was a weapon New Delhi could have done without.

What happened in your meeting with Prime Minister Modi, I asked him? Did he get a sense that tectonic shifts would follow 72 to 96 hours after that fateful meeting on 1 August?

He answered the question in his baritone voice.

'I thought India was going to war with China. The troops kept flying into the Valley.'

But what did Modi say?

'He told us that he had no intention of destabilizing Kashmir.'

Hasnain Masoodi, the third member of the National Conference delegation, (who was a part of the same meeting), was more forthcoming about their conversation with Prime Minister Modi. Masoodi, a former judge of the Jammu and Kashmir High Court, was also a part of a 2015 order which had ruled that Article 370 was 'beyond amendment, repeal or abrogation'.

Masoodi was the one who had requested for the meeting with Modi.

'Advisories had started circulating and we felt that a constitutional assault was going to happen. We told the prime minister about the atmosphere of suspicion in the Valley,' he told me, sitting in the lawn of his home in Srinagar in November 2024, when I interviewed him for this book. He was more than willing to set the record straight.

Did you talk about the fear of Article 370 being abrogated?

'We told him that the state's special status should not be altered. We also told him that there was relative peace and that the Amarnath Yatra was going on successfully. I remember the conversation. We also told him why would you want to disturb the status quo....'

What did he say?

'He assured us and said he had no such intention. He sounded very convincing. In fact, he told us that he was planning to hold assembly elections in the state.'

Did you ask him about the troop build-up?

'Yes. He said the troops were tired because they had been deployed for the Yatra and the 2019 Lok Sabha election. In fact, he said that the fresh troop deployment was being sent to replace the ones who were fatigued.'

So, would you say that the prime minister lied to you?

'I would say he misled us.'

On 5 August 2019, Masoodi got the chance to speak in the Lok Sabha as the MP from Anantnag, Kashmir. He called it a 'black day' and an 'assault on the Constitution'.

On returning to Srinagar, he tried to call on Farooq Abdullah but was refused entry. Masoodi had to approach the court to get permission to meet his party president.

Gulshan Mufti, Mehbooba's ageing mother was also denied permission to meet her incarcerated daughter. 'We wrote a letter to the Jammu and Kashmir Police asking for a short meeting. We even said "you can frisk her". It has been 21 days, and we have no word on the arrested leaders. Why are mothers and daughters not being allowed to meet? How will that impact the ground situation?' asked Mehbooba's daughter Iltija Mufti, when I called her.

Mehbooba and Iltija found an ingenious way of communicating. Six months after the reading down of Article 370, when internet connections were slowly being restored, Iltija revealed how she had kept in touch with her mother. In one of her posts on Twitter, she said, 'I spent days riddled with anxiety until I received a crumpled and tersely worded note, the first of many furtively exchanged letters. I found it in a tiffin box that contained home cooked food sent for her.'

Mehbooba's note for Iltija warned her against using her Twitter profile on her behalf. 'They have taken an undertaking that I won't be using social media to communicate. In case someone else does it, he will be booked on charges of impersonation. Love you and miss you a lot,' Mehbooba had written, in one of her first notes.

Many notes followed. Explaining how she managed to send notes to her mother despite the tight security, she said, 'My grandmother found an enterprising solution. The letter I wrote was folded into a tiny square and carefully sealed, rolled and locked inside the middle of a chapatti.'

The common Kashmiris were not so fortunate. They had to take permission to even walk to the neighbourhood mosque to offer Friday prayers. Hazrat Bal and Jamia Masjid, the two main mosques had been locked and Mirwaiz Umar Farooq, the Valley's chief priest and chairman, Hurriyat Conference – was not allowed to lead Friday prayers for over four long years. Even in 2025, six years since the abrogation, the local administration decides whether he can be allowed to lead the Friday sermons, on a weekly basis. He has learnt to read the signs. If security cars don't draw up and block his residential gate by 10 a.m., he knows he can take his seat at the Grand Mosque's pulpit. Six years since the abrogation and the promise of a 'Naya Kashmir' have not led to 'azadi' for the Mirwaiz, or his followers who ask him why New Delhi is afraid of congregations and why Delhi has a problem with them offering namaz.

I had, over the years, seen colonies in Srinagar being cordoned off but in 2019, the entire city had been shut down. People were seething with rage – the graffiti reflected the depth of their anger. Their conversations, too, were loaded with contempt and rage, I was able to measure the quantum of their fury when I landed in Srinagar, a few weeks after the momentous announcement on 5 August 2019.

'We've had enough. We are not even considered human. India says it wanted to integrate Kashmir, but it is an ugly country. You are a sham democracy,' a young man on a street in a South Kashmir village, told me.

He refused to share his name.

'I will not tell you. Your forces will come after me. We don't even have the liberty of free speech. I want independence, I want you to leave me alone. I was going for a railway recruitment board interview but there is no public transport.'

The irony of wanting an Indian government job was lost on him and when I pointed it out, he only got angrier.

'What can I do till you don't leave us alone?'

'You can't keep killing our people and expect us to be a part of you. You think all of us who use mobile phones are terrorists.'

The fact that I worked for an 'Indian' newsroom angered him even more.

'You will go back and join the "everything is normal" brigade. Why don't you go back to India? I don't want to talk to you,' he said and walked away.

The anger was not unexpected. It wasn't new.

The ground had shifted once again, and a new reality was taking shape. The soldiers, out in large numbers, were ensuring an uneasy, if tenuous peace, I had reported, for *Hindustan Times*.

One month after the Valley had been stripped of their rights and their dignity, a civil resistance had taken shape. The government had announced the opening of schools, but attendance was thin. It was the same story at government offices. The wires had been rolled back in several public places and Section 144 had been lifted but most shops remained defiantly shut.

Only neighbourhood grocery stores, tucked away in by-lanes, opened in Srinagar and across districts. Local officials were told to help speed the process by holding meetings with traders' associations. A South Kashmir district commissioner, who had held several such meetings, told me, 'They just refused and said, "You cannot force us. You have chosen to break the link with us by removing an Article [370] that gave us our identity. Now let us decide our own future."'

There were no open protests like the Valley had witnessed in 2010, after the fake encounter in Machil, or the one in 2016, when Burhan Wani was killed. Instead, militants were pasting posters on mosque walls, calling upon their 'mujahid brothers' to enforce strict restrictions on the movement of traffic. They did not want civilians driving around the city, giving the impression that their anger had subsided or that normalcy was slowly returning.

Another notice, pasted on colony walls, said, 'Only patients going to hospitals may be allowed to move on the road.... After *maghrib* (evening) namaz, people are requested to turn off the streetlights so that our mujahid brothers can move around freely.'

The one disturbing change I witnessed was the return of a sympathetic sentiment towards Pakistan.

The neighbouring country had not stopped sending mercenaries across the LoC, but Kashmiris had gone cold on Pakistan. They had realized that they were being exploited and being used as pawns. But in the weeks after the nullification of Article 370, people in the state were eagerly watching Pakistan's moves.

Cable networks had been shut down but those with access to dish antennas were tracking Pakistan Prime Minister Imran Khan's moves, closely. Within 48 hours of the altered reality, Khan downgraded diplomatic ties and suspended trade with India. Ajay Bisaria, the Indian high commissioner to Pakistan was given only 72 hours to pack his bags and leave Islamabad.

In Srinagar, a locality called Soura, reflected the pro-Pakistan sentiment. The neighbourhood had always resisted the state but this time it morphed into a separate enclave that erupted every Friday. Soura is where I, and other journalists, went to, in 2019. The colony had become the symbol of resistance. Its residents took out the first big protest march on 9 August, just days after Article 370 was repealed. The government initially denied it but finally accepted that some people did take to the streets.

Security forces had used pellet guns to quell the protest, but Soura's residents, consumed with rage, had dug up all roads leading into the locality and blocked access. They were not happy to see 'Indian' journalists, but it gave them a chance to vent their ire.

'We love Pakistan,' shouted Ruqaya Nabi, barely 50 metres from a shop that had 'Pakistan army Zindabad' painted across its shutter. Nabi was preparing for a master's in education when communication networks went down. Another resident, Fehmeeda Jan, was bitter that Eid could not be celebrated. 'We wish you a similar Diwali. Only Pakistan understands our pain. You are pushing our brothers into militancy,' she said, daring me with, 'Let me see if you go back to Delhi and write what I'm telling you.'

I did. The sentiment was conveyed through an article I wrote for *Hindustan Times*, where I then worked.

It had more information on how the Centre was trying to convince the local population of the benefits of a move through which they thought they were integrating Jammu and Kashmir. Across villages, the army distributed pamphlets on the 'benefits of the removal of Article 370 and 35-A'. Printed in Urdu, the flyers said the people would now have the right to education, freedom from corruption, mid-day meals at government schools, new hotels, tourism centres, and health benefits under Ayushman Bharat, a flagship programme aimed at providing healthcare coverage to the economically vulnerable.

The governor announced the creation of 50,000 jobs. At the time, no promise appeared to calm the community which felt completely bereft and forlorn.

The wound was deep and was being reflected through different voices. Very few were willing to come on record. They were afraid of being arrested. They were scared they'd be sent to jails, miles away from home. They were staring at a future that was both dark and uncertain.

Apart from political leaders, political workers and separatists, scores of Kashmiri men had been arrested under the PSA and flown out of the state. No state functionary was willing to put a number to just how many had been flown out.

I met one such family in South Kashmir's Kulgam. Their son had been sent to a jail in Uttar Pradesh, and they did not have the money to travel and meet him. His fate lay consigned in a file. One of the documents in the file read, 'You have been found working as an active overground worker of active terrorists whose only aim and objective is to secede Jammu and Kashmir from the Union of India. You have been instigating the youth to resort to stone pelting.'

On the face of it, the government can legitimately claim that it did not have to fire a single bullet on 5 August, but all these years later, the Centre also knows – though it will not admit – that the people have not accepted the sweeping changes delivered with stunning stealth. The people were neither considered worthy of discussion nor debate. They were just recipients of a 'shock and awe' operation that is still being sold in the name of development.

The stealth with which the government went about its move, in fact, points to a festering fault line: it inherently does not trust Kashmiris. It was not willing to give Kashmir common liberties. For over six years now, New Delhi has tried to stamp its authority through the liberal use of draconian laws like the PSA and the UAPA, which has strict provisions for granting bail. Journalists and human rights activists have been arrested, government officials suspended or simply dismissed without explanation. Scores are still waiting for the police to verify their passport applications. Others remain in dread of a phone call summoning them to the police station to explain a comment they may have put out on social media.

The problem is compounded because the Kashmiris don't trust New Delhi either. With the passage of time, resistance faded and people returned to their shops and businesses. As several Kashmiris told me, 'We have families to feed, we also want to educate our children. Why do you expect us to make all the sacrifices? What has any political party ever done for us?'

Over time, the mainstream politicians including Omar, Farooq, and Mehbooba were also released. The Abdullahs gained freedom after seven months. Mehbooba was the last one to come out of confinement in October 2020, 14 months after she had been pulled out of her Srinagar home.

It was in October 2020 – soon after their release – that the Valley's political parties, including the National Conference and the PDP, joined hands to form the People's Alliance for Gupkar Declaration. The main aims, as spelled out by Farooq, who headed the new platform, were to continue a peaceful struggle for the restoration of Jammu and Kashmir's special status, and to boycott future elections.

Different leaders made different promises. Omar said he would not contest elections till statehood was restored. Mehbooba swore never to be a part of any election till Article 370 was restored. Several parties also petitioned the Supreme Court against the abrogation of Jammu and Kashmir's special status.

When the apex court finally gave its verdict in December 2023, very few were surprised that the Supreme Court had endorsed the resolution passed by Parliament on 5 August 2019. While the court did not address the issue of why the state had been downgraded, it asked the Centre to restore statehood as soon as possible and hold assembly elections by September 2024.

The Centre told the Supreme Court that the abrogation had led to 'unprecedented development, progress, security and stability to the region' and that 'life has returned to normalcy in the region after three decades of turmoil'. It also claimed that the status change had helped dismantle the terror network. While it is true that the youth were no longer pelting stones in the Valley, probably out of fear of being arrested, terror had found a new address in the Jammu region. Terror bases shifted from the Valley to the Jammu region. The security forces had focussed their attention on the Valley – where the counter-insurgency grid had been strengthened, while gaps had been left in Jammu, where violence had abated over the years. But does the absence of violence translate into peace?

The 'peace' was shattered in Pahalgam and I will come to that later in this chapter.

The abrogation was a political move, aimed at strengthening the Hindu vote bank. Not only had the Modi government gone ahead with its political agenda of abrogating Article 370, the writing down of the special status had helped bolster the very muscular, '56-inch chest', image the prime minister has always liked to project.

That was not a view the Kashmiris shared. They felt completely betrayed. The BJP leaders in Delhi are aware that their 'awe and shock' move had not won any hearts in Kashmir, but they continued talking about a 'Naya Kashmir'.

If the Modi government was so convinced about the 'unprecedented development, progress, security and stability,' the BJP would not have refrained from contesting the parliamentary elections from the Valley in 2024.

Modi only went to Kashmir for the first time after the abrogation four years later, in March 2023. While there, he described Jammu and Kashmir as the 'mastak' or the head of India. He elaborated on what he meant. A 'head held high is a symbol of respect and development,' he said.

Yet, several years after hailing his government's move as one that would herald peace and development, the BJP did not have the confidence to contest elections from India's 'mastak'. It did not field a single candidate for the Valley's three Lok Sabha seats of Srinagar, Baramulla, and Anantnag-Rajouri.

The party which was seeking a third successive mandate for itself had set an '*Abki baar, 400 paar*', target for the NDA alliance. The BJP reminded voters that it had fulfilled its promise to bring Jammu and Kashmir at par with the rest of the country. The Article had been added to the Constitution in 1949, bestowing on Jammu and Kashmir special rights which allowed it to have its own constituent assembly. The assembly had the powers to reject laws passed in India's Parliament. It also had its own flag and anthem. On 5 August 2019, the BJP finally fulfilled the demand made by the Bharatiya Jana Sangh founder, Syama Prasad Mookerjee, who often said, 'One constitution, one flag, one prime minister.' Until 1965, the Jammu and Kashmir chief minister went by the nomenclature of prime minister.

Referring to the revocation of the special status, Modi said the 'shackles had been removed'. According to him, the abrogation of Article 370 had paved the way for development and '*bandishon se azadi*' (freedom from hurdles).

Until the revocation, the BJP had contested all Valley seats in every general election held between 1996 and 2019, but decided to back proxy candidates in 2024. Was the BJP afraid of losing? Its absence from the electoral fray only pointed to the stark ground reality: the Valley was extremely unhappy with what the BJP did in August 2019. The striking down of the special status and the humiliating slicing of the state into two union territories was an unpopular decision. The BJP knew it, but how could it voice it?

Neither the BJP, nor the Prime Minister, however, shied away from using Article 370 as an election pitch in the rest of the country. In an interview to *The Times of India*, Modi said, 'Article 370 has been a very emotional issue for us, our karyakartas and the people of India. People have waited for generations for this to happen. Abrogation of Article 370 has been a driving force for our karyakartas for decades. When people saw that our government did this, it made them very emotional and the feeling among people was that we should give 370 seats to the party which abrogated

Article 370. And hence, the slogan, "*Abki baar, 400 paar*" for the NDA emanated from among the people.'

The 'people' didn't include residents of Srinagar, Baramulla or Anantnag-Rajouri. It is a sad commentary on a fault line that still continues to fester. The BJP's absence from the Valley's electoral fray only punctured the 'Naya Kashmir' pitch the government has been trying to portray. Home Minister Amit Shah, while speaking of the revocation in Parliament, had said that it would see an end to violence and bloodshed. He had promised development and peace as the Valley's new realities.

But by not fighting elections, the BJP only conceded to the fact that the party, its politics, and its controversial abrogation stood rejected by the Valley's inhabitants. Amit Shah tried to explain his party's absence, saying, 'The BJP is not in a hurry to see the lotus bloom in the Valley.... We are not going to conquer Kashmir as projected by our adversaries. We want to win every heart of Kashmir.'

It is clear that the Kashmiris went out of their way to ensure that the lotus does not bloom in the Valley. They lumbered through long curfews which then made way for the long lockdown due to the coronavirus. They waited patiently, even if grudgingly, for the return of internet connectivity. It came in spurts, first only for prepaid connections and finally returned after 18 long months. The union territory, a backyard of New Delhi, was run by the governor and on instructions from Delhi. The Valley went through spurts of violence, but the tourists started returning. The surface normalcy returned. The Kashmiris, who had for decades learnt to live with challenges and impediments, finally got a chance to speak when the union territory went into election mode.

When the assembly elections, mandated by the Supreme Court, were finally held in 2024, the percentage of voters soared. By the time the three-phase elections were held, the Central government had, through a delimitation exercise, increased the number of seats from the Jammu division.

It had also played another card. In an attempt to splinter the vote in the Valley, it not only encouraged proxy candidates, it also did not stop candidates from the banned Jamaat-e-Islami – who had returned to the election arena after 1987 – from contesting the election. In a surprise move, Sheikh Abdul Rashid, also known as Engineer Rashid, was granted bail and allowed to campaign for the assembly polls. He had been arrested in 2019 under UAPA on terror funding charges.

In a stunning victory, the separatist voice and founder of the Awami Ittehad Party, defeated former chief minister Omar Abdullah from the Baramulla parliamentary seat, while being imprisoned in Tihar jail, by over one lakh votes.

Rashid's release gave the National Conference some anxious moments. Unlike the PDP, which had seen a split in its ranks after many of its members left, the National Conference stayed together and focussed on a manifesto that appealed to Kashmiri voters. The release of political prisoners and the restoration of Article 370 were high on its list of promises.

Omar Abdullah finally threw his hat into the ring, after

initially averring to stay away from the electoral arena till statehood was restored.

A year before he finally relented, he had told me in an interview, 'I'm not fighting an Assembly election, and I stand by that. As far as I'm concerned, I've been chief minister of an undivided Jammu and Kashmir, with the most empowered assembly in the country. I'm hardly likely to go back to an assembly where the lieutenant governor will decide who the chief minister's peon is going to be. I have a little bit more self-respect than that. I want to fight for the restoration of what was taken away from Jammu and Kashmir to the fullest extent possible. And that's what I'm doing. And I don't need to come into the assembly for that.'

In the end, he filed his nomination papers from two constituencies. His predicament was simple. How could he campaign for his party and ask people for votes if he sat out? 'Seeking votes from the people while not being a candidate myself seemed contradictory,' he told me. Omar won both seats. He gave up Budgam and retained the Ganderbal seat from where he had also won in 2009, going on to become the union territory's first chief minister.

His party, the National Conference had also stitched up a pre-poll alliance with the Congress. Both were also a part of the India Bloc, a group set up prior to 2024's Lok Sabha election. The National Conference was banking on the Congress to pull its weight, particularly in Jammu. More importantly, the alliance was needed to send a message to its vote bank in the Valley that it was not going to sup with the BJP. Mehbooba had paid a price for that, and Omar wanted to send out a clear message, in advance.

Kashmir's altered landscape had no appetite for the BJP. The BJP contested 19 of the 47 seats in the Valley but could not win a single one. The voters had not forgiven Mehbooba and her party either. The PDP won only three seats. Mehbooba did not contest and was unable to secure a victory for her daughter, Iltija.

The assembly elections were not just the first after the state was bifurcated. It was also the first election – after insurgency first took root – for which no boycott calls were issued. After the infamous 1987 election, the militant outfits and the separatists who combined to form the All Party Hurriyat Conference in 1993, issued regular boycott calls.

People came out in large numbers in the Valley. They did so to keep the BJP at bay. They also did so to register their protest against the abrogation of what many call, 'an article of faith'. The votes became the stones that were not pelted in 2019.

The election results show that Jammu and Kashmir continues to be a fault line, but they also hold the promise of a better tomorrow. Omar, who was sworn in as the chief minister on 16 October 2024 has tried to address the gaping divide between the Valley and Jammu – which voted overwhelmingly for the BJP – by appointing a deputy from there. But the distance between Srinagar and New Delhi too needs to be bridged.

Will the Modi government restore statehood as recommended by Jammu and Kashmir's cabinet on 18 October, two days after Omar's swearing-in? Will it pay heed to another resolution that was passed on the floor of the assembly, calling for the restoration of its special status and constitutional guarantees?

The National Conference was careful to not specifically mention Article 370 in the resolution. Omar is trying to negotiate a relationship with New Delhi and is treading cautiously.

Will New Delhi respond and seize the window of opportunity, or will the chief minister have to take on the role of being the chief rebel? Will the battle be taken to the courts again?

Before any of these questions could be asked – or answered – the Valley was stained with the blood of 26 tourists, including a local horseman. Terrorists emerged from the woods in Pahalgam's Baisaran meadow on 22 April 2025 and mercilessly shot dead 'guests' after ascertaining their religion. The men were killed in front of their families. The sight of a young woman sitting beside the listless body of her husband became the defining image of a strike so brutal, it brought the common Kashmiris out of their homes and on to the streets. Himanshi Narwal lost her husband, a Naval officer, within a week of their marriage.

A 'Naya Kashmir' took birth on 22 April after the Pahalgam attack. People poured out of their homes and lit candles and took out 'tiranga yatras', a sight I had never seen since 1989. The 'Not in Our Name' message was delivered loud and clear. One placard which said, 'Peace not pieces' summed up the mood of the ordinary Kashmiris. They, in fact, were the first responders, carrying the injured tourists on their shoulders to the nearest hospital – almost an hour away – by foot. Chief Minister Omar Abdullah, also the tourism minister, made a visibly emotional speech in the assembly, after reading out the names of each of the victims. He rued the fact that he had to send tourists back in coffins.

On 22 April, Omar was on his way to Jammu from Srinagar, when reports of the terror strike at Pahalgam first started trickling in. 'I was told one had died and several had been injured but by the time I reached Jammu, I was told 26 had been killed,' Omar told me when I spoke to him, in May 2025. He had by then received a call from Union Home Minister Amit Shah, and he soon returned to Srinagar to meet Shah.

When the Modi government responded with Operation Sindoor and used the Air Force to fire missiles that hit the headquarters of the LeT and the JeM, it was Omar once again, who was left staring at the debris of conflict.

The pendulum swings without notice in Kashmir. It swung on 22 April at the Baisaran meadow and as Omar said, 'A very dark cloud hovered over Kashmir.' The terrorists, who asked tourists to recite the *kalma*, had also aimed their guns to provoke a communal conflagration and deepen the Hindu-Muslim fault line. The Kashmiris who have never taken to the streets to protest terror attacks – or even the migration of the Kashmiri Pandits – spoke up against the blood of their 'guests' being spilled on their soil.

The Kashmiri response was not debated in television studios. It was not, as the Mirwaiz Umar Farooq told me, 'even acknowledged in Prime Minister Modi's *Mann ki Baat.*' Far from acknowledging the solidarity shown by the Kashmiri street, several hardline voices forced Kashmiri students and professionals to return to the Valley. Himanshi Narwal, who lost her husband, was viciously attacked after she pointedly said, 'Don't attack Kashmiris and Muslims.' Jammu and Kashmir signalled for peace and stability and despite Omar's categorical statement that not all Kashmiris are terrorists, New Delhi has paid scant attention to the one-in-a-lifetime opportunity to reach out to the alienated population.

That has been Kashmir's greatest tragedy. The windows of opportunity have always been frittered away. Everyone talks about Kashmir but nobody talks TO (*emphasis mine*) Kashmir. All through the India-Pakistan military exchanges between 7 and 10 May, the border areas of Poonch, Kupwara, and Uri bore the brunt. As the country went into a hyper-nationalist mode, few spoke about the lives and livelihoods lost in the border areas. The leaders adopted a belligerent tone and television anchors conveniently played war games. Their microphones sounded like missiles. Some even aimed their 'missiles' at Omar, lending credence to the whisper campaign that tourist guides had accessed the Baisaran meadow without permission.

In an exclusive – and revelatory – interview with me for this book, Omar set the record straight. He'd perused all the files and said, 'Let me set the record straight. Only last year [2024], the current lieutenant governor's [Manoj Sinha] government issued a tender for Baisaran for three years and made it a ticket destination. The contract was given to a local businessman from South Kashmir, who in turn paid the LG's government one crore rupee per year for ticketing rights. You don't offer one crore a year for some place that's only open for a month. It was open for eight to nine months in the year. The only time it closed was after heavy snowfall and during the Amarnath Yatra. There was an effort to feed sections in the media with the line that the tour operators opened it without permission.'

I asked him the question again, saying, 'Let me clarify this once again, no permission was needed to open Baisaran?' His reply was unequivocal.

'I asked for all the papers, all the records. There is not a single piece of paper to suggest that written permission or any sort of permission was ever sought. And again, I make the point, Baisaran was bid and sold as a ticketed destination. I mean, my numbers are correct. More than 40,000 or 50,000 people had already visited Baisaran by 22 April. The number could be higher. Now, if it had been opened without permission, was the administration sleeping? Couldn't they see 50,000 people trooping up the mountain on ponies? Show me a piece of paper where the police have said that Baisaran should have been closed or why it was open without permission... those demanding my government's head in the studios are just ill-informed. They don't know any better. They're also cowards because it's much easier to demand my head than to seek actual accountability.'

Conflict is a great teacher. The din of the television studios drowned the voices seeking accountability.

Nations and governments are free to respond to terror strikes but if another attack is to be prevented, hard questions must be asked. Why was there not a single man in uniform anywhere near the Baisaran meadow? Kashmir is still a conflict zone. Why was the popular destination left unguarded? Why was there scant intelligence about the attack? Had the administration fallen victim to its own narrative of 'everything is now normal in Kashmir'?

Complacency is dangerous.

The erstwhile state's future lies buried, not just under the weight of its past, but also in the uncertainty of its tomorrow. Pahalgam served as a reminder that Jammu and Kashmir remains a fault line that cannot be papered over. The levels of violence may have been down; its streets bereft of protests and stone pelters, but that cannot be mistaken for normalcy. The number of tourists visiting the Valley each year cannot be the yardstick to measure levels of normalcy. The absence of violence does not signal the advent of peace. The alienation is still crying out for a political initiative. There are indices, before and after Pahalgam that hold a mirror to the ground reality: the arrest of human rights defenders, the killings of Kashmiri Pandits and migrant labour, the liberal use of the PSA, and the weaponizing of dissent. There is a difference between dissenters and those who wield weapons.

Kashmir has always responded to outreaches by prime ministers, be they Jawaharlal Nehru, I. K. Gujral, P. V. Narasimha Rao, Atal Bihari Vajpayee, or Manmohan Singh. It is Modi's turn to make one.

In the separate ruling, delivered by the Supreme Court

upholding the scrapping of Article 370, Justice Sanjay Kishan Kaul called for an impartial investigation into human rights abuses in Jammu and Kashmir since the 1980s, when militancy took root in the beleaguered state.

'I recommend the setting up of an impartial Truth and Reconciliation Committee to investigate and report on the violations of human rights both by the state and non-state actors perpetrated in J&K at least since the 1980s and recommend measures for reconciliation,' Justice Kaul said.

'To move forward, wounds require healing. Inter-generational trauma is felt by people. The first step towards healing the wounds is the acknowledgment of the acts of violations done by the state and its actors,' he added.

Jammu and Kashmir stands at an emotional crossroad, begging for attention. Several experts have recommended the way forward. Former R&AW chief, A. S. Dulat, author of several books, proposed – in an interview with me for *The Times of India* in 2023 – that Narendra Modi should go to Srinagar, drive around its streets and announce the restoration of statehood. 'I can tell you, that if Modi does that, he will never feel the need to be protected by security guards after that,' he said.

Lieutenant General Dua, the corps commander, who got a good taste of Kashmir when it exploded in anger after the killing of Burhan Wani, is also of the view that the alienation needs political redressal. In his book, *A General Reminisces: A life under fire in Kashmir*, Dua sticks his neck out and recommends what he calls a 'bold suggestion'. He articulates an exit strategy for the army in Jammu and Kashmir and explains what he means thus: While recommending that the army continue be deployed on the LoC, he proposes that it be withdrawn from the hinterland. 'The army can remain in a hand-holding role and continue to underwrite peace by remaining in their hubs and bases in case the situation turns ugly.... This transition cannot happen in a hurry, but merely by articulating it, we will create more stakeholders in the peace process. Today, sadly, every aspect of the situation in Kashmir seems to be outsourced to the army.... The political process must start as soon as possible, giving expression to the political aspirations of the populace....'

Soldiers seldom speak of political processes or political aspirations, but there are several ways forward if New Delhi is seriously committed to making the territory of Jammu and Kashmir into the Union of India. For the present, the task lies at Modi's door. Lieutenant General D. S. Hooda, who headed the Northern Command and has studied Kashmir closely, also recommends a political outreach and warns against the use of force to settle what is essentially a problem that requires New Delhi to gain the trust of people. 'It cannot be viewed just as a piece of real estate,' he cautions.

Will Modi make a bold move or has Pahalgam shut the door to that initiative? When I read about External Affairs Minister S. Jaishankar having spoken to his counterpart in Afghanistan, I couldn't help wonder why the government was willing to speak to the Taliban, a force once guilty of shielding Osama bin Laden, but not to its own citizens in Kashmir.

It is difficult to write the last word on the destiny of Jammu and Kashmir that has continuously swung between hope and hopelessness. The surgical strikes after Uri (2016) and Pulwama (2019) did not deter the terrorists or their masters. Will Operation Sindoor put an end to terrorism? Omar is of the firm belief that 'Jammu and Kashmir is not normal and you can't just wish normalcy. Normalcy has to be created, and the fact is that you can't also normalize Jammu and Kashmir without taking the people along with you.'

The people made their voices count. The anti-Pakistan sentiment was crystal clear after Pahalgam. An anguished Farooq Abdullah, in an interview with me, said, 'Pakistan will not get Kashmir. They can keep trying for a thousand years.'

The last word on Jammu and Kashmir lies in the distant future. It, in fact, may not be written in my lifetime.

My Tryst with the Turbaned Army and their Edicts

Freedoms are empowering. They are not available in Afghanistan. They come with great costs to life and liberty. There is no silver lining on the horizon. The Taliban are the police. They are the army too. The country is in the firm control of their diktats.

The Taliban is good at executions, and on the night of 27 September 1996, as they entered the capital city of Kabul, they knew exactly who to target.

The chilling brutality of the Taliban was on full display.

An army of Talibs, flush with victory, stormed into the well-guarded United Nation's compound, where former president Mohammad Najibullah had taken shelter since 1992 and pulled him out. They shot him in the head, tied his body to a car, and dragged it through the streets. But even that was not enough. They then strung his body to a pole.

The body of the former Afghan president was left hanging for three days. His wife, Fatana Najib had managed to move to India in 1992 with their three young daughters. The family received news of his brutal killing through news reports. Najibullah, was president from 1987 to 1992, after which he was forced to make way for a transitional government, sponsored by various rebel factions, who proclaimed an Islamic republic.

Afghanistan saw tentative peace, but it was short-lived, as Burhanuddin Rabbani took over the reins of the country but refused to step down and leave the president's office, in accordance with the power-sharing formula agreed upon by the different Islamic factions. Other mujahideen groups, led by Gulbuddin Hekmatyar, then started pounding Kabul with artillery fire. The Afghans spent the next few years amid strife, as different warlords, representing different tribes tried to assert control.

The Taliban, a predominantly Pashtun force, was born amid this chaos. Its ultra-conservative interpretation of Islam had many takers and it soon flourished as an alternative. Led by Mullah Mohammed Omar, the Taliban established its writ over the province of Kandahar, also the birthplace of Omar, famed for having fought to throw the Soviet Army out. In the process of the 'jihad' he waged against the external forces, he lost his right eye in an explosion. When the Taliban marched into Kabul in 1996, he was the undisputed leader of the student militia, who had not just fought the Soviets but also taken on the Northern Alliance led by Ahmad Shah Massoud.

The Taliban, a group of armed mercenaries, had announced their arrival in Kabul. The unbelievable had happened. The Taliban, bred in madrasas in Kandahar and in Pakistan, where many had crossed into during the years of strife and chaos, were openly roaming the streets of Kabul.

As soon as the news of Kabul's fall was relayed, journalists from around the world made their way to the war-torn country.

I was one of them. Aroon Purie, my editor, had no qualms in sending me. The gender lens was crucial to understand the militia. I was denied my rights as a journalist, but being a woman mattered. My gender helped me absorb the full import of Taliban's strictures and their orthodoxy and how that, in turn, affected half the country's population.

Getting to Kabul was not easy. The journey entailed a flight from Delhi to Lahore and onwards to Peshawar. The only way to travel to Kabul from Peshawar was to get a seat on a small aircraft operated by the International Committee of the Red Cross (ICRC). After landing in Lahore, I took a connecting flight to Peshawar. A day later, I was on my way to Kabul.

Aid agencies were being allowed into Kabul, and I'd been told to carry a small suitcase.

Right on top of my suitcase was a burqa. The kurtas I packed had to be long-sleeved, and shoes were a must because women were not allowed to expose even their feet.

The Taliban had raced into Kabul, in tanks and ammunition-laden Toyota Hilux trucks and stormed the Arg, as the presidential palace was called. They had stared in wonderment at the ornate furniture, the crystalware, the glistening chandeliers, and the oversized hallways in the 83-acre palace.

Bred in battlegrounds and fed on a severely hardline interpretation of Islam, they had led a completely different lifestyle from the other Islamic factions. The only time they put their guns down was to pray five times a day.

Storming Kabul was a heady moment for them.

In 1996, when it finally stormed the capital, we watched in utter amazement as the Talibs decorated their guns with roses. They were celebrating their conquest of the country. Soon, bone-chilling edicts started flowing.

Women were ordered to stay indoors. They were permitted to shop for provisions provided they wore the hijab and were accompanied by either their husband, a brother, or father. No woman could walk the streets alone. No woman could walk the streets with a male neighbour or a male friend.

The strictures were relentless, and they came, one after the other, like bullets exiting gun chambers.

Men were ordered to wear skull caps and grow beards.

Girls were forbidden from attending school.

Death by stoning for those taking drugs, found drinking or having illicit sexual relations.

People caught stealing would have a hand amputated.

Music, TV, and, videos banned.

Playing of chess and cards banned.

Men ordered to pray in a mosque five times a day and ensure their women pray inside the house.

All guns, personal and official, to be handed back.

I was aware of the strict code of conduct before I set foot on Afghanistan's soil. The Taliban had issued the same edicts in Herat, Kandahar, and other provinces, which they had captured over the two previous years.

When I arrived within days of the Taliban takeover, Kabul was a city on edge. Its residents were still struggling to understand what a Taliban rule entailed. Would it lead to peace? Would the constant rain of rockets striking the city and its mountainside cease? Massoud had fled north towards the Panjshir Valley. Would he lie low, or would he try to retake Kabul?

All of us had the same questions.

Wrapped in a chaddar that draped my head, I arrived tentatively in Kabul. The city was teeming with international journalists and there were no hotel rooms available. There was no Indian embassy to go to. Sensing the advent of the Taliban, the staff had upped and left shortly before the storming.

My male photographer colleague, Saibal Das, and I were offered rooms by one of the aid agencies that was hosting other reporters too.

The fortnight that I spent in Kabul ranks as the most claustrophobic assignment of my career. It was not just the attire that was suffocating. Most of the time, I was viewed less as a journalist and more as a woman. The Taliban had no concept of professional women. It still doesn't.

The armed gunmen who occupied ministerial offices in 1996, walked the silk carpets of the palace and the ministries with trepidation. Up until then, they were accustomed only to mosques and battlefields. The Quran –

as they interpreted it – was their weapon and they brooked no interference from anyone.

Arabic translations of the United Nations Charter were available, but the Taliban had neither the time nor the inclination for diplomatic nuances and international political norms. They had their own code of governance and got down to the task of implementing it. They were not interested in the fact that Afghanistan had, in November 1946, joined the United Nations or that it was bound by the Charter which envisioned peace, stability, and human rights for all its member countries.

The press soon got a taste of the Taliban's style of functioning. Kabul had just become their prized possession, and they invited the media to witness what they called a 'bottle smashing ceremony'. We gawked as a tank rolled its blades into a giant heap of brandy and beer bottles. There were other ways of banning liquor, but the Taliban did it their way. They made their point forcefully – which they continue to do. That day, they chose to ignore their ban on photography. They wanted us to relay their message to the world.

In less than a week of the takeover, the 1.2 million residents of Kabul were not the only ones worried. The Taliban, controlling 20 of the 32 provinces, had established its writ over 75 percent of the country, and were ruling at gunpoint.

The international community – represented by the UN, the ICRC, and over a dozen NGOs – had left Afghanistan on 26 September, hours before the Taliban came knocking on the doors of Kabul. They rushed back within the first three days of Taliban rule to continue aiding the civilian population. By then, war had in some ways given way to tentative peace.

Iran's clergy came down heavily on the Taliban, terming them 'heretics' who were enforcing 'fossilized policies'. India, whose embassy officials had taken the first flight out of Kabul, struggled for words, saying, 'We will watch and see.'

Pakistan, Saudi Arabia, and the United Arab Emirates were the only countries quick to recognize the Taliban. The rest treaded cautiously, watching the horror that was unfolding. America called for a representative government – one that would represent all tribes – Pashtuns, Uzbeks, and Tajiks.

The treatment being meted out to women was among the reasons for the call for a representative government. Mullah Mohammed Rabbani – the chairperson of the caretaker council for Kabul and second in command to Taliban founder Mullah Omar – refused to let women reporters attend his first press conference. He had decreed that female government employees should sit within the confines of their homes.

Offering to send them their salaries, Amir Khan Muttaqi, minister of culture and information, said: 'We are restoring the honour of our Afghan sisters by keeping them at home. Islam hasn't changed over 1,400 years. These principles are eternal. If the women want to work, they can leave the country.'

Along with other women reporters, I was told to get up from around the conference table where we were seated and to stand at the far end of the hall. 'No questions,' we were told, 'or you will not even be able to stand in the conference room,' was the firm diktat.

On the streets of Kabul, the six-member shoura (religious council), passed other strictures, reflective of their military ways and their hardy lifestyle. The soldiers-turned politicians forced shopkeepers to stay open late to prove that the public was safe from robbery, common in the earlier years of civil strife. Electricity was restored to the beleaguered city and the prices of essentials were controlled. Food and fuel, once tougher to find than missiles and rockets, became freely available and at lower prices. A loaf of bread that cost 1,000 Afghanis was now available at half the price. Onions dropped from 10,000 to 8,000 Afghanis and potatoes to 15,000 from 18,000 a kilo. The dollar, which fetched 20,000 Afghanis, came down to 14,000.

The Taliban ensured this drop in prices in their own unmistakable way. A butcher's fingers were chopped off for selling meat above the fixed price of 15,000 Afghani per kilo. The terrifying message spread rapidly as armed Talibs swarmed markets, Kalashnikovs casually strapped on their shoulders, to ensure that their orders were being followed.

A woman was beaten up because her toe showed through her shoe, and a married couple was lashed for sitting too close on a bicycle. The Taliban also instructed imams at mosques to give them names of men not turning up for prayers.

Although these extreme actions were condemned by

the international community, the Talibs were too steeped in their interpretation of Islam to worry about sanctions even though Afghanistan was heavily dependent on aid. I met several women who worried about their future. Their lives had been sequestered, and they were being forced to live cloistered lives. 'War was better than this kind of peace,' a school teacher told me. Scoffing at the idea of being paid to sit at home, she wanted to know what would happen to her students and their future. Women comprised 50 percent of the staff in government departments alone, but the corridors of power were firmly shut to them. They were now strict, 'no women allowed' zones that could not be breached.

The Taliban had grown in numbers and there was no dearth of bearded gunmen who remained constantly on the prowl. In 1996, when it stormed Kabul and hit the streets like lightening, the numbers had swelled to 40,000 soldiers.

The story among the foot soldiers was that Mullah Omar, the one-eyed supremo, had picked up the gun again after he saw the Islamic mujahideen that preceded them, force women into a check-post located outside his house in Kandahar's Singesar village. According to one Talib, '*Amirul momineen* (head of the believers) could not live with the manner in which those women were being passed around under his very nose.'

'Women were like roses, meant to be smelt only by their families, and home was where they belonged,' one Talib told me. Fired by the need to usher in a purer form of Islam than was being practised by the Burhanuddin

Rabbani regime dislodged in 1996, Omar had a willing army from among the religious students, who forced across the borders of Kandahar into refugee camps in Peshawar, were brought up on the teachings of Quran in madrasas.

Largely believed to be backed by Pakistan's ISI, the Talibs were able to stamp their authority over the province of Kandahar in 1994. It came under the control of the Taliban mainly because it was being run as the private fiefdom of four rival mujahideen groups. The constant sniping paved the way for the militia's growth and advance. And as they moved from one province to another, they took with them the mujahids from different factions who either swam with the tide or were charmed by the Taliban's interpretation of Islam.

'Anyone who is religious and sports a beard can join the Taliban. Once they are enrolled, they are given training in the use of weapons,' Deputy Foreign Minister Sher Mohammad Abbas Stanekzai explained to me. He was the only high-ranking Talib who deigned to speak to me in his office, on the condition that I would not look him in the eye.

That was a difficult ask. I believe in making eye contact, an essential tool, that helps ease the equation between the interviewer and the interviewee. The Stanekzai interview was the only interview I ever did, while staring at a wall.

The military garrisons in Kandahar and Herat were used for training, he revealed. The tanks, gunships, and ammunition they captured went towards building the arsenal. Left with no choice, the captured pilots and maintenance staff simply switched loyalties.

A lethal mix of training – provided by the ISI – and religious fervour enabled the Talibs to strike Kabul like lightning. When they said, 'we are ready to die for Islam' they meant it. Admired and dreaded in the capital city, 70 percent of which had been pounded and destroyed in the past decade, the Taliban soon had to continue the war to prevent retaliation from the popular resistance leader, Ahmed Shah Massoud, who had fled north towards the Panjshir Valley.

The streets reflected the tension of war. Kabul's war-weary residents were forced into a life dictated by the clerics. Massoud was trying to edge his way back, but the rockets which once whizzed past residential areas – when different mujahideen factions were trying to exercise control – were no longer pounding the city.

'I wish I had been killed by a rocket. This is slow death,' was the refrain in many households in Kabul. Prices of food and fuel had decreased but so had the earnings of most, for each home once had at least one female member bringing in a monthly salary. And then there were homes with only women, war widows who didn't know how they would sustain their families, each of them with an average of four children to feed. The country's economy, which could boast of neither imports nor exports, survived on considerable help from international agencies.

Afghanistan – and Kabul in particular – had chugged along with the help from NGOs – medicine from the ICRC, plastic sheets from Oxfam in winter, or free bread for 50,000 homes in Kabul from French

NGO, Acted, for instance. The total international aid had added up to $55 million a year before the Taliban marched in.

The ultra-conservative brand of Islam being preached by the Taliban put a serious question mark over the continuance of this massive aid. The then UN Secretary-General Boutros Boutros-Ghali's threat – that he will be forced to withdraw aid if the Taliban does not relax its rules – had little effect. The Taliban, who had not faced such an outcry till they reached the capital, could not understand why the West was making such a big noise about 'women being protected'.

I spoke to several aid agencies in Kabul. Aid had not dried up but was beginning to peter out. Sue Emmott, head of Oxfam told me, 'We have already had to suspend some of our programmes because we've always had a strong gender policy and we are not willing to let go of our principles.' The 15,000 families that were supplied plastic sheets would not be getting them that winter because Afghan women could not leave their homes to distribute them. 'Half the population is being taught not to be resilient,' said Emmott. She was facing the same dilemma as other NGOs: to suspend operations altogether or to continue by employing men.

Their immediate concern was for the women working with them. They tried to work out arrangements so these women continued to get paid. While one NGO had employed the male relatives of the women who were working for them, yet another, which had four women employed as cooks and cleaners, was sending laundry to them to wash and iron at home. Each woman mattered because entire households were dependent on them.

The risk no one was willing to take was to antagonize the Taliban. Kabul was adjusting itself to a new set of rules born out of both fear and resentment, I had reported for *India Today*. Hospitals were not spared either. Even in children's wards, girls and boys were segregated. Male doctors were not allowed to treat women and lady doctors and nurses were scared to report to work, even though they had been exempted.

The militia, too, was adjusting itself to a new role – of running a country. The Taliban had two important tasks: to strengthen their hold on Kabul and gear up for a bloody battle in the North, where the mountains were reverberating with the sound of gunfire and columns of smoke rising from the thud of shells. Massoud was not going to give in easily.

One morning, Saibal and I drove up North, towards the Panjshir Valley. Once outside the border of Kabul, where the Taliban were more particular about an adherence to the code of conduct issued by them, it was easier to speak to the turbaned gunmen. The Talibs were curious about women journalists being in a conflict zone and were willing to answer questions, even as they engaged Massoud's mercenaries who had shed their old-time rivalry and tied up with Abdul Rashid Dostum, a military commander, popular amongst Uzbeks. The Tajiks – represented by Massoud – and the Uzbeks, shed their old-age ethnic differences to take on the Pushto-led Taliban.

The debris of war was visible all around us as we sat down for a chat with a few Talibs. Others were visible in the distance, aiming their guns and firing; dodging splinters which poured like metallic rain.

Here, in the middle of the battleground, they didn't have a problem looking me in the eye or talking to me. Except for one Taliban soldier who walked away when he learnt that my photographer colleague was neither my husband nor brother. 'You are not supposed to be out with strange men,' my translator said, quoting the Talib who had walked away. The translator's voice was nervous and edgy, but I continued my interviews with the others.

'Have you heard about Kashmir?' I asked out of curiosity and was taken aback with the answer: 'Heard about Kashmir! I've been there and back,' said one and then another. So many of them had added to the list of 'foreign mercenaries', a noting that had begun appearing in army and IB files since 1994 when 'guest militants' had first been welcomed into the Valley.

'I trained and worked with Maulana Masood Azhar and Nasrullah Langrial,' one said. I was familiar with both names. Masood Azhar and Langrial, a foreign mercenary, had been arrested in Kashmir in the mid-90s, for waging war against the Indian state.

Happy to hear that I was a frequent visitor to Kashmir – where a Talib said he would return for jihad once their hold over Afghanistan was complete – he wanted me to request the Indian government to release the two he described as 'Islamic preachers'.

Arrested in the Valley in February 1994, Masood Azhar was released in Kandahar in exchange for passengers aboard the hijacked IC 814 flight. Langrial, a senior member of the Harkat-ul-Jehad-e-Islami, was lodged in an Indian jail and was involved in various acts of terror in which he killed at least nine BSF men.

I had laughed then, at the audacity of the young Taliban soldier's request. But it hits me differently today. Masood Azhar and Langrial were both trained in Afghanistan and therefore well known to the Taliban. Azhar's JeM was responsible for the attack on the convoy in Pulwama in 2019, that killed 40 CRPF troopers.

The cauldron, in fact, had been brewing for years. Ahmed Omar Saeed Sheikh, another militant who was released in Kandahar, is supposed to have wired $10,00,000 to Mohammed Atta, one of the suspected hijackers who crashed a plane into a tower of New York's World Trade Centre. Sheikh is best known for his role in the kidnapping and murder of *Wall Street Journal*'s Daniel Pearl in 2002.

The audacious attack on America on 11 September 2001 changed Taliban's fortunes. Two planes had erased New York's iconic Twin Towers, and another had damaged the Pentagon in Washington. The dastardly attacks claimed 3,000 lives and remain one of the deadliest terror strikes worldwide.

In less than a month, on 7 October, the US announced a global war against terror. Its firepower was aimed at Afghanistan where it believed Al-Qaeda leader Osama bin Laden had been given shelter by Mullah Omar. By December, there was no trace of the Taliban. The militia, which was governing most provinces, melted into Pakistan or simply went underground.

The pounding by military jets was only the beginning of a prolonged conflict that would carry on until 2021.

The Americans waged a protracted and complex war for two long decades. It came at a significant cost to both the US and Afghanistan. Code-named Operation Enduring Freedom, America and the UK military put boots on the ground and set up military bases.

Several steps were initiated to set up a police force and an army. In June 2002, a Loya Jirga or 'great council' was convened to select a transitional government to rule the country until a new constitution was adopted and national elections could be held. Hamid Karzai, an English-speaking president was a stark contrast to the Taliban that had been sent scurrying into rural Afghanistan – and across the border into Pakistan – after America's war against terror. Karzai won the elections held in October 2004, two years after he had been made the head of the transitionary government.

I went back to Kabul in 2003, soon after the US opened another front, through its invasion of Iraq, to dislodge Saddam Hussein, who it accused of amassing weapons of mass destruction. I briefly worked with Saeed Naqvi, an eminent journalist who was producing a show on world affairs, broadcast on Doordarshan, India's government-run channel.

Kabul was a changed city. The contrast was stark. The Americans – with Karzai's help – were trying to fashion Afghanistan into a modern state where democracy could grow its roots. Kabul still looked war-scarred. It had suffered decades of strife, but the capital was no longer in the grip of the Taliban and their suffocating edicts. The women had thrown their burqas away and the men were back in salons, getting their beards trimmed. Afghans, who had crossed over into Pakistan, had returned. The Indian embassy too had reopened, and women were back to work in government offices, with NGOs, and in privately-owned enterprises like beauty parlours, hotels, and gyms. Diplomats were back to hosting cocktail parties.

In 2003, I could breathe in Kabul. Though I was accompanied by a male colleague, my videographer, this time I could roam the streets alone without the fear of being lashed. I also got an interview with President Hamid Karzai, who I approached through the Indian embassy in Kabul. Karzai had studied at the Himachal Pradesh University in Simla, from where he completed his master's in political science in 1983. He was happy to give an interview to an Indian journalist. India was deepening its engagement with the war-torn country and investing in development projects to try and bring Afghanistan out of the morass of war. Its aim was also strategic: to grow its diplomatic importance in a region that Pakistan considered its backyard. The ISI had contacts with the Taliban and other terror organizations like the Haqqani brothers, responsible for inflicting damage to lives and properties. Note the name Haqqani. It will make a chilling appearance, again, later in this chapter.

In the following years, the turbaned Talibs, slowly began to emerge out of their hiding places in Pakistan.

While there, some amongst them had also started a group called Tehreek-e-Taliban Pakistan (TTP). They started aiming guns at their own benefactors in the Pakistani army for the help the country was providing to the US troops. Conflict zones are indeed murky. Enemies change swiftly and quickly.

On the ground, in Afghanistan, elections were held in October 2004. Karzai won a popular mandate, and women were accorded voting rights. He ruled till 2014 amid growing attacks between the US troops, the newly trained Afghan army, and the Taliban. The war against terror, launched by the George Bush administration, continued through two terms of Barack Obama's tenure. In the run-up to his presidency, Obama had promised to pay more attention and commit more troops. He put more boots on the ground in Afghanistan, but the Taliban was making strides, gradually gnawing its way back. The one trophy that Obama could claim, came through a stealth operation, code-named Neptune Spear, conducted on the night of 1 May 2011. Helicopters carrying US SEALs left from the US-controlled Jalalabad air base in Afghanistan. They arrived at the Abbottabad compound in Pakistan, on 2 May in the dead of the night. After years of hard work that involved building contacts and using surveillance techniques, the US believed that the man they were looking for was hiding in Abbottabad, a military garrison, a mere two-hour drive from Islamabad, Pakistan's capital city.

That night, US commandos entered the house they had zeroed in on and, killed Osama bin Laden and managed to take off with his body before the Pakistani establishment reached the scene. Bin Laden was buried in the Arabian sea. Along with him were buried several questions: Did Pakistan, a US ally know about the covert operation or had the US reached a stage where it didn't trust its ally anymore?

Double games and covert operations lie at the heart of conflict zones.

The death of bin Laden was a setback for the Al-Qaeda, but it added to the Taliban's determination to retake the country from the 'foreign invaders' who by then had also angered local Afghans by killing civilians in the hundreds and bracketing them as 'collateral damage'.

The astronomical numbers linked to the global war against terror tell an astonishing story of how much money was spent; how many Afghan civilians were sacrificed as 'collateral damage', and how many embalmed body bags flown back to America.

Research by the Watson Institute for International and Public Affairs, Brown University, estimates losses in the Afghan security forces at 69,000; the number of civilians and mujahids killed at about 51,000 each, and more than 3,500 coalition soldiers dead since 2001, nearly two-thirds of them Americans. More than 20,000 US soldiers were injured.

According to the United Nations, Afghanistan has the third-largest displaced population in the world. As per the Watson Institute report, the US spent $2.3 trillion on the war.

Neither money nor the best military might could buy tentative peace in Afghanistan. Two decades later, when the US eventually withdrew from Afghanistan, Kabul was taken over swiftly by the Taliban – the very force the Americans had set out to destroy after the 9/11 attacks.

The Taliban are artful dodgers who stayed in the shadows as the war lumbered on for 20 years. The US made the mistake of drawing a distinction between 'good Taliban' and 'bad Taliban' and even though they worked out a deal, hammered out in Doha, for a phased withdrawal of troops in return for a more representative government and 'an agreement of bringing peace', the superpower had to shut its embassy in Kabul and virtually flee. Before they left and lowered their flag, they had to destroy hundreds of sensitive documents and literally break computers and hard drives.

No one expected the Taliban to reach the gates of Kabul on 15 August 2021, a fortnight before the US had said it would withdraw its troops. To the contrary, the hope was that the Afghan army and police – trained by the US and its allies – would be able to stave off an attack from the rampaging Taliban for at least another few months.

American President Joe Biden conceded as much in a statement put out by the White House on 31 August 2021. He said, 'Last night in Kabul, the United States ended 20 years of war in Afghanistan – the longest war in American history. We completed one of the biggest airlifts in history, with more than 1,20,000 people evacuated to safety. That number is more than double what most experts thought was possible. No nation – no nation has ever done anything like it in all of history. Only the United States had the capacity, and the will, and the ability to do it, and we did it today.... And they did it facing a crush of enormous crowds seeking to leave the country. And they did it knowing ISIS-K [Islamic State Khorasan Province] terrorists – sworn enemies of the Taliban – were lurking in the midst of those crowds.... Twenty service members were wounded in the service of this mission. Thirteen heroes gave their lives.'

Expounding on the 20-year-long war, Biden said, 'In April, I made the decision to end this war. As part of that decision, we set the date of August 31st for American troops to withdraw. The assumption was that more than 3,00,000 Afghan National Security Forces that we had trained over the past two decades and equipped would be a strong adversary in their civil wars with the Taliban. That assumption – that the Afghan government would be able to hold on for a period of time beyond military drawdown – turned out not to be accurate. So, we were ready when the Afghan Security Forces – after two decades of fighting for their country and losing thousands of their own – did not hold on as long as anyone expected. We were ready when they and the people of Afghanistan watched their own government collapse and their president flee amid the corruption and malfeasance, handing over the country to their enemy, the Taliban, and significantly increasing the risk to US personnel and our Allies.'

The Afghan president, Ashraf Ghani – who replaced Hamid Karzai in 2014 – referenced by Biden, had fled the presidential palace, afraid perhaps that he would be hunted down like Soviet-backed Najibullah was. He feared he would meet a fate similar to Najibullah, who was killed and left hanging from a pole in 1996. The Taliban were not even willing to let him rest in a grave in Kabul. His body was handed over to the Red Cross.

Neither the US nor Ghani, Afghanistan's caged president had anticipated the lightning advance of the turbaned marauders.

It is over four years since the Taliban took control. In all this while, there has been no real threat to their supremacy or to the fact that their reign will continue. The threat from the Islamic State (Khorasan), a terror organization which wants to set up a Caliphate across Iraq, Syria, and Afghanistan, is not taken seriously by the Taliban. They don't see themselves being dislodged by a different militant ideology or by a foreign power, particularly after the US' departure.

The battleground-fed seminarians, therefore, have gone back on all the guarantees they gave in the Doha agreement. Prime amongst them was the one to not allow Afghan soil to be used for terror activities.

The Agreement for Bringing Peace to Afghanistan, commonly known as the United States-Taliban deal or the Doha Accord was signed on 29 February 2020. The agreement obligated that the Taliban would cut all ties with Al-Qaeda and other terrorist groups and instead, focus on intra-Afghan peace talks to decide on the 'future political map of Afghanistan'.

Yet, in July 2022, the US targeted and killed Al-Qaeda leader, Ayman al-Zawahiri in a drone strike in the heart of Kabul, a few blocks away from the presidential palace. Zawahiri had taken over Al-Qaeda's leadership after bin

Laden's death and had a bounty of $25 million on his head since 2011.

The world – India included – had hoped that the Taliban would mend its ways but it is clear that the war-hardened fighters, who undertake long journeys in the name of religion, are wedded to their own radical interpretation of the Quran. Their edicts flow from the same, unyielding interpretation and they play only by that rule book. I call it the terror toolkit.

Within the Taliban, there are a few faces who try and present a different picture. They make themselves available for interviews and roll out propaganda they hope will cloak the chaos and destruction that struck Afghanistan on its face in August 2021, when the Taliban whiplashed their way back into power.

I interviewed Suhail Shaheen, one such sophisticate, who is the head of the militia's political office, based in Doha. His two daughters were afforded the luxury of being educated in Qatar, but he made no such concessions for the daughters of Afghanistan. The fact that his daughters were educated was known but he was not willing to talk about it. He did, however, answer many other questions for the interview I did for *The Times of India*, one year after the Taliban had rolled into Kabul.

Shaheen is clearly adept at giving interviews. He tried to nuance the 'terror toolkit' in his interview with me. There were several hard-hitting questions the Taliban needed to answer – they still do – and Shaheen was willing to get headline space in India, a country it is now trying to reach out to for assistance and recognition.

Q Why are girls still not allowed in classrooms beyond Grade 6? Why should Afghanistan's girls not have a right to education?

A Private secondary schools for girls are open all over the country but opening public schools is pending until further notice from the leadership.... Assistance from the international community is needed in this regard. For the record, I would like to say, we are not against girls' education in general, provided they observe wearing hijab.

Q But why has the leadership not been able to decide on education for girls in public schools in an entire year?

A We are a country which has just come out of the morass of war. We are not a match to a country which has not seen war for the last four decades. Still girls are receiving education.... Efforts are underway to reach the level of any other country. However, it will take time.

Q Some Indian diplomats have returned to its embassy in Kabul and there seems to be some movement forward, but India says it wants 'humanitarian engagement' for now and that should not be mistaken for recognition. What assurances have you given India?

A We are committed to providing a safe environment to the routine functioning of embassies and to diplomatic activities of embassies of all countries based in Kabul. This includes India.

Q How does the Taliban view Kashmir and the changes to its special status under Article 370?

A Kashmir is an issue between Pakistan and India. We hope they resolve it through peaceful means.

Q India, and other countries, are worried about the fact that Al-Qaeda leader Ayman al-Zawahari was killed in a recent strike in the capital city of Kabul. In the past, Indian assets have been attacked by foreign terrorists. Doesn't Zawahiri's killing in Kabul mean that Afghanistan was allowing its soil to be used by terror groups? It is also against the Doha agreement.

A We are fully committed to the Doha Agreement. Our leadership was not aware of the presence of Ayman Zawahiri in Kabul. Thirdly, it is just a claim now. The Islamic Emirate of Afghanistan is investigating the claim and will share the findings with all. No one is above the law.

Q You say the leadership was not aware of Zawahiri's presence in Kabul. Is that not a huge intelligence failure? It is like Pakistan saying it was not aware of Osama bin Laden's presence in Abbottabad.

A Let's put it this way: tens of incidents did occur in India in the past, but the Indian government was not aware until they happened. It doesn't mean they were not committed to prevent them. The core question – is our policy to not allow anyone to use our soil against others, in place or not? Yes, it is in place, and we are determinedly adhering to it. This is of significance for all.

Q Would you call Zawahiri and bin Laden terrorists?

A There is no single definition of terrorism in the world. However, based on Doha Agreement, we will not allow anyone to use the soil of Afghanistan against any other country. That is our commitment.

Q The Haqqani group – banned by the US – has targeted Indians and Indian assets in Afghanistan. Your interior minister, Sirajuddin Haqqani now says he wants better relations with India, but can India take him for his word?

A There was occupation in our country, and we were fighting against the invaders. The Islamic Emirate of Afghanistan has never targeted Indians because of them being Indians. Now, we are an independent country, and we want to have positive relations with India and other countries. Secondly, there is no separate entity titled "Haqqani group" as portrayed by the media. The IEA has a sole leadership and unity in its hierarchy.

Q The Taliban promised a general amnesty, but extra-judicial killings of former security and government officials continue. Why are people being picked up and killed?

A This is a part of malicious propaganda against us. We declared general amnesty and so far, nobody has been targeted because they worked for the previous regime. Our leadership has set up a commission to facilitate return of officials of the former regime to the country, assuring them that they can lead a normal and secured life.

Q Former President Hamid Karzai has appealed

to the Taliban to break away from Pakistan's influence. Does the Taliban want to?

A We have de facto diplomatic relations with several countries including regional countries.

Q As a woman journalist myself, I must ask you this: Why are Afghan women journalists losing their jobs?

A There is no restriction on female journalists from the government. However, because of deteriorating economic situation many media outlets have shut down their channels. Freezing of Afghanistan assets has direct impact on journalists and media workers as well because banking system is not functioning normally. So, it should be clear that the reason behind Afghan women journalists losing their job is economic.

Since my interview with him, the restrictions on women have increased. They are now not allowed into universities. They have also been ordered to sequester windows in residential areas so that they are not visible. Under-construction homes are now not allowed to frame windows into their walls. It is 'haraam' for men to even see a neighbouring woman, if even by mistake.

The world is unsure of how to deal with the Taliban. Some, such as Russia and China, have welcomed Taliban leaders to their countries.

Unlike in 1996, when the Taliban got formal recognition from three countries, not one came forward to do so since its return to power in 2021, except Russia which recognized the turbaned army in 2025. India, which had shunned all diplomatic ties with the Taliban since it first came to power in 1996, evacuated all staff from its embassy in 2021.

A few months later, it sent a technical team to oversee humanitarian assistance. India realized it can neither afford to lose the goodwill among the common Afghans nor cede strategic space to Pakistan, by withdrawing completely. In January 2025, India upped its public 'embrace' of the Taliban. The announcement came through a statement put out by the Ministry of External Affairs, dated 8 January. It said, 'Today, Foreign Secretary Vikram Misri had a meeting with the Acting Foreign Minister of Afghanistan, Mawlawi Amir Khan Muttaqi, in Dubai. The two sides discussed various issues pertaining to bilateral relations as well as regional developments. The Foreign Secretary underlined India's historic friendship with the Afghan people and the strong people to people contacts between the two countries. In this context, he conveyed India's readiness to respond to the urgent developmental needs of the Afghan people.'

Both sides evaluated the ongoing Indian humanitarian assistance programmes. The Afghan minister appreciated and thanked the Indian leadership for continuing to engage and support the people of Afghanistan. Given the current need for development activities, it was decided that India would consider engaging in development projects in the near future, in addition to the existing humanitarian assistance programme.

'In response to the request from the Afghan side, India will provide further material support in the first instance to the health sector and for the rehabilitation of refugees....

The Afghan side underlined its sensitivities to India's security concerns. The two sides agreed to remain in touch and continue regular contacts at various levels.'

The contact between India and Afghanistan went up a notch after the Pahalgam attack when foreign minister S. Jaishankar spoke to his Afghan counterpart, Muttaqi, to appreciate the Taliban's condemnation of the killing of civilians at the Baisaran meadow in Pahalgam on 22 April 2025.

Short of officially recognizing the Taliban as the rulers of the Islamic Emirate of Afghanistan, the call and Misri's meeting signalled several markers. The meeting came at a time when Afghan-Pakistan relations have nosedived. The Taliban has established its rule in Kabul and is no longer beholden to either the ISI or the Pakistan Army, which wants it to rein in the Tehreek-e-Taliban. In the shifting sands of diplomacy and geo-politics, India is willing to make space for the turbaned army to checkmate Pakistan, bogged down by an economic crisis and the mayhem being caused by the TTP.

By reaching out to the Taliban, the Indian government also underlined its concerns regarding the continuing presence, in Afghanistan, of a large number of terrorists belonging to the Lashkar and the Jaish. India should also be concerned about the fact that Sirajuddin Haqqani, Afghanistan's interior minister was responsible for an attack on the Indian embassy in July 2008. Two senior officials and several security officials drawn from the Indo-Tibetan Border Police (ITBP) were among 59 killed after an explosive-laden truck rammed the gates of the

Indian mission. Sirajuddin, a proscribed terrorist, with a bounty of $10 million on his head is now occupying a portfolio that involves security and peace. His ministerial colleague, Abbas Stanekzai, the country's deputy foreign minister made a strong pitch in favour of more freedom for women and girl students, annoying Taliban Supreme Leader Hibatullah Akhundzada, who continues to be based in Kandahar. Like the rest of the world, India too has been trapped into not shutting its door to the Taliban. The 'door half open' policy suits the Taliban but does deep injustice to the women of Afghanistan who wait behind closed doors. They remain the pawns on a geostrategic chessboard.

The Taliban has only increased its curbs on women's rights. Women now don't have access to education. They cannot work even in the maternal healthcare sector (Afghanistan has one of the highest maternal mortality ratios in the world). Women are being erased from society. No woman will now graduate to become a teacher, an engineer, a lawyer, a nurse, or a doctor.

Who will treat sick women in hospitals? The Taliban is not interested in answering such questions. What they're clear about is this: women cannot go to college, or visit beauty salons, work for international aid agencies, wear nail polish or other cosmetics or access gyms. They cannot even go to public parks. They cannot sing. They cannot even be heard by family members while praying.

Several agencies have published reports pointing to the dire ground reality in Afghanistan. Heather Barr, associate director of the Women's Rights Division at Human Rights

Watch has said that the Taliban seem perfectly comfortable with the idea that women and girls are dying because of a lack of healthcare professionals, but the Taliban is undeterred. It prefers to shut its eyes to reports that are now pointing to increased child marriages, sale of children, and sale of organs.

Amnesty International and the International Commission of Jurists (ICJ) have also asked for the Taliban to be investigated for crimes against humanity, for their brutal crackdown on the rights and freedoms of women but there have been no changes in women's conditions in Afghanistan.

Men, too, are not spared. In a throwback to its early days in power in 1996, the Taliban has resumed executing men in football stadiums, where they are shot, stoned or lashed.

Afghanistan is a country still at war.

The Islamic Emirate of Afghanistan, as the Taliban like to call it, has not been recognized as a legitimate government but is gradually getting recognized on the world stage.

The citizens of Afghanistan are the worst sufferers. Staring down an abyss, they remain silent – and frightened – spectators to a reality that is unlikely to change in the foreseeable future.

While returning from the Panjshir Valley in northern Afghanistan in 1996, I had an urge I could not resist. I requested my cab driver to let me take the controls of the car for a few kilometers, which appeared desolate and deserted.

I rolled down the windows, pressed the accelerator and drove at high speed. The wind swept the chaddar off my head and rustled my hair. I took a deep breath.

Freedoms are empowering. They are not available in Afghanistan. They come with great costs to life and liberty. There is no silver lining on the horizon. The Taliban are the police. They are the army too. The country is in the firm control of their diktats.

A War in the Barren Mountains

When Kargil Vijay Diwas is celebrated each year in July, to commemorate the victory in Kargil, the most overpowering memory that rushes in, unannounced, is the one of the freshly pinched face that had been hammered into a tree.

One afternoon in June 1999, I made my way to the Brigade headquarters in Dras. The mood was sombre. Artillery shells were flying from Kargil's barren mountains, inflicting casualties. Indian Army soldiers were dying, and the officers were not clear about who the enemy really was.

The Brigade headquarters is where we often went, for information and for a hot meal, a luxury in the battlefield that Kargil had become since early May. That afternoon, a senior officer, suddenly said, 'Would you like to see something that won't let you sleep for three nights?' I may not even be able to eat for a few days, he told me, walking me out to a courtyard.

Summoning a soldier, the officer asked him to remove a sack that was hanging on a tree trunk. What did he want to show me, I thought to myself. What is it that would keep me from sleeping? I'd seen bullet-ridden bodies of soldiers and civilians in Punjab and Kashmir.

What I saw, when the sack was removed, left me stunned. The head of a Pakistani soldier had been pinned to the tree like a grisly trophy. After three weeks of fighting in the frigid heights of Kargil, the Indian Army finally knew that it was up against regulars from the Pakistani army and not armed terrorists as they had earlier thought.

Frustration had built up among the jawans and so had the thirst for revenge. After capturing Point 4700, one of the many peaks that had been occupied through a deep infiltration that had gone undetected for months, the Indian Army had finally laid their hands on the enemy. One of them took out his knife and slit the head of a Pakistani soldier in one stroke. The head was sent down to the Brigade headquarters at Dras and pinned to a tree trunk. The enemy had not yet been captured alive – but this was proof that it was only a matter of time.

The enemy head had become an exhibition piece for anyone who had the stomach to look at it. The sight of the pinched face, hair intact, had served the macabre purpose of motivating the troops. Or at least, that's what some brigade officers believed. By then, the enemy was neither invisible, nor invincible.

After spending a better part of three months covering the Kargil war, I returned to the high-altitude war theatre to talk to the jawans and the officers, to write a book. *A Soldier's Diary: The Inside Story* was my way of dealing with the nightmares that stayed with me long after the short but sharp war had ended. The trip back, in September, a few months after the mountains stopped reverberating to the sound of gunfire, helped me understand what the soldiers had actually endured.

I got several letters from angry retired army officers after the book was published. The letters, pointed in particular, to my references to the head pinned to the tree. The Indian Army does not do this, was the tone and tenor, of the letters, but mine was a first-hand experience.

A quarter century has passed since India fought to reclaim the freezing heights but each year, without fail, when Kargil Vijay Diwas is celebrated in July, the most overpowering memory that rushes in, unannounced, is the one of the freshly pinched face.

In the jagged heights of Kargil, the signs of battle have long been obliterated. India fought against challenging odds in a rugged, remote, and inhospitable corner that few had even heard of. Kargil, Dras, Mushkoh, Batalik were mere names till the media brought them into ordinary drawing rooms.

Even the names of locations in the war theatre bore testimony to just how desolate and isolated this part of India was: Point 4875, Point 5140, Point 4812. They were just geographical references, restricted to strategic maps in the offices of army commanders, until Kargil exploded into life, in full colour on television screens.

For my generation of journalists, Kargil was the first taste of war. India emerged victorious in 1999 but paid a heavy price – the Indian Army and the Air Force lost over 500 men. As many as 1,109 were wounded. Several post-mortems were done after Nawaz Sharif, the then prime minister of Pakistan was ordered by the president of the United States of America to withdraw his troops from Indian territory. Within 72 hours of the army declaring victory on 26 July 1999 – referred to as Vijay Diwas – the government set up its first committee, under the chairmanship of K. Subrahmanyam. The committee was formed to 'review the events leading up to the Pakistani aggression in the Kargil district of Ladakh in Jammu and Kashmir', and recommend measures, 'considered necessary to safeguard national security against such armed intrusions'.

The committee was scathing in its report. 'The Review Committee had before it overwhelming evidence that the Pakistani armed intrusion in the Kargil sector came as a complete and total surprise to the Indian government, army and intelligence agencies as well as to the Jammu and Kashmir state government and its agencies. The Committee did not come across any agency or individual who was able clearly to assess before the event, the possibility of a large-scale Pakistani military intrusion across the Kargil heights,' it said at the outset. None of the intelligence agencies had any inkling that Pakistan was putting an audacious plan into action, in the peak of winter, braving avalanches and blizzards.

Kargil will remain, amongst my most difficult and

challenging assignments. It was also an important one, for it gave me an insight into the courage and bravery of the infantry soldiers. I wrote my book as a soldier's diary. That was the only way, I felt, I could do justice to how they had fought and conquered the unforgiving heights, despite the lack of preparedness and the cavalier attitude of the top brass.

The book got widely read and reviewed. One day, in 2002, my phone rang, and I answered it even though I seldom respond to calls from unknown numbers. A lady introduced herself saying, 'Hi, this is Preity Zinta....'

'Ya sure,' I said hanging up, reprimanding myself for having taken the call. The phone rang again, and I answered it thinking I'd rebuke the prankster. 'Hi, this IS (*emphasis her's*) Preity Zinta. I've just read your book on Kargil and would like to meet you,' she said. She had been cast to play a war correspondent in the movie, *Lakshya*, directed by Farhan Akhtar. Set in the backdrop of the Kargil war, the movie released in 2004 and in several interviews and social posts, Zinta called it her 'toughest film ever'. Shooting at heights of 18,000 feet was not easy and she recalled her experience as being both 'beautiful and brutal'.

Wars are brutal. Shooting a movie in the unpunishing heights is vastly different from taking on an enemy.

I think it necessary to reproduce select excerpts from *A Soldier's Diary*, that continue to serve as an important reminder of what wars entail. It was written through the voice of one of the officers involved on the battlefront.

~

13 May
The scene that greets us is chaotic. This is the Traffic Check Post (TCP) at Sonamarg. Ahead, the road twists and turns, leading to Kargil. Both sides of the road are choked with endless convoys of army vehicles. Like us, all the units that have been rushed here have done so virtually overnight. Most have been hastily pulled out from CI Ops, army shorthand for Counter-Insurgency Operations, in the Kashmir Valley. Some, like 1 Naga, were awaiting transfer orders after a gruelling stint in Siachen. Most of their men were on leave. They have arrived here at just about half strength. We are all here because of a typical army-style briefing. In tones terse and cryptic, we were told: "Some rats have come in."

Translated, it meant that there had been some incursions into Indian territory by Pakistan-backed militants. This, however, was clearly no routine crossover. The large number of vehicles and the number of units that had been rushed here – 8 Sikh, 1 Naga, 12 Jammu & Kashmir Light Infantry, and 18 and 16 Grenadiers, which was the holding unit for the Dras-Kargil sector – clearly implied that this was more serious than usual. Yet, in all our briefings so far, the attitude of senior army commanders had been exactly the opposite. Back in the Valley, a Major-General, the man in charge of CI Ops in the area, repeated in his briefing that we were being sent to Kargil to evict "some Paki rats", the phrase underlining the assessment by Army Headquarters in South Block and Srinagar, that we were dealing with a minor intrusion. In fact, so lightly was the threat treated that officers and men of 16 Grenadiers still had their families with them. Even in our unit, most of us had written or sent messages to friends and relatives saying we would be back soon.

The sense of unease among the officers huddled by the side of the road at the Traffic Check Post (TCP) was growing by the hour. What was going on? Why were we being told nothing? Where were the intelligence inputs? Where was the detailed briefing on enemy strength, positions and fortifications? There were other questions that needed answering. Why the unusual point of ingress? Why through Kargil? Why through a Shia-dominated area where shelter is difficult? Here, the local population is not sympathetic to the so-called independence movement. They have lived in near-total isolation from the Kashmir Valley where shutters are hastily downed a little before sunset. Kargil and Dras are, figuratively, a million miles from the slogans and chants of *hum kya chahte, azadi* (we want independence). Far from the scenes of violence and the omnipresent gun barrels and sandbags. Why, then, had the infiltrators chosen these desolate mountains? It was a question to which our field commanders had no initial answer. In fact, the real answer was to become, for an excessive number of brave soldiers, their epitaph.

Our convoy snaked its way past the bends, the three tonners groaning as they crawled up the narrow Zoji La pass at 11,600 feet. For the superstitious, the date had an ominous ring. As our convoy moved past the TCP and along the road that represents Kargil's lifeline, there was an even more ominous warning. The driver of my vehicle suddenly braked. Our convoy had been waved down by a Colonel camped alongside the road. He thrust his head into the commanding officer's or CO's vehicle and shouted hysterically, "Don't go ahead, you will all be killed. They are dominating the road... you will all be butchered." The Colonel, an artillery officer, had already had a taste of the enemy firepower. He had been under an incessant rain of shells fired from across the border and from the heights now occupied by the "rats".

We were given our share soon enough, our vehicles shaken by huge explosions which carved out chunks of the mountain. There was dust everywhere, barely settling before another shell sailed in, and another, and another. The terrain was already pockmarked with craters. The earth shook. Through the haze, I could still hear the Colonel's voice repeating, "Don't move forward. Believe me, you will all be butchered. Soon it will be dark and you cannot drive with your headlights on. That's an invitation to death." We asked the Colonel where we could find the brigade commander, Brigadier Surinder Singh, the officer in-charge of the Kargil sector. He gave us directions and we found the Brigadier sitting in a bunker in a tracksuit, a blanket thrown around his legs. We reported the arrival of our unit and Surinder Singh, as always wearing a ready smile, said, "Don't worry, some *atankwadis* (militants) have come in. We will catch them by the scruff of their necks and throw them out."

"We don't know the terrain, sir," our CO replied.

"Don't worry, the commanding officer of 16 Grenadiers will brief you. I will give you a task tomorrow morning," he said, bidding us good night.

We stayed on the roadside that night, most of the unit huddled in their vehicles. Sleep was impossible amidst the thunder of artillery fire and the roar of guns. It was a foretaste of what we were headed into, a deadly killing zone where the enemy was not just artillery shells and fanatical soldiers, but the weather and terrain as well.

All of us officers and company commanders feel a sharpened sense of responsibility. We are leading men who will follow us to hell, bound by tradition and faith, unquestioning, ever-obedient, unmindful of the danger or threat to their own lives. I am filled with a sense of dread.

14 May

We conducted a quick survey of the arms and ammunition we were carrying. The unit we had relieved had handed over their weapons to us in a crisis situation, the handover lasting till 3 a.m. It was the only way we could have moved, as we had been ordered to, by 13 May. Like many other units which converged hurriedly on Kargil, we were woefully short of weaponry. We don't have enough rocket launchers and only one of the five radio sets is functional. Automatic Grenade Launchers (AGL), Machine Guns, Faggot missiles. They are all listed but the numbers under the column "Deficit" far outweighs the column for "Authorization". Batteries… we are even short of batteries. We are also short on news about the intrusions, the enemy force, their strength or their defence. "There is some problem in Kargil" is all that 15 Corps, the Srinagar-based operational headquarters, told us. The official word, even two days after our arrival, was that "some militants have crossed over".

Finally, news has started trickling in. The "infiltrators" had first been noticed on 5 May. Three days later, when a patrol was sent to investigate, they returned with four of their men in body bags.

A clearer picture emerged after I met officers from 1 Naga, the infantry unit which was among the first to move into Dras. Their experience was to prove a dangerous portent of what was to follow over the next few days: the army brass and the Defence Ministry playing down the threat while soldiers continued to die under circumstances which should never have been allowed to happen. What this resulted in was total and suicidal confusion. The commanding officer of 1 Naga had this to say in his After Action Report (in which the unit outlines its tasks and experiences during the battle, spells out the lessons learnt and makes recommendations): "On 12 May, the unit had not even started acclimatizing when it was asked to deploy one company in small groups in Tololing nallah and Bimbac nallah. The rest were asked to be ready to move at short notice. The same day again, orders were received for one company to move to Mushkoh Valley in 4754 and occupy defences. In the evening, further orders were received from 121 Brigade Headquarters (commanded by Brigadier Surinder Singh) to move one company to Kargil, which also left immediately. One remaining company was asked to move and be deployed on the southern spur of Point 4590. On 13 May, at 2000 hours, orders were received to again concentrate all companies at Dras, including the company which had moved to Kargil. By first light on 14 May, the officiating commander was briefed by Commander 121 on the impending task of the unit…"

It was clear from this that confusion prevailed. His report raised some serious questions. Where was the command and control? How many infiltrators were there? More importantly, where were they? How many troops were needed to tackle them, and where? 121 Brigade certainly didn't know. Neither did 15 Corps. Nor did Northern Command at Udhampur, or the Army Headquarters in Delhi. In fact, in a bizarre sequence of events, the army chief, General Ved Prakash Malik, was away in Poland the day our unit arrived in Dras. The very fact that he was out of the country and in no hurry to rush back only added to the dangerous sense of complacency at the top.

15 Corps was the hub, the operational headquarters overseeing the war theatre. It got its inputs from 121 Brigade and disseminated information up the line to Northern Command at Udhampur and Army Headquarters in Delhi. But it also had its own independent sources of information. What was its intelligence wing doing? Were they as much in the dark as everybody else?

The entire chain of command seemed to be in the dark. It was the only explanation for their indecisiveness.

Why send one company to Mushkoh and dispatch another to Kargil and then get them all back again between 2000 hours on 13 May and first light, 14 May? Driving the 60 kilometers stretch from Dras to Kargil was not without peril.

The artillery shells meant driving through a hail of steel. One officer returned from the 15 Corps headquarters at Srinagar and the briefing he had had from the Corps Commander, Lt Gen. Krishan Pal and his team was not very different. "Some people have come in. It is a localized affair. Take them on and throw them out," were the orders he had been given. For a long time after our arrival, we continued to address the enemy as "they". In briefings, we were continuously told "they" were "militants" and "mercenaries".

It is the kind of situation that is every soldier's nightmare. To go into battle with a total lack of information, under confused leadership, conflicting orders, no intelligence about the enemy force, their motivation, their numbers, their defences; their weaponry. Or even their identity: were they regular soldiers or mujahideen?

13 June

This is a red-letter day. Ravindranath was able to go up, stand on the top and radio the brigade commander of the first major victory, a victory that became the psychological turning point of the war. Tololing had been taken at last. Celebrations were called for, but Ravindranath wept. He had lost 10 men, and 25 others had been seriously wounded, including the unit doctor who now had a splinter lodged in his foot. And Bhanwar Singh, of course. He succumbed but not before he had reached the top as he had promised. They had grossly miscalculated the number of stretchers that would be needed. They had taken 12 but needed 25 for the injured and another 10 for the dead.

But they won Tololing back and also counted nine enemy bodies. The rest had obviously fled, leaving behind what was the first physical proof of what the enemy had been equipped with. The reverse slopes were full of administrative bunkers which had been fortified with iron pickets and corrugated iron sheets. Approaches to each bunker had been covered by three to four MMGs firing from different positions. Our soldiers used the many tins of ghee they found on Tololing to keep themselves warm after they'd got to the top. They made a feast of butter and honey that was there in large quantities and managed to smile in temperatures hovering between –5 and –10. They also found another piece of vital equipment, issued to the enemy but denied to his Indian counterpart – splinter-proof jackets. If our soldiers had been equipped with these jackets, many lives would have been saved.

Now, it is time for the post-mortem. All four companies and the reserve troops had had a harrowing time and learnt several lessons. The officers have started writing notes, listing the shortcomings and the lessons learnt. These will go into the After Action Reports of all the units that are taking part in this war.

We will all make recommendations for the future. We have all learnt costly lessons. Don't ask the officers at Army Headquarters. They are busy revelling in the patriotic fervour the media has helped unleash. They are playing petty games, denying that the intruders have built bunkers. Even banning the press from crossing the barricade at Sonamarg, embarrassed that the reporters are beginning to bring out the truth: no winter clothing, no snow boots. Special clothing is only one small aspect. There are so many shortcomings, numerous lessons learnt.

Here are some that are listed in the After Action Reports submitted by different units:

There was a lack of powerful binoculars required for close reconnaissance. We were unable to gather information about the objectives (the different heights which have been occupied) even after reaching as close as 600 metres because the resolution provided by the service binoculars was not sufficient.

Continuous soil erosion over a period of time had changed the configuration of the terrain. The changes had not been incorporated in maps and this led to great difficulty in identifying the routes and the objectives. Most maps had become outdated. There weren't enough of them available, and many units had to make do with Xerox copies.

Lack of night vision equipment severely hampered troop movement. The night vision equipment presently under use has a limited range and is meant for engaging targets. The units were not authorized any long-range night vision devices (NVDs), which can be used for reconnaissance and surveillance. The night vision equipment which was issued uses different types of batteries which were mostly in short supply. The result: the equipment remained unutilized.

One of the most critical shortcomings, whether in Mushkoh, Dras or Batalik, was the lack of bunker bursting equipment. The army has no dedicated weapon system for destroying concrete bunkers. Rocket launchers are ineffective. Rocket after rocket was fired but they made no difference to the enemy bunkers, solid as they were. The bunkers were made of cement and mortar. Which means that the enemy had come equipped with construction material and tools. They must have taken months to prepare these bunkers. What this implies is that the incursions were taking place even as Prime Minister Atal Bihari Vajpayee was in Lahore, on the historic bus ride on 19 February.

Lack of bunker bursting weaponry: 18 Garhwal's After Action Report says that "some of the enemy bunkers had overhead protection with CGI (corrugated iron) sheets and huge boulders on top of them". The report brought out by 56 Brigade says: "The sangars proved to be very strong fortifications. Automatic grenade launchers, rocket launchers, and flame throwers had very little effect on these sangars whereby the enemy can withstand repeated attacks on his fortifications." Under "Recommendations", the report goes on to say: "Bunker bursting capability is a very crucial aspect in gaining a foothold in mountains.

Suggested equipment: Laser designators for guidance of aerial bombs accurately to the target. Cannon Launched Guided Projectiles (CLGPs) can enhance the accuracy of projectiles on targets and help in bunker bursting. Penetrating capability of flame throwers needs to be enhanced."

Milans and Faggot missiles used did not give the desired results as the life of the warheads had expired.

Intelligence gathering was almost nil. Quality air photos, which are so crucial for planning attacks at unit levels, were not available. In some cases, there was a prior aerial recce of the heights which had to be recaptured, but this was only helpful in getting a better overview. It did not help any of us either in assessing the enemy disposition or in choosing the axis on which to launch our attacks. It is difficult to plan an operation without such basics.

In Mushkoh, 79 Mountain Brigade's AAR says: "During active operations, any photo more than seven days old was found to be inaccurate." The Pakis kept changing the location of their tents, so the photographs, so important for intelligence gathering, ended up being useless pieces of bromide. In fact, the Pakis often pitched tents to fool us, for the tents were not even inhabited. It was a brilliant ploy on their part for we'd have wasted precious effort and time – planning an operation and then sending troops up heights that are eating men, tiring out the others and doing little for morale. As the brigade commander R. K. Kakkar noted, "No contact intelligence about the enemy was available.

The Brigade therefore had to operate in an environment which was characterized by an information void, lack of logistical infrastructure and tenuous axis of maintenance susceptible to enemy interference."

Unit after unit was deficient in weapons. Our unit was short of machine guns. 12 JAK LI (Jammu & Kashmir Light Infantry) was short of AGLs. Supposed to be authorized with eight, it had none. The Nagas were given INSAS rifles at the last moment. 2 Raj Rif was also short of AGLs. It was given new equipment like laser ranger finders but just before the build-up for an assault. This is what the unit's CO put in his report: "Last minute issuing of equipment absolves the staff of their responsibility of sending troops fully equipped but does not increase our fighting power as there is no time for training... if infantry has to be effective, then marrying up of man and equipment must take place before the assault and the soldier must be trained in its use. The use of equipment also has to be integrated into the tactical plan or the effect of modern equipment will continue to be marginal."

The CO of 1 Naga wrote later: "Due to the deployment of the unit in counter-insurgency operations, supporting weapons have not been issued for almost a year... adequate detachments of fire support weapons are not available. Prior to induction, the unit holding of MMGs was nil and these were issued just prior to the attack. The detachment could not even fire them, which could have given them the required confidence in the weapon. Unit is issued AK-47s during counter-insurgency operations. INSAS have been issued to the unit but due to non-availability of training ammunition, weapons cannot be fired and zeroed. A large number of young soldiers were posted to the unit in CI Ops to make up strengths and were not trained in INSAS. No time was available to the unit to run any kind of cadre or to get weapons zeroed."

Food and water were major limiting factors in the planning of operations. Lack of pre-packed meals and water added to the already high administrative burden of moving ammunition up for attack. The load carrying capacity of an individual is limited to 15 kg. In case extra weight is given, their speed of movement is drastically reduced.

Troops often went without food for more than 24 hours. Raj Rif learnt this lesson during its Tololing experience and realized that hot food for fighting troops raises the morale to a great extent. Besides, the troops located at firebase have to be sustained for over 72 hours and hence it is impractical to ferry food from the base to the roadhead. They decided then to establish a cookhouse halfway to the firebase, but that meant extra time spent looking for a safe area where the shells wouldn't take a further toll. Areas were selected under cover and in the dead zone of enemy artillery fire.

After mid-June, when the snow melted, water became a major problem. Says 12 Mahar in its war summary: "The points being totally arid, even water had to be carried up. The water situation is so precarious that throughout the two months of fighting, all including officers and JCOs, holding onto captured positions, sustained themselves on barely one litre of water per day in an area where dehydration occurs rapidly due to extremely dry climate."

At one stage, all the 58 battalions involved in counter-insurgency operations had been de-inducted from Kashmir. Yet, at our individual unit levels, we struggled because fighting troops were involved in other important battle tasks like Casualty Evacuation (Cas Evac) and as fighting porters. Since Cas Evac takes place mostly on foot, it not only consumed manpower but delayed evacuation as it took eight to ten hours to bring the injured down. Then, eight to ten soldiers were required to evacuate each of the injured. This often meant that the momentum of the attack suffered due to lack of adequate fighting troops. Brigadier Kakkar says in his report: "A large part of the fighting strength was employed on fighting porter duties, thus reducing the effective fighting strength. Over the arduous terrain obtaining in the brigade sector, net availability was reduced to 50 percent as one man can carry out porter duties only on alternate days."

Casualty Evacuation whether in Mushkoh, Dras or Kargil, became a major problem. Says Brig. Aul, in his report, "Cas Evac from forward locations is a tedious process and took eight to ten hours for casualties to reach the Advance Dressing Station. Cas Evac by helicopters was hampered due to enemy shelling and bad weather.... The need for quick evacuation of casualties needs no emphasis. Persons with stretchers need to be earmarked for this purpose before the commencement of operations. During recce, areas of helicopter evacuation need to be identified."

The lack of Artillery Locating Radar. Around 80 percent of casualties, fatal and non-fatal, were due to enemy shelling. So many lives could have been saved if, three years ago, Army Headquarters had gone ahead with its decision to purchase artillery locating radars. This vital piece of equipment traces the trajectory of approaching shells and calculates the location from where they have been fired. A team had visited the United States of America and almost placed an order worth ₹200 crore. Then, the DRDO said that these could be made indigenously. But nothing happened. By the time a decision was taken on their import, the nuclear tests at Pokhran on 11 May 1998 had forced the US to impose a ban on military purchases. The non-availability of these radars was sorely felt.

The bullet-proof jackets issued for counter-insurgency operations were too cumbersome for the mountains and could not be worn because of their weight – every bit of which counts at high altitudes – and also because it is difficult to kneel and crawl forward.

8 July

We are numb and exhausted, too exhausted even to sleep. Or rejoice. There will be no celebrations for us up here. Too many of our men have given their lives to retake barren pieces of land. The morning dawned on soldiers sprawled out across the feature. Some were completely exhausted, lying there with eyes wide open, unable to sleep. The rest were dead. Lt Balwan was in a daze. When he had set off for the assault, he had 20 soldiers. Now only two are still alive.

Below, the commanders are rejoicing. The taking of Tiger Hill was one reason. Now, it appears they had another. We got the story later from our fellow officers, that from Batalik, two days before we began our final assault on Tiger Hill, the first enemy soldier had been taken alive. He was captured by 12 JAK Light Infantry. His name is Inayat Ali and his passbook and other papers identified him as belonging to the Northern Light Infantry battalion based in Skardu. The flurry of frantic activity his capture unleashed is unbelievable. Senior officers in the Military Intelligence (MI) Directorate and Military Operations called every hour. They were in a hurry to lay their hands on the prize. "Get him, bring him down... airlift him. Just send him. Make sure there is no firing." The messages came thick and fast. Ali was their proof of Pakistani involvement. The biggest catch of the war. The diplomatic value would be priceless. They are so keen that he arrives safely that, incredibly, the generals even agreed to temporarily suspend operations. So long as Ali was dispatched to them alive, in one piece.

A special helicopter was arranged for him and, under heavy guard, he was brought down to the helipad. Throughout the six hours it took to bring him down the mountain, the frantic calls kept coming. Army Headquarters were monitoring his position almost step by step. His photographs needed to be splashed across the world. There was also the interrogation that would provide the answer to those vital questions: When did he first set foot on Indian soil? When did the first intrusion take place? What equipment was issued to them and by whom? How many other regular army battalions were involved?

My fellow officers in the Batalik sector already know the answers. They had accompanied Ali down the mountain and he had told them, while scrambling down, that he had crossed over into Batalik way back in November! He thought some others had crossed over even earlier. They needed to be in position before the snow came, so they could find the rocks and boulders they used to construct their bunkers. After November, this area is covered in at least 20 feet of snow.

This gave lie to the official version being put out by the defence ministry and the army spokesmen, that the intrusions had taken place in April. It suited the army brass and the government to stick to the story. The Opposition parties, we read in the papers, had been asking uncomfortable questions; accusing the government of having gone to Lahore at a time when the Pakistani Army had already occupied Indian territory.

Up here, we are starting to get the real story. By now, we have cleared enough of their positions to make an analysis of what they had left behind while fleeing. We have a bagful of documents: soldier's pay books, register entries, leave slips and personal diaries that give detailed accounts of the intrusion, the identity of the intruders, and their instructions. We also have their weapons with markings and numbers of the army units to which they belonged.

Reading the personal diaries of the Paki soldiers gave us a strange sort of satisfaction for they wrote of the hardships they had faced. But they also tell how they had been sitting on those heights for months and how the operation had been planned long before Prime Minister Vajpayee's bus rode into Lahore. Long before the handshakes and the warm embraces. We found scores of letters the Pakistani NLI soldiers received from their families that date back to August 1998. Lt Muhammad Maaz Ullah Khan, a young Pakistani soldier of the 8 Northern Light Infantry (NLI), whose personal diary was recovered from Point 4812, had left for Kargil from Rawalpindi as early as 1 January 1999. Interestingly, he began his diary with a verse from Ghalib: "*Ragon mein daurte phirne ke hum nahin kayal, Jo aankh se na tapka woh lahu kya hai….*"

The extracts of Lt Maaz Ullah Khan's personal diary prove, beyond any shadow of doubt, that the Pakistani Army had put its Kargil plan into action well before the year 1999 started. Lt Maaz Ullah was in only one of the Northern Light Infantry units which reached the LoC in early February – well before the Lahore bus journey made by the prime minister.

More shocking is the discovery that the Pakistani army chief, General Pervez Musharraf, had actually visited Mushkoh. The man who planned and set in motion the intrusion was actually on Indian soil! This was revealed in another personal diary, written by Capt. Hussain Ahmad and recovered from a bunker in Mushkoh. According to the diary, he came to Hussain post, located on Point 4815 in Mushkoh on 7 February 1999. Posted from 17 Frontier Force to 12 NLI, Capt Ahmad (I-card no: 064394) lists his CO's name – Lt Col Syed Ahmad Bashir – and talks of the Pak Army Chief Pervez Musharraf's visit to Mushkoh.

28 September
We try to equip ourselves as well as we can but already, we are having to deal with more bodies of soldiers dying of high-altitude pulmonary oedema (HAPO). Some others are being treated for frostbite. In this intense cold, taking off your gloves for a minute, necessary to obey calls of nature, is an invitation to frostbite.

The men are exhausted from erecting the new bunkers, made of fibre-reinforced plastic. But first, the men have to go out to clear the snow. We have already had the first snowfall in the higher reaches. It has to be beaten down so the tracks don't disappear. This is an avalanche-prone area and the bunkers have to be strategically located. Obviously, not every inch of the LoC can be guarded by foot soldiers. There are gaps between bunkers and for a patrol party to walk through the snow and cover a distance of only one kilometer takes between five and seven hours.

That is mostly what we are doing now, to protect the peaks. Teaching our boys the use of mountaineering equipment and snowmobiles. Teaching them to survive on meagre rations, in case the weather does not permit supplies to reach us at the forward posts. To subsist on what we call compo ration, which comprises 125 grams of vegetable pulao, 100 grams of *suji halwa* and some tea bags. There is also an emergency survival kit comprising a chocolate bar and some *chikki,* which is manufactured in Hyderabad and packed by the Defence Food Research Laboratory in Mysore.

If you fall sick, you have to pray that the hepter (helicopter) can land through the clouds which envelop us ever so often. HAPO bags and emergency medical kits have been kept in all the posts but they don't always suffice. Every unit has only one doctor each and he can't possibly be in all the posts or even handy when needed. There are nursing assistants too, but then there is little that they can do when your body gives up after being perpetually exposed to freezing winds, blizzards, and avalanches.

Even when the hepters come into land, the men have to furiously beat the snow and unroll the fibre-reinforced plastic so the chopper can make its descent. The only time I see some semblance of a smile on the faces of the men is when the mailbag arrives. It is the only thing that gives them warmth – those letters from home which bring them news of their families, their children, and their parents.

15 October

Guard duty is the worst possible assignment. All night,

the men have to sit in the freezing cold, eyes glued to the night vision devices which we have belatedly been issued. The army has been doing some hasty shopping. Apart from the NVDs, we now have decent Extremely Cold Climate Uniforms and proper alpine snow boots. It's on these peaks, at heights ranging between 12,000 and 18,000 feet, that we have now made our homes. The posts and structures had to be in place and equipped before the snow started. So, everything has to be carried up by mules or airlifted – food, kerosene oil, medicines, arms and ammunition.

18 October
Every day is a nightmare; brigade commanders total up the number of sorties made by the Mi-17s carrying supplies. Every evening, a report is submitted to Maj Gen Puri, who in turn informs Corps of the progress. Maj Gen Puri is in charge of the entire sector from Kaobal Gali in Kupwara at one end to Chorbat La at the other. Mules make their way up tracks, as far as they can go, after which supplies have to be carried by the troops. This exercise will carry on through October. So many helipads have to be constructed for airlifting supplies. Just carrying the fibre-reinforced plastic sheets is a task that seems to take forever. Each hut that houses four to six men weighs around 1500 kg. Each Mi-17 carries a load of about 1,000 kg. So, three sorties have to be made for every two huts.

In terms of rations, each man requires 1.7 kg of food and 2.7 litres of kerosene oil per day. Add to this the 500 g of special rations comprising soup packets, dry fruit, and Frooti tetra packs, which constitute high-nutrition food. For approximately 200 days of winter, it is necessary to stock one tonne per person and there are at least 20,000 troops now committed to holding the heights. And these don't include men drawn from support battalions like supply, ordnance, and medical, etc.

There is a new Forward Surgical Centre which has come up at Dras now. A centrally-heated underground hospital, which from experience is considered necessary in this sector. One thing is certain: the winter will take its own toll.... The doctors will continue to struggle to save frostbitten toes and fingers.

It is a no-war, no-peace situation. Artillery guns are in battle-ready mode and we are on constant alert. In this sector, far more treacherous than Siachen where there are roads that take you at least up to base camp, the approaches go through deep gorges. It is these gorges and peaks that an entire division of the army is now going to protect, unlike earlier when a brigade was in charge. During the war itself, five additional brigades had to be brought in to rescue Indian territory.

Territory is now being measured in terms of financial cost. Siachen, they say costs an approximate four crore a day, Kargil will need at least 10 crore a day. It's worth it, they'll tell you, to defend the nation's honour. And as they keep telling us: always be on guard, Pakistan now has a military executive heading their country. The same General Pervez Musharraf who conceived of the Kargil intrusion.

> We did our bit. We went beyond the call of duty. We fought in frozen wastelands where the snow often turned red. We struggled with faulty weapons but we did not turn back. We climbed dizzy heights, sometimes only to bring back our dead. But, we continued. We will continue to guard our borders and suffer the vagaries of weather. There is just about enough space for our men to sit in these snow habitats; lying down is a luxury, but they will continue uncomplainingly. This is, after all, the Indian Army. And we are, after all, doing our duty. It has to be done because, even though we forced the intruders out, we really didn't win the war. If we had, we wouldn't be sitting here – eyeball to eyeball.

~

The army top brass and the government learnt important lessons, but have the security gaps been filled? Is India better placed to take on the enemy if Pakistan devises another plan as sinister as Kargil? Has the ministry of defence, in charge of assessing and addressing battle-preparedness, been able to procure the vital, war-changing arms and ammunition that the armed forces would need?

The authors of the After Action Reports minced no words when it came to listing the impediments that made the battle tougher and contributed to more body bags.

A quarter century later – and going forward – we have cleared the fog of war over what really happened in the frigid heights of Kargil. The fog, however, persists over India's preparedness.

The peaks which were regularly vacated during the winter months till the war broke out in 1999, now cannot be left abandoned.

Can Kargil be repeated?

The Subrahmanyam Committee answered the question through the following observation: 'Pakistan's action at Kargil was not rational. Its behaviour patterns require to be carefully studied in order to gain a better understanding of the psyche of its leadership.'

Understanding Pakistan's 'behaviour patterns' is an important, critical aspect. There are several others.

Has India learnt its lessons from Kargil? The continuing assaults on India – over the two and a half decades since Kargil – provide some answers. India has been hit multiple times. In less than two years after the Kargil conflict, Pakistani-trained terrorists attacked the Indian Parliament in December 2001. The assault on the temple of India's democracy brought India and Pakistan to the brink of war once again and the armies of the two nations were caught in an eyeball-to-eyeball confrontation for several months.

Despite a complete analysis of the need to shore-up the country's intelligence-gathering abilities, 10 armed terrorists sailed to Mumbai, all the way from Karachi and held the financial nerve-centre hostage for over 72 hours, killing 166 innocents. The gaps in India's security establishment were prised open once again and many post-mortems done. Several prime ministers, I. K. Gujral, Manmohan Singh, and the more muscular-oriented Narendra Modi have been tested by Pakistan and its proxies.

Modi took the risk of allowing an ISI representative to be part of a Joint Investigations Team that visited India after another audacious attack on an Air Force base in Pathankot in January 2016, but Pakistan has done little – if nothing – to bring the terrorists to book. After the Pathankot attack, the advisor to the Pakistani prime minister admitted to the fact that the terrorists had made telephone calls to the Jaish-e-Mohammed headquarters in Bahawalpur, but the investigation made no headway.

Pakistan continues to hit India through non-state actors. The suicide attack on an army camp in Kashmir's Uri in September 2016 forced Modi to take political ownership of the surgical strikes that followed, but the strikes have failed to deter Pakistan.

The assaults have also exposed the chinks in India's armour. Fedayeens, determined to destroy and die, have repeatedly managed to find their way into well-guarded installations. They did that in Pathankot, where they even spent a night, undetected. Suicide squads managed to cut the wire and kill 18 unsuspecting soldiers in Uri. In January 2018, another squad breached the security to enter an army installation in Jammu's Sunjuwan.

In another brutal assault in February 2019 – months before the general election – a suicide bomber killed 40 CRPF troopers. A local Kashmiri belonging to the Jaish rammed an explosive-laden car into the CRPF convoy in South Kashmir's Pulwama.

Modi, who had redrawn the security matrix after Uri, used the Indian Air Force to carry out punitive strikes at a Jaish facility in Pakistan's Balakot. The Modi government has sent out clear signals of a zero-tolerance policy and refuses to engage with Pakistan. Talks and terrorism cannot go hand in hand, he and his ministers have reiterated. After the killings in Pahalgam, he put the Indus Water Treaty in abeyance and said, 'Blood and water cannot flow together.'

He and his government have now taken on a more belligerent tone and the new mantra is, '*Ghar mein ghus ke maaregein*' (We will enter your house and kill you).

In 1999, Pakistan had entered the 'ghar' in the hope of internationalizing the Kashmir issue. In 2025, Subrahmanyam's words rung alarmingly and devastatingly true. They are worthy of being repeated. 'Its behaviour patterns require to be carefully studied in order to gain a better understanding of the psyche of its leadership.'

The 'psyche' of Pakistan's leadership was playing out on television screens and ought to have been analysed by India's security managers. Pakistan was pointing fingers at India soon after the hijacking of an entire train that chugged out of Quetta in Balochistan, a mineral-rich province that has for long been up in arms against Pakistan's rulers, the military in particular. The dramatic hijacking, in March 2025, in which at least 29 security personnel were targeted and killed by the Balochistan Liberation Army, ought also to have been deeply analysed after several Pakistani ministers spoke of the 'India hand'. In a prescient column written in *FirstPost*, senior diplomat and strategic expert, Vivek Katju virtually predicted an attack on Indian soil, three weeks before the terrorists walked out of the woods in Pahalgam.

'...each army chief has to show that he is up to giving a "fitting" response, especially to an attack (the train hijacking) the institution he leads perceives or rather misperceives, has come from India. As such, it is possible that the Pakistan Army will attempt to sponsor a terrorist event in India within the foreseeable future.' The foreseeable future unfolded in Pahalgam on 22 April. A few days before that, Pakistan Chief of Army Staff General Asim Munir, in a provocative speech, reiterated the two-nation theory and underlined the cultural differences between 'Hindus and Muslims'. Like his predecessors, Munir referred to Kashmir as its 'jugular vein'.

The Modi government responded with Operation Sindoor and drew new red lines. Unlike the strikes after the attacks in Uri and Pulwama, the Indian Air Force hit at the heart of the Pakistan Army's domain in Punjab. Missiles targeted and damaged the headquarters of the LeT and JeM in Muridke and Bahawalpur respectively. The three-day military escalation that started on 7 May also hit Pakistan's airports and runways. To underline its 'zero tolerance for terror' stance, the government also sent seven all-party delegations to 32 different countries. Beijing was not amongst the list of India's global outreach.

The bottom line is simply this: Several strategic experts are predicting another attack and if and when that takes place, will Donald Trump jump in again as the crisis manager? Are India and Pakistan now going to be caught in a dangerous tit for tat escalation that will necessitate the intervention of foreign capitals because two nuclear neighbours remain in a state of heightened tension?

India cannot afford to lower its guard. It is now also facing a challenge on its border with China, even though there are some signs of a thaw. The question then is, what is the level of India's preparedness? To answer this question, it is necessary to dig deeper into the previous decades.

In a signed column, written sixteen years after Kargil, General V. P. Malik – who was the chief of army staff during the Kargil war – said, 'Our western border is much better manned than before. More troops have been deployed on the LoC and a border fence has been constructed. We also have surveillance satellites, unmanned aerial vehicles, thermal imagers, radars and ground sensors, which were non-existent in 1999. But apart from that, we do not seem to have learnt any important lessons from that war. The modernization of the armed forces continues to lag behind. The existing state of weapons and equipment could be sufficient for border skirmishes, but if they escalate, which can never be ruled out, deficiencies of weapons and ammunition and the lack of modernization will make the present day Chiefs repeat what I had said long ago – "We shall fight with whatever we have." Over the years, our capability to deter the adversary has been seriously eroded.'

The vulnerability is more than evident. His words remind me of what I witnessed for the two months that I was in Kargil. In 1999, young officers and men won the day for the nation, despite unimaginable odds: shortage of men and machines, guns that didn't open up, missile warheads that didn't fire.

Twenty-five years after Kargil – and now after Pahalgam

– the question, have we learnt our lessons, remains relevant. General Malik provided some answers but here is what a 2017 report by the Comptroller and Auditor General of India (CAG) found: 61 of 152 types of ammunition, considered critical by the Indian Army to fight a war, were available for just 10 days. The report, tabled in Parliament in July pointed out that the army is meant to hold ammunition to fight a 20 day war.

Ironically – and worryingly – that is the last report on the preparedness of the armed forces in the public domain. CAG is still doing its audits and submitting their reports to Parliament but not uploading them on its site. The only clue to India's current preparedness is contained in a statement put out by the audit agency in 2023. It said, 'The Comptroller and Auditor General of India has flagged that the replacement of existing artillery guns with state-of-the-art guns has been progressing at a "slow pace" for over last two decades.'

The reason why the reports are not being made available was revealed by Rajiv Mehrishi, the head of the audit institution, who retired in 2020. He said it was his decision to not upload reports relating to defence audits. He detailed how the 2017 report regarding the lack of ammunition caused a controversy. Posted in the home ministry then, Mehrishi in an interview later to *The Indian Express* said, 'When I was in Home [Ministry], there was a lot of tension with Pakistan. At that time, there was a CAG report detailing a shortage of ammunition. Basically, if there is a shortage, then at least the enemy should not know about it.... At least we are not making it available on the tap of a button. *Koi Washington me dekh raha hai, Beijing me bhi dekh raha hai, Islamabad mein bhi dekh raha hai* (The report was being seen in Washington, Beijing, and Islamabad). Therefore, we took a decision.'

For the sake of transparency, it is imperative that governments keep Parliament, and their citizens informed. Transparency is vital for a democracy. It cannot and should not be kept cloaked. That only adds to the fog of information as also to the fog of war.

The Deep, Dark World of Illegal Immigration

When we flew from London to Brussels, making sure to pack what we called 'refugee clothes', we had no idea how we would be able to make our first contact with an agent. Hindi and Punjabi were my only armour but was that enough to unravel a carefully crafted racket that involved getting past border controls and immigration authorities?

In December 2023, a chartered plane landed at France's Vatry airport. The 303 Indian passengers aboard Legend Airlines' flight had cleared security immigration and customs in UAE and were on their way to Nicaragua.

The halt at Vatry was not expected to take longer than an hour. The plane was being refuelled when, a tip-off revealed that the passengers on board were being trafficked to Nicaragua, from where they would probably be taken to the United States or to Canada.

The 60-minute halt stretched to four days. It was clear that the plane was a 'donkey flight', a catch-all term that references illegal movements. Most of the passengers had paid large sums, in the range of ₹40 to 60 lakh each. While a few remained and applied for asylum, most of them returned to Mumbai. The plane was directed back to India because neither UAE nor Nicaragua was willing to let it land on their soil.

As I scoured the newspapers for more details, I was reminded of a sting operation I had done on illegal immigration almost 30 years ago. I was struck by how the quest for foreign shores remains unchanged and how the modus operandi had undergone a sea change from the time I did my first sting operation while on a scholarship in London.

The Chevening scholarship, for which I spent three months in London, in 1994, entailed an internship. Vinay Kamath, from the *Hindu* newspaper, and I were taken on board by UK's Independent Television (ITV). The channel was investigating a story on illegal immigration for its popular programme, 'The Cook Report'. That Vinay and I spoke Hindi and Punjabi worked to our advantage. The channel provided us spy cameras that we learnt how to use.

Posing as immigrants who wanted to illegally cross into the UK from Belgium, we were able to infiltrate the vast network of agents. The dangerous business of sending illegals was run mostly by South Asians. Operating from countries like Belgium, France, and Germany, which are separated from mainland UK by the channel, the agents we met were transporting immigrants by the hundreds every month.

When we flew from London to Brussels, our bags packed with 'refugee clothes' (a shirt and a salwar, in my case), we did not know how to make the first contact with an agent. How do you begin to penetrate the netherworld in a completely new country? While I had language as my armour, was that enough to unravel a carefully crafted racket that involved getting past border controls and immigration authorities?

'Talk to other South Asians. I'll drop you off at the Grand-Place [central square in Brussels],' the ITV producer who had travelled with us, said. She had hired a car after we landed in Brussels and told us exactly where she would park and wait, as we tried our luck at finding a contact who would help us in our mission.

To my utter surprise and horror, we hit pay dirt as soon as we walked around the square. The square had several outlets including a big shop that sold Godiva chocolates. I stopped at a lace shop and chatted up a salesgirl. 'Were there any Indians who I could speak to,' I asked her, and she pointed to what are popularly called 'night shops'.

We entered the night shop pretending to be customers. Indian music playing in the background gave me the comfort to walk up to the salesman to strike up a conversation.

'Why is it so difficult to go to England,' I asked him, in Hindi, in a hushed whisper. He neither looked at me nor did he bat an eyelid. He had other customers seeking his attention. I stood there holding my breath till he glanced at me and said, 'You want to go to England. No problem. Who said it is difficult?' It was almost as if I were one of the customers who he was doling out provisions to.

I was waiting for him with trepidation. His colleague at the night shop, Zulfikar, I was told, was at that precise moment, on his way to England. 'Come back tomorrow and speak to Zulfikar yourself. He's gone there to get married and will be back in the morning. That, we discovered was only one of the tricks of the trade used by immigrants to secure citizenship. Zulfikar went to England illegally, exchanged marital vows and came back and deposited his marriage certificate in Brussels, to claim citizenship. Registering marriages in England was far easier than it was in Belgium.

Zulfikar was happy to become a Belgian citizen. All he needed to do was find a woman who was willing to be called his wife on paper. We got our first lead but still needed to find out how the illegals made their journey from Brussels to London. The salesman at the night shop provided more details.

A majority of the illegal immigrants had set their dreams on London, for multiple reasons. Many already had friends and relatives in London. UK was safer than Belgium, France or Germany, for another reason. It was easier to pick up odd jobs there as well as to escape the police dragnet. Given the number of Indians and Pakistanis living in Britain, the chances of getting caught were almost nil as the illegals would easily assimilate with their countrymen.

We bid goodbye to the salesman after he gave us the name and number for an agent and quickly made our way out of the night shop. The producer who was waiting a little distance away was apprehensive about why we had returned so early.

We had a number, we told her. 'Get out of your refugee clothes. We're going out for dinner,' she said with a broad smile as we filled her in with the details of what we had found.

After the first vital input, we moved briskly. Each agent we met put us on to another, each explaining painstakingly how they would help us reach London. All we needed was to make an advance payment of £2,000.

Finding an agent was as easy as buying lace in Brussels or diamonds in Antwerp.

Finding an agent to transport me illegally from Belgium into England, I discovered, was much simpler than trying to get in with valid papers. Forget visas, you didn't even need a passport. A passport in fact, was a deterrent. You should have nothing that even remotely connects you to your country of origin, be it a passport, a driving licence, or any kind of identity card, we were told. Now, all we needed to do as the agents who transport immigrants in lorries revealed, was to cook up a story about how some political party in India was hounding us by slapping fake charges. You could also say that you dared to differ with their ideology. That was enough to apply for asylum in Belgium.

Vinay and I were quick at finding our own 'story'. We were a runaway couple, we said, elaborating that our families were against an interfaith marriage. The agents were not interested in quizzing us to verify our story. Not one of them even asked us how we had reached Brussels. All they were interested in, was the £2,000. We were just one of many illegals who they hoped to make money out of.

As we dug ourselves into the rabbit hole of research, we came across a wide cast of characters. We also managed to unearth the modus operandi through spy cam conversations with several agents.

One among them was Mohammed Shafi, a resident of Lal Chowk in Srinagar. He worked at one of the late-night stores and had applied for political asylum in Belgium on the grounds that he was being harassed by the security forces in Kashmir. He had said he feared ending up as a victim of 'custodial deaths'. Shafi had worked his way into Belgium through Romania, Poland, and Germany, crossing the borders of each country with the help of agents.

Tusavar Shah, an Antwerp-based agent who had made it to Belgium from Pakistan also had a story. 'I told the authorities that Benazir Bhutto's Pakistan People's Party (PPP) would have put me in jail only because I was a supporter of her opponent, Nawaz Sharif.' The more imaginative the story, the better, it appeared.

It didn't matter even if you were not granted political asylum. It was enough to have a record to show that you had applied and that your papers were being processed. That single piece of paper was worth its weight in gold. It ensured that in the event of being caught by the immigration authorities on either side (in Belgium or in England), you were not put in a detention centre before being deported to India but sent back to the country from which you attempted to cross into the UK.

The course of action was simple, though not without risk. Once a contact in England had agreed to pay £2,000, all you had to do was put yourself in the hands of one of the agents, get into a lorry packed with other illegals and sail across one of the border ports. Judging by the number of people who successfully entered the UK using this route, the chances of getting caught were only about one in a thousand.

Ram Avtar Rana, one of the agents, tried to address my apprehension when I questioned him about the inherent dangers and the likelihood of getting caught. 'Don't worry. Your main concern is reaching England. In the last five years, only one lorry was apprehended and even then, the immigrants were sent back to Belgium,' he said.

Rana, a resident of Punjab had come to Belgium two years before I met him in 1994. He worked closely with Nirmal Singh who lived in another Belgian town, Liege. He would send illegal immigrants in lorries and cars that left Brussels at least once every week. Singh had made this lucrative 'profession' his source of livelihood. He earned a minimum of ₹60,000 a week, while Rana got a commission for every immigrant he passed onto Singh.

Given the profitability and the low risk involved, it was not surprising that Indian and Pakistani agents had converted it into a thriving business. After our first conversation at the night store, we had little trouble penetrating the dark underbelly of illegal immigration.

Most Indians and Pakistanis we met were willing to give us the telephone number of an agent. Several, including Tusavar Shah, offered to personally put us into a lorry. They were also generous about providing food and shelter. Portions of the transcript below were used by ITV and also reproduced in *India Today*. The article was a part of the submission I made at the end of the Chevening scholarship.

Harinder Baweja (HB): Can you please help? I have lost my passport and need to get into England.

Shah: It's okay, don't worry. Treat this as your own house. It will cost you money, but I will see that you reach there. I send many people across – at least 30 to 35 every week.

HB: How much will it cost?

Shah: Around £2,000. But do you have a relative in England who'll pay the money for you?

HB: Yes.

Shah: Why don't you talk to him and give me his number because we also have to be satisfied.

HB: How are the immigrants transported?

Shah: In trucks. It will be a very big truck.

HB: How soon will the truck leave?

Shah: You can be in London tomorrow if you speak to your relative today.

HB: Where do the lorries leave from?

Shah: You are not supposed to know all that. I'll drive you down to the port. Why are you getting worried? Leave everything to me.

HB: Won't there be any checking?

Shah: No, no.

HB: Isn't it dangerous?

Shah: No, not at all. Trucks go every week and it is my responsibility to see that you reach safely.

HB: What if the truck is stopped?

Shah: Since you have come to me, it is only fair that I give you the right advice. Why don't you apply for political asylum? It only takes a day. God forbid, if you are stopped, then they'll send you back here and not deport you to India.

HB: On what grounds will I get to stay?

Shah: Just say that you had problems with the political party in India.

HB: Won't they recheck the story from India?

Shah: No, no, there's never any inquiry.

HB: Where will the truck leave from?

Shah: Don't worry. We can't disclose such information. It could be from Liege or some other port.

HB: How many hours does the crossing take?

Shah: About six to seven hours.

HB: Are you sure the truck won't be stopped?

Shah: Why are you so worried? The truck is shut and before you realize, you'll be in England.

Money. That is all the agents were interested in. Each one, in fact, saw me as a prospective customer who would be billed £2,000. They were not only polite and helpful, they even offered to put me up at their homes saying the accommodation and food would be free. The most effective strategy was for me to tell them that I had been robbed of all my travel documents and money. That, for them was the most exciting bit of information, for other than using their services, I had no other means of reaching England. They even called my friend Altaf – who had been briefed in advance – in England to confirm that he would pay the money once the lorry ferrying me reached the UK. What happens to immigrants whose relatives fail to turn up with the money, I asked, and

Shah, the Antwerp-based agent, gave away his criminal leanings, saying: We have our ways of setting the police on them.

The agents themselves, ironically, were not scared of being found out by the police or of their lorries being impounded by the immigration authorities. As Shah explained: We use lorries registered in England, so the immigration officers just wave them by. That was an assertion I found difficult to believe until I spoke to the press officer at the Immigration Desk myself. According to official figures, only about 500 immigrants were detected, each year, trying to enter the country in lorries. A minuscule number, given the fact that each agent was sending approximately 1,500 immigrants into England each year. Belgium, as we discovered, was teeming with agents.

Vinay and I were very pleased with our investigation but the ITV producer who accompanied us to Brussels wanted me and Vinay to hand ourselves over to one of the agents. I was doing most of the talking and was more than just a little aghast. How could she, a colleague, expect me to be a part of a journey that was totally illegal? We'd already escaped being outed when, at one of the many night stores, I found Vinay furiously gesticulating at me. I couldn't understand why, until he came forward to whisper that one of the wires of the spy cam had fallen and was visible under my 'refugee kurta'.

You have to keep your composure and playact a role while conducting sting operations. Strapping on the spy cam was the easy part; supressing the journalist in me was not. I had to learn to be subtle and resist the temptation of shooting questions, one after the other. Arousing the suspicion of the person you are recording is risky business.

However, there are lines even I wouldn't cross. I was absolutely clear I would NOT put myself into one of those lorries. The producer hinted at two options, both of which were insulting, annoying, and racist. She presumed we 'South Asians' would be willing to take money from ITV to complete the journey.

I was neither an 'illegal' nor was I going to agree to be a part of any unlawful activity. I conveyed my thoughts to the producer in no uncertain terms.

I was not willing to be human cargo.

The only reason I haven't mentioned her name is because, sadly, I have forgotten it.

I understood that she wanted to close the loop on the investigation, but we were not going to help with that, by becoming illegals. I had my scholarship to complete and a job and family to return to in India.

We returned to London to transcribe the Hindi and Punjabi conversations into English. Soon after, I learnt that ITV had hired Tariq, a Pakistani national, to pose as an immigrant and journey to England in a lorry. Armed with a camera concealed in a handbag, Tariq sat in the back of a lorry amidst a dozen other immigrants, with no water or food for 22 hours until they reached England. He had a tough time breathing, while some of the other immigrants vomited and gasped for air inside the 40-foot-long trailer, meant ostensibly for carting cargo.

The lorry Tariq travelled in, entered the UK border undetected, adding 12 more to the growing number of illegal immigrants entering England. According to our conversations with the agents, Belgium alone was transporting at least one lakh illegal immigrants annually. Each agent was sending 20 to 30 immigrants every week. There were, according to our investigation, a minimum of 100 agents making a quick buck through immigrants desperate to reach England where they worked as labourers earning two pounds an hour. Their day ended with about 20 pounds in their pockets. The pound in the mid-90s was approximately equal to about 50 rupees. A thousand rupees at the end of each day added up to more than they could have earned in India.

It was this desperation that the agents were exploiting.

The network of agents has expanded and so has the desperation of those willing to risk their lives. Entire families try and reach Canada or the USA. The flight that returned from Vatry to Mumbai is a testimony to just how determined scores of Indians have become in their pursuit of setting foot on foreign soil. They are willing to risk sneaking past border controls and sniffer dogs. The agents have mastered the art of finding the loopholes. Only a handful of them are outed and arrested. The most heartbreaking account of the Vatry flight came from French prosecutors who told the media that 11 of the passengers aboard that flight were unaccompanied minors, who were put under special administrative care. Where were their parents? Were they on another chartered flight? We may never know the answers.

Police officials investigating the Nicaragua case are familiar with the reasons why the agents seldom get outed. As many as 150 passengers aboard the chartered plane were from Punjab. According to one police investigator I spoke to, the main problem is that such cases 'end in a compromise between the immigrant and the agent'. The immigrants were reluctant to reveal the names of the agents, and the police found it hard to proceed against the passengers because most of them had valid visas for Nicaragua. The reason why the passengers didn't divulge information is also because despite being sent back, they still hadn't given up on their dream of trying to reach a First World country.

A first information report (FIR) filed in Amritsar details how the agents ensnare young men bewitched with the idea of going abroad. Damanpreet Singh, 24, a resident of a village near Amritsar told the police that an agent approached him and said, why don't you try and go to Europe. You have another brother who can stay back to help your father who is a farmer. The agent promised to send Singh to Portugal for a fee of ₹11 lakh.

The sum was huge, but Singh was told he could pay in instalments. On an initial payment of ₹60,000, Singh was soon on his way to Dubai, where he was received by a sub-agent. He waited in Dubai to travel to Portugal, but was instead sent to Azerbaijan on a tourist visa. By then, Singh had paid another instalment of one lakh rupees. The Portugal dream was cut short when Singh was told to check in but not show up at the boarding gate. 'My lawyer will meet you,' he was told by the sub-agent.

There was no lawyer, and Singh was left in the lurch. The sub-agent had vanished, and Singh was deported to India where he was grilled by immigration authorities. But as per the FIR, he did not reveal the name of his agent. On his return to his village in Amritsar, he called the India agent and asked him to return his money. This time, the agent offered to send him to Australia. Still hopeful, Singh agreed.

The agent accompanied Singh to Delhi and booked him on a flight to Bangkok and handed him an E-visa for Australia. He was finally on his way out of India, Singh thought, until the authorities at Bangkok airport told him that the Australian visa was fake. He would have to return to India.

Singh was back in his village for the second time. The agent now gave him a cheque when Singh pressed him to return his money, but the cheque bounced. The agent finally returned ₹70,000, and this time promised to send him to America. Singh reached the UAE, from where he boarded the flight to Nicaragua. The refuelling halt at Vatry sealed his fate. He was forced to return to his village for the third time. When Singh filed an FIR this time, he named the agent. Tarsem Singh was arrested but is probably out on bail because as the official investigating the case said, 'They usually get bail after spending about three months in jail.' In India, charges of fraud are easily bailable.

The agents aren't deterred. They are soon in search of fresh recruits, who are not hard to find. They know the journey is perilous, but the power of the European and

American dream is so strong, it overtakes the fear of what they know could also end in death.

Two years after I returned from my scholarship in London came news of a terrible tragedy. Illegal immigrants from India, Pakistan, and Sri Lanka died in the hundreds after a 'slave ship' sank in the seas between Malta and Sicily on Christmas night 1996. I was still working at *India Today* and flew to Athens where a few survivors had been apprehended by the Greek authorities.

The survivors described the night when they finally saw the twinkling lights of Italy and how desperate they were to walk on land. They had been sailing for over two months and the lights bore the promise of a better tomorrow.

But disaster was soon to follow. It was a full moon night, and the sea was choppy. The waves, one survivor said, were 'two storeys high' and the Ionian Sea was buoyant and angry. The temperatures were sub-zero but the 464 illegals aboard the ship named *Yiohan*, were not far from docking. They could see the blinking lights of the smaller boat making its way towards them. A new life, a better one, was finally within reach.

Balwinder Singh stared at the lights, dazzled and bewitched. He had spent ₹2.80 lakh to undertake a journey from his village in Punjab and had already been sailing for over two months. The destination was finally in sight, he thought to himself.

Suddenly, everything went horribly wrong. He found the sea lashing at his legs. The crew aboard *Yiohan* had informed them in broken English that three smaller boats would take them to their last stop. The twinkling lights

Balwinder had seen belonged to the ferry that was making its way towards their ship.

Let loose from the hatches – otherwise used to store refrigerated fish – the immigrants made a dash and jumped into the ferry, in a mad scramble. However, instead of three, only one ferry had come.

'The crew didn't stop us. Nor did they warn us that the ferry had been loaded beyond capacity,' recalled Jaspal Singh, one of the other survivors.

According to some of the Indian survivors who I later interviewed, the crew of the ferry were drunk and while it attempted to sail, it hit the *Yiohan*. 'We weren't worried then,' recalled Jaspal. There was a crack, and some water started seeping in, but the crew told them not to worry.

Within the next half hour, the men in the lower berth crept up as the water started filling up. Soon they were knee deep in it. The crew asked them not to panic and told them to scoop out the water using buckets.

Sucha Singh, another survivor, recalled some of them stuffing extra bits of clothing into the crack, but soon the captain of the ferry was radioing *Yiohan*, sailing in front of the ferry. Youssef al Halal, *Yiohan*'s captain, returned and threw a rope towards the ferry but the sinking boat's captain used it to haul himself to safety rather than to moor the sinking ferry.

The ferry's engine had packed up and it was losing momentum, swirling in the waters. Once again, it hit *Yiohan* and this time some of the human cargo fell into the water. Screams of '*bachao, bachao*' (save us) rent the cold night and fell silent as the winds wailed past a sinking boat.

Pandemonium had struck. Though the news broke only on 30 December, at least 283 men, women, and children drowned that night – making it one of the worst maritime disasters in the Mediterranean Sea.

Balwinder, one of the survivors, was among those who had managed to catch hold of a rope thrown by those aboard *Yiohan* and tie it around his wrist. 'But I couldn't haul myself up because I was wearing four layers of clothes which were wet and heavy. I was lucky that the boys on top noticed me,' he told me later when I met him in Greece.

Italy was where they were supposed to reach. Instead, the survivors were told they would now have to go to Greece and that the journey would take another three days. After five days, and what seemed like a lifetime, 175 of the 464 illegal immigrants saw land and sighed with relief. 'During these five days,' recalls Jaspal, 'most of the sailing was done by night and as before, the crew kept changing the ship's colour and name.'

Onshore at Sipia beach, in the Greek district of Nafpleon, the immigrants threw themselves on the ground and kissed the earth. Balwinder, set foot on dry land for the first time in nearly four months, since 3 October 1996, the day he had set sail from Adana in Turkey.

The moment of freedom, the survivors discovered, was short-lived, for soon two Indians and three Pakistanis arrived. Every new destination, every new stop has a different set of sub-agents. Closed trucks had already been parked at Sipia beach, to take the survivors in four batches of 40 to 45 to different destinations. They were taken to a farmhouse tucked away in a grove where they were asked to wait for three days before they would be put on another ship to Italy. The word 'ship' terrified them. 'We were scared that we would be put into containers and dumped in the sea,' said Jagtar, sitting in Greece's Nafpleon police station.

How did they end up here?

One night in the farmhouse, the starving survivors had decided to throw caution to the wind. They were not willing to hit the high seas again. And so on 30 December, Ermioni, a small Greek village with a population of only 2,100, woke up to find a group of South Asians wandering about the village, queuing up outside a food store. Others approached taxi drivers to drive them to Athens.

Alerted by the taxi drivers, the Nafpleon police soon swooped down on the immigrants and arrested 107 of them, while a batch of 68 managed to escape.

The survivors narrated stories of how desperation had led them to hope.

I remember Paramjit, in particular. A resident of village Narangpur in Punjab's Jalandhar, he said he was 'Class X pass' and tired of earning ₹1,600 a month as a welder in a factory. From a small village which had only 20 houses, Paramjit's family was only one of the three which had not sent sons abroad. 'The remaining 17 homes are happier and richer, and I wanted to improve my home too, after my father's death,' the 22 year old had told me, clutching his few belongings – a tracksuit, a toothbrush, and some writing pads and a pen – all provided by the local gurdwara authorities who came to the Nafpleon police station to help them contact their families. I had travelled to Athens and onward to Nafpleon, with the help of embassy officials. The nightmare endured by the survivors was detailed in *India Today* magazine in February 1997. The magazine invested time and money to unravel the racket in illegals.

Paramjit was happy to have survived but was not looking forward to going back to Narangpur. Two and a half of their three acres of land was mortgaged so that he could pay the ₹2.80 lakh the agent had demanded.

Paramjit sat with me at the police station and sobbed silently. Italy is where he wanted to be. At that moment, he didn't know where his future would take him. All he knew was that he was being dragged back to the past. Narangpur is not where he wanted to be.

I tracked the case for a few months. *Yiohan* had not been found. It had probably changed its name, flag, and its colour. According to the maritime authorities in Greece, this was common practice.

The survivors revealed the route the agents had used. They had been flown to Amman and onwards to Istanbul. From the Turkish capital the illegals were taken to Adana, from where sub-agents took them to the port. They then set sail on *Yiohan*. Those lucky to survive the choppy seas and escape the sinking ferry were finally rescued by the Indian embassy in Greece.

Embassies have to step in to help citizens both legal and illegal. The Indian embassy in France was roped in after the chartered flight that landed in Vatry was suspected of carrying human cargo. More recently, the government has had to help desperate Indians who were flown to Moscow by greedy agents on the promise that they would be employed in various Russian ministries for a monthly salary of ₹1.5 lakh. The lure of such a big amount saw several make their way there but once they reached Moscow, they were forced into fighting the war at the Russia-Ukraine border, that began in February 2022. Hapless Indians found themselves signing forms in Russian, a language they could neither read nor write. After rudimentary training in the use of weapons, they were forced to dig trenches at the frontline. Several videos of desperate Indians stuck in the war theatre have been circulating on social media. According to the Ministry of External Affairs (MEA), 96 Indians have been discharged from the Russian Army while 12 have died in Russia, and 12 have been classified as missing.

The MEA provided facts and figures after the death of Binil Babu in January 2025. The 32-year-old electrician from Kerala died on the Russia-Ukraine border amid desperate calls for help. Before he was killed, Binil was sending voice notes to the *The Indian Express*. 'Mentally and physically, we are exhausted.... We are now in difficult terrain in the Russia-occupied territory of Ukraine. Our commander says that the contract was for a year. We have been pleading with local commanders for our release. The Indian Embassy is of the view that unless the Russian Army relieves us, they cannot help. The embassy says we should be taken back to Russian territory,' he told the newspaper.

Binil is one amongst many who were not released by the Russian Army – despite the grave issue of Indians being used as slave labour in an external war – being taken up at the highest levels.

The allure of a foreign country and the desperate urge to overcome economic distress lie at the heart of human trafficking. The network of agents adroitly uses social media and YouTube links to lure the dreamers. The same online world is also full of videos of young men stuck at the Russia-Ukraine frontline, but that hasn't shortened the queue of those who want to fly abroad.

Several young men who have returned from Russia have narrated heart-rending stories of how they were duped but the chance of increasing one's monthly earnings from ₹30,000 to ₹1.5 lakh is an offer they find hard to resist.

Agents have become smarter. They advise their clients to first visit countries where it's either easy to get visas or there is an option to get one on arrival. 'Build your travel history,' the agents advice and that's how so many were sent to Moscow on a tourist visa. Those who went to Moscow were also told they would be helped with work permits. They were tricked into believing that they would be appointed as helpers in government offices.

It was only after landing that the men realized that the 'government office' was in fact a battlefield.

Many returned after Prime Minister Modi took up the matter with his counterpart, Vladimir Putin, but there are unfortunate ones who died or received injuries that required reconstruction surgeries.

I have been in touch with the family of 22-year-old Gagan from village Sirsala, 7 kilometer from Kurukshetra, Haryana. His parents, Gulabchand and Neelam last heard from him on 13 April 2024. Their anxiety levels have shot up since the MEA put out the number of those missing. Is Gagan in the 'missing' category or is he a part of an unknown statistic? The family is desperate for an answer.

The netherworld of illegal immigration, populated by greedy agents, has swallowed several youths who have died in jungles, in the battlefield, and in snow-clad wastelands.

The perils of illegal immigration continue to make headlines. I helped crack the modus operandi of those wanting to enter the UK, 30 years ago.

In February 2025, three decades later, a US military plane landed in Amritsar carrying deportees who had been handcuffed and shackled. The process of deportation, started by President Donald Trump's administration, is likely to continue. Only 104 came back with their legs chained. According to official data released by the US authorities, there are 7 lakh illegal Indians in America. Many made it past the Mexico border while several were arrested by security patrols.

The business of illegals will continue, despite the deportees narrating harrowing experiences of how they were cheated by their agents as they walked through frigid wastelands.

Families with minor children are willing to make the arduous journey, an investigating officer told me. 'The lure is too strong. They think they are going legally but stumble upon the harsh realities of dodging border patrols. By then, it is too late to turn back.'

The 'I have a dream' principle that drives Indians to undertake perilous journeys often reminds me of the song by pop group Abba...

I have a dream, a fantasy...
To help me through, reality...
And my destination makes it worth the while...
Pushin' through the darkness, still another mile...

The number of Indians pushing through the darkness – by land, air or sea – are selling their homes and falling deeper into debt but are unwilling to give up on the dream.

Despite the journey being fraught with danger and many casualties, 90,415 Indians tried to enter the United States via Mexico or Canada without valid papers between October 2023 and September 2024, as per data compiled by the US Customs and Border Protection agency. According to *The Times of India* which published the data, about 10 Indians were caught every hour trying to cross the land border into the US without a visa. How many actually made it across, undetected, will never be known.

The youth of Punjab are not the only ones aspiring for a better future. Roughly 50 percent of those who tried to enter the United States were from Gujarat. The shocking report of a family from Gujarat who froze to death at the US-Canada border in January 2022 made international headlines. The Canadian police found the family of four, including two children aged 11 and 3, lying frozen in an empty field on 19 January. They had died 12 metres from the US border after being caught in a blizzard in temperatures that were 35 degrees below freezing.

Indians from all states are pursuing the dream of a better future. Those who found themselves digging trenches for the Russian army included residents of Karnataka, Kashmir, and Telengana.

The geography has expanded. The network of agents and sub-agents spans continents. Their tentacles have spread far and wide and their rates have shot up from 2 lakh to 60 lakh rupees.

The lyrics of the Abba chartbuster 'I have a dream' has another line, 'I believe in angels… I'll cross the stream.'

In the dark world of illegal immigration, the agents are not 'angels'.

Above: Bhindranwale's warriors atop Akal Takht in the Golden Temple complex on the eve of Operation Blue Star. Courtesy: Sondeep Shankar.

Below: The author with J. F. Ribeiro, DGP, Punjab in 1986.

India Today editor-in-chief Aroon Purie celebrating the release of the Kargil book.

Dawood Ibrahim with Chhota Rajan before the underworld kingpins' split.
Courtesy: *India Today* magazine.

Officers of 18 Grenadiers celebrating the capture of Tiger Hill in Kargil, July 1999.

The author with army troops who fought the war in Kargil.

The Taliban after they took control of Afghanistan in 1996.

The Taliban laying down arms to offer prayers on the outskirts of Kabul.

Prime Minister Nawaz Sharif soon after Pakistan went nuclear in 1998.

The only Indian journalist to visit the Lashkar-e-Taiba headquarters in Muridke, Lahore. It was targeted and destroyed during Operation Sindoor in May 2025. Courtesy: *Aaj Tak.*

Kuka Parray, the leader of Ikhwan-e-Muslimeen, the Indian Army's rogue army. Courtesy: *India Today* magazine.

A soldier guarding a Srinagar street soon after the Valley was shut down in August 2019, when the state's special status was changed.

Kashmiri Pandit migrants in Jammu's refugee camps after they left the Valley fearing for their lives in 1990. Courtesy: *India Today* magazine.

Muzaffar Wani (centre) at the grave of his son, Burhan Wani, a Hizbul Mujahideen commander killed in an encounter in 2016.

Kar sevaks atop the domes of 16th-century Babri Masjid in Ayodhya on 6 December 1992, the day it was demolished. Courtesy: Prashant Panjiar/*India Today* magazine.

The author at the Brussels square in Belgium, where finding illegal immigration agents was as easy as buying lace.

EPILOGUE

'Who is your role model?'

It is a question I have been asked often. Each time I try and answer it, my mind throws up names of people I've met in the course of my life through conflict. I visualize several faces and most come attached with a location.

The faces and locations swirl in my head. The powerful memories refuse to fade. Time doesn't always allow the pain of conflict to recede. I think of the many families I met in Delhi's dharmshalas where frightened Hindus from Punjab took refuge. I think also about the thousands of Kashmiri Pandit families who were forced to live wretched lives in Jammu's tents. Just how do they accept the unpalatable fact that their homes – once situated in the picturesque towns and villages of chinar-lined roads and apple orchards – are no longer home?

I think also of a group of women who assembled without fail, in a Srinagar park near the iconic Lal Chowk, every week. Representing an organization called Association of Parents of Disappeared Persons (APDP), the group was led by Parveena Ahangar, whose son Javaid, disappeared one night in August 1990. She is the active face of the group comprising what Kashmiris refer to as 'half widows'.

Conflicts add words and phrases to its dictionary and 'half widows' – unique to the Kashmir Valley – are a group of women whose husbands have gone missing but have not been declared dead. Uncertainty is always more difficult to deal with than the finality of death. The 'half widows' received support from civil society and advocacy groups but their – and their children's – lives remain caught in a twilight zone, compounded by economic hardship and psychological stress.

Over the years, governments – at the state and the Centre – have paid scant attention to the deep psychological wounds inflicted by conflict. I remember Parveena telling me one evening, when I sat with her in the park, in her halting mix of Urdu and Hindi, that while the women were hunting their men down in police stations, detention centres, jails, and burial grounds, all they were told by the police and the soldiers was that they are a part of Kashmir, which is an 'atoot ang' (integral part) of India; and that their sons and husbands would not have gone missing if they had not strayed into violence. But the question of how they went missing is still unanswered. The families don't know if they were taken by militants or by the security forces. I've always remained alive to the fact that people need to be made to feel like they *are* (emphasis mine) 'atoot ang'. Unfortunately, the phrase has always applied to the territory rather than its inhabitants. Instead of saying, '*Kashmir hamara heh,*' (Kashmir is ours), the line can be changed just a little; it can be tweaked to, '*Kashmiri hamare heh*' (The Kashmiris are ours). The lack of that approach has only widened the schism between the people and the authorities. Parveena can't sit in the park anymore. The abrogation of Article 370 in August 2019 does not allow sit-ins. They're seen as a form of dissent.

The men in uniform have suffered too. So many have died in the line of duty and the images of their wives and children saluting coffins is another memory that troubles the mind. It underlines the principle that while more troops are needed on the ground, those extra pairs can only walk in the direction of containing the levels of violence.

Conflict resolution and the difficult, often vexed, process of peace-building requires courage, determination, and clear intent. Peace can take root only when there is an earnest attempt at reaching out to injured communities, be they the Pandits or the Muslims in Kashmir or the Meiteis and Kukis in Manipur. The sense of alienation can only be addressed by governments who are willing to change the status quo. To do that, they must deviate sharply from the oft-held view that they will be able to shoot their way through a crisis.

Two prime ministers worked hard at finding solutions to the raging insurgency in Kashmir and to improving the India-Pakistan relationship. Atal Bihari Vajpayee, in the context of Kashmir, often said, '*Yeh guthi suljhani heh*' (This knot has to be disentangled). In its pursuit, he not only invited Pervez Musharraf, the architect of Kargil, for a summit to Agra, but also sent his home secretary Kamal Pande to Srinagar for a meeting with Hizbul Mujahideen terrorists, who came with their faces masked. That was in the year 2000.

His successor, Manmohan Singh, worked the back channel with Pakistan to work out an agreement that was almost formalized but went into cold storage because Musharraf got sucked into a domestic crisis after deciding to unseat the Chief Justice of Pakistan. According to the agreement, 'Pakistan agreed to ditch its long-held position seeking a Kashmir solution through the implementation of a UN resolution for a referendum and agreed not to redraw borders during secret negotiations with India in 2007,' Singh's special envoy, S. K. Lambah revealed to me in an interview with *Hindustan Times*, in October 2015. At a press conference in 2014, before demitting power, Singh confirmed that India and Pakistan were close to an important breakthrough. Kashmir has stayed at the heart of the India-Pakistan conflict. Prime Minister Narendra Modi's government has stood firm on its position that talks and terror cannot go hand in hand. After Pahalgam, the position has changed to, 'We will only talk about Pakistan-occupied-Kashmir.'

A critical problem that underlines conflict resolution is the fact that there is no continuum. Each prime minister exhibits a different style of functioning, and each has his or her own personality traits that guide their decision-making processes. Each is also curtailed by the ideologies of the party they represent.

Narendra Modi, Singh's successor demonstrated the appetite for peace with Pakistan in the first year of his prime ministership, when he invited his counterpart, Nawaz Sharif for his swearing-in, and through a pit stop at Lahore, when he went to congratulate Sharif on the occasion of his granddaughter's marriage. The bonhomie didn't last long. Modi changed the security paradigm after terror strikes in Uri, Pulwama, and Pahalgam, as I've mentioned in my introductory chapter.

In the Preface, I have written about hate being the new fault line, and to return to the question of role models, I must confess that Bilkis Bano – the young pregnant mother who was gang raped during the 2002 riots that shook Gujarat – ranks high on my list.

I respect her indomitable spirit and the zeal with which she chose to walk the road to justice, after losing her first-born child and six other members of the family. Put yourself in her shoes and answer a few questions: Would you be able to summon the courage to walk to the police station after seeing your child being bludgeoned to death? Would you be able to go from court to court, knowing that you are pregnant and about to give birth to another child in a society riven with communal divides? Would you be able to keep moving homes because the accused and their ecosystem ensure you never feel safe? How would you feel, when you see the convicts – guilty of murder and rape – walk out of jail, aided by an outdated remission policy – only to be feted and garlanded by members of the Vishwa Hindu Parishad?

At some level, the sight of convicts being offered sweets,

became the spark that lit an outreach initiative. Around the same time, members of the Muslim community were being lynched, and their homes and shops were being bulldozed. The brazenness with which the fault line was being drawn and the callous candour with which communal fires were being politically fanned, is also the time when five Muslim intellectuals joined hands and sent an email to RSS Chief Mohan Bhagwat. Bhagwat responded within a month and the meeting made instant headlines in 2023. Neither side revealed that they had met, but the news leaked about a month after their meeting on 22 August.

I personally know two of the five and I spoke to both: the former Chief Election Commissioner S. Y. Quraishi and Shahid Siddiqui, editor and author. I wanted to understand the reasons why they had sought the meeting. It is difficult for me to forget what they said.

Quraishi admitted that he was apprehensive about how the news of their meeting with Bhagwat would be perceived.

'Why were you apprehensive?' I asked.

His answer was loaded.

'We were worried we'd be accused of selling out.'

A moment's pause later, he added, 'But what do we have to sell-out?'

Shahid Siddiqui pointed to Bilkis Bano's convicts being garlanded, to the calls for economic and social boycotts, and to the constant attempts at 'othering' the community. 'In the past too, we have had riots, in the past too, we have been singled out as "maulanas" and "love jihadists", but now the community has been pushed to the wall and is at its most insecure.'

The meeting – several more followed the first one – opened a window of dialogue. Crucially, the meeting led to a conversation. More such initiatives are needed to walk the long road to peace.

Frankly, the outcomes cannot be prejudged and there are many – even amongst the five who met Bhagwat – who concede that the Hindu-Muslim divide is a well-practised and honed technique of winning electoral battles. Yet, they keep endeavouring, because while the pursuit for peace can be a lonely and difficult fight; it is a fight that cannot be given up.

Do I despair, Priya Kapoor, the editorial director of my publishing house asked me, when she sent me feedback on my manuscript. I thought about the question and understood that yes, I was given to despair, but I am not the only one. I understood, also, that I'm a firm believer in the power of individuals; of groups and organizations who continue to wage daily battles to end civil strife; to fight for a united, pluralistic and secular India that is fundamentally enshrined in our Constitution.

I am not hindered by those who want to label us as 'liberals' and 'sickulars'. I've stayed focussed – through my journey across battlefields – on pointing to the reasons for why conflict takes root. I've focussed also – and continue to, through my writings – on why governments need to heal wounds, not deepen them.

I reiterate here what Justice Sanjay Kishan Kaul said in a separate judgement, while deliberating on the case involving the hollowing out of Article 370. He put it simply but precisely, when he said, 'To move forward, wounds require healing. Inter-generational trauma is felt by people. The first step towards healing the wounds is the acknowledgment of the acts of violations done by the state and its actors.'

It is difficult, sometimes, to read reports about how communities are deliberately provoked; how mere 'hearsay' can lead to detentions and arrests and how policemen, paid to uphold the law, have become paid masters of their political bosses.

When I hear comments like, 'Holi comes once a year, namaz 52 times…,' I tune out and then tune in to a voice I've worshipped since my childhood.

Mohammad Rafi's mesmerizing voice is my 'rational anthem'. The words are in quote marks because they are borrowed from my friend and journalist, Priya Ramani, who authors a column under that branding.

Rafi's lilting voice is soulful and the lyrics of the 'rational anthem' carry deep meaning.

'*Tu Hindu banega, na Musalmaan banega…*

Insaan ki aulad heh… Insaan banega.'

It is from the movie, *Dhool ka Phool*. In the movie, the song is sung by a Muslim father who is bringing up a Hindu child. The movie was made decades ago, in 1959.

That's the 'note' I'd like to end on. That's the only 'chord' that can take us forward.

Acknowledgements

The book had been taking shape in my mind for some years. It had also occupied chambers of my heart and my subconscious over time. Covering conflict is never easy. It is a nerve-wracking, heartwrenching experience that takes a toll. Each time I'd sit down with friends to chapterize the book, I would also push it to the backburner. Till one day in late 2023 when Priya and Kapil Kapoor, the able duo at Roli Books reached out to me to discuss another project they wanted me to co-author. 'I have an idea of my own,' I told them and we discussed it briefly.

I wanted to chronicle my journey through conflict. I had, over the years and decades, been a witness to seismic events that have shaped and changed India. I wanted the book to reflect on how conflicts are born; how they're stoked, and how they're handled and mishandled by different governments.

I'm not particularly comfortable with bringing myself

into the story but narrating my personal experience, in this instance, has hopefully added value to a book that spans my career over four decades. It has definitely been a cathartic process. It has also been a process of self-examination.

The morning after my conversation with the Kapoors, Priya sent me a contract. The finality of the deadline set me off with the writing. I thank them both for egging me on.

I thank all the editors I have worked with; Aroon Purie in particular. *India Today* was the perfect learning ground. Each of the subsequent editors has helped me become a better journalist through all the bouquets and brickbats they've thrown my way. I'm grateful to *India Today*, *Tehelka* and *Hindustan Times* for allowing me to source my articles and quote from them, as also to the team at *The Times of India* and *The Quint*.

A journalist, reporters especially, are as good as their sources and contacts and I've had the fortune of earning their trust and in some cases, also their friendship. A heartfelt thank you to all of them.

I must acknowledge all my colleagues at *The Sunday Observer*, *India Today*, some at *Tehelka*, and the ones in *Hindustan Times*, who have journeyed with me. So many are not just close friends; they're family.

A big shout-out must go to Poonam Saxena, editor, author, and friend who gave me her time and her advice. She read each chapter as I wrote it, and I am deeply indebted to her for her generosity and her patience. Her feedback and gentle persuasion helped me complete the book, my second after the one I authored on the short but short war in Kargil.

Thank you Roli Books – Priya and Neelam Narula, for editing the manuscript and giving it final shape.

Not all my friends are journalists and to them too, I stay grateful. Each one of them kept me going with companionship and food for my soul.

Finally, my mother, who spent long hours alone as I locked myself in my room to write the book. Heartfelt gratitude to her, my sister, and the children who are caring, supportive and argumentative, as they should be. They've been eager listeners to the many stories I've brought back from Punjab to Pahalgam.

The timing of the book is fortuitous. It is a reminder of the many conflicts and the many fault lines we continue to negotiate. Conflict is up front and centre. It is a reality that will continue to stare us in the face.

INDEX